# theturning world

# theturning world

## STORIES FROM THE
## LONDON INTERNATIONAL FESTIVAL OF THEATRE

**Rose de Wend Fenton
and Lucy Neal**

with
Rustom Bharucha
Lyn Gardner
Naseem Khan
Dragan Klaić
Peter Sellars

CALOUSTE GULBENKIAN FOUNDATION

Published by the
Calouste Gulbenkian Foundation
United Kingdom Branch
98 Portland Place
London W1B 1ET
Tel: 020 7908 7604
Email: info@gulbenkian.org.uk
Website: www.gulbenkian.org.uk

ISBN 1 903080 03 7
    978 190308003 0

British Library Cataloguing-in-Publication Data
A catalogue record for this book is available from the British Library

Copyedited by James Loader
Designed by Helen Swansbourne
Printed by Expression Printers Ltd, IP23 8HH

Distributed by Central Books, 99 Wallis Road, London E9 5LN
Tel: 0845 458 9911, Fax: 0845 458 9912, Email: orders@centralbooks.com
Website: www.centralbooks.co.uk

Cover image: *File O*, Xi Ju Che Jian Theatre, China, LIFT'95 (page 80). Courtesy of LIFT
archive. Photo: Han Lei.
Frontispiece: *Garden of Light*, Groupe F, France, LIFT'01 (page 45), Victoria Park,
Hackney. Courtesy of Groupe F. Photo: Thierry Nava.

# Contents

To
Margaret and West
Michael and Barbara

# Authors' acknowledgements

The process of writing this book has been a surreal mix of endings and beginnings. As we delved into the stories that made up LIFT's history, we were also launching the LIFT Enquiry and helping our Board in the search for our successor. Keeping us at the writing wheel while we were beset with distractions were Siân Ede and Felicity Luard of the Calouste Gulbenkian Foundation, both of whom we thank for their sustained energy and patience in editing this book. We were honoured that Rustom Bharucha, Lyn Gardner, Naseem Khan, Dragan Klaić and Peter Sellars agreed to join us as contributors.

For every production we have described in *The Turning World*, there were a hundred more we could have chosen, and it was a painful and almost impossible task to decide which to include. LIFT is a story of collaboration and risk-taking – of jumping in at the deep end – and we honour and offer a fanfare of thanks to all the artists, organisations and individuals we have worked with collaboratively over the years.

We are extremely grateful to our LIFT colleagues who have held the fort and put up with absences from the office at critical times during the writing process, in particular Angela McSherry and Tony Fegan, who also generously read our first manuscripts, as did Julia Rowntree, Anna Ledgard, Margaret de Wend Fenton, Michael Neal and Simon Maggs. Chuck Mike, Dragan Klaić, Malu Halasa, Penny Brooke, Rabih Mroué, Rose Issa and Ahdaf Soueif all provided invaluable guidance on certain chapters and, along with Barbara Heinzen and Helena Kennedy, gave us book-writing advice as we embarked on the endeavour to capture a quarter of a century of LIFT life.

Finally, sincerest thanks to our families, who surrendered long ago to the idea of LIFT as a houseguest in their lives – late into the night, at weekends and on holidays. For accommodating a book on top of a festival, thank you!

Rose de Wend Fenton and Lucy Neal

# Foreword

The Gulbenkian Foundation's arts publications seek to reflect a spirit of change, rarely by dictating what should happen but by presenting readers with an engaging narrative, with speculations and suggestions, so they may ponder on the peculiar compulsions which inspire the making of art and, more prosaically, consider the implications for future strategy-making and support. In commissioning this book our first intention was to take a closer look at what was happening in British theatre in the context of increasing globalisation in the world in general and in the arts in particular. British theatre has clearly been hugely successful in finding numerous ways to reinterpret the well-constructed English text. Many adventurous British companies have travelled abroad and returned exhilarated and influenced by the different work they have encountered. British-based theatre people from other cultures have created their own distinctive modes of expression. There has long been change in the air, but until recently not a lot of consistent international exchange. We very rarely feature the activities of any one organisation but it seems clear that the history of LIFT over the past twenty-five years embodies many of the changes that have transformed British theatre, internationalising it, breaking down its conventions and art-form boundaries and *vulgarising* it in the best sense of the word. Whilst funding bodies have been slowly creating policies to demand of the arts that they become more 'multicultural', or 'culturally diverse', or 'intercultural', or 'inclusive' (whatever the subtle change in emphasis), Rose Fenton and Lucy Neal have been venturing overseas, driven by curiosity and instinct, making swift decisions and then seeing their hunches through to full production on London stages or streets without losing face, cool or faith.

There is a palpable sense of risk to many of the stories in this book. And yet they pulled it off. Conventional London stages were transformed. Public spaces became sites for unusual goings-on. The activities of international theatre companies paradoxically made the aspirations of London's own experimental theatre-makers and hidden communities more visible and vocal.

During the writing of most of the book Rose Fenton and Lucy Neal were still Directors of LIFT, often arriving at our office straight from Heathrow, or, encumbered with suitcases and lap-tops, on their way to Beirut or Cape Town or Bucharest. Discussion would be interrupted by urgent mobile messages from production managers, fund-raisers or exam-taking daughters; photographers arrived to snap them for PR shots; writing tasks were listed in giant jotters already filled with production details, phone numbers and flight options. Recording LIFT's many and varied activities over more than two decades has been hard and we have had to make difficult choices and omit many good things. At an early stage we removed all the artworks from the walls of the Foundation's Committee Room and stuck up giant post-its in different colours which represented dozens of countries, and on them superimposed the many LIFT-commissioned productions that had emerged from a rapidly changing world. The solution to organising the book was probably inevitable. There would be four sections – London, International, Festival and Theatre. We fully acknowledge that our decisions as to which productions should go where were often arbitrary because, of course, they have all taken place in London and interacted with its local communities; they have all conveyed new international perspectives on the world; they have all been festive; they have all pushed the boundaries of what we traditionally think of as theatre.

LIFT's history is told here as narrative. Both Rose Fenton and Lucy Neal are able to make bold statements about the power of theatre but the truths underlying their conviction become vividly evident when they start to reminisce (they seem to have photographic memories), so we insisted that we leave others – our invited contributors and the reader, of course – to ponder on the wider implications of what they created. Their task was simply to describe their experiences in their own compelling way, reflecting on the story of art-making through the art of story-making, with no summary declarations or homilies. 'Just tell the story,' was one of our catch-phrases; 'no abstract nouns'. Interestingly, while Rose Fenton and Lucy Neal have quite different personalities, their vision seems always to have been unquestioningly shared and their memories seem to be as one. They have both contributed stories to each section and their accounts merge seamlessly – indeed, there have been times

*Yerma*, The Company, India, LIFT'93. Photo: Simon Annand. Neelam Mansingh Chowdhry's production transposed Lorca's classic to a Punjabi village, its traditions, rhythms and dances performed by folk singers, 'urban' actors, musicians and naqqals – traditional female impersonators (page 193).

when we couldn't remember who had written what – though we have since quietly identified the writer when necessary to satisfy the more curious reader.

We were delighted that four extraordinarily discerning commentators agreed to write essays in response to the four sections, each of them uniquely expert in their fields and each a long-term follower of the LIFT project. For over thirty years writer and policy adviser Naseem Khan has observed the evolution of multicultural London and its arts constituencies and been actively engaged in the often difficult political debates ensuing. Rustom Bharucha, who comments on the shifting meanings implicit in the idea of international, is an independent writer, director and cultural critic based in Calcutta. He is currently involved in conducting workshops with indigenous and local communities on issues relating to land, memory, development and globalisation. Theatre scholar and cultural analyst Dragan Klaić has studied the ins and outs of international performing-arts festivals. Lyn Gardner is steeped in theatre of all kinds as a critic for *The Guardian*, much respected by practitioners and admirably qualified to see what LIFT has effected in the wider context of theatre.

The title *The Turning World* comes from T.S. Eliot's *Burnt Norton,* the first part of *Four Quartets:*

> *. . . After the kingfisher's wing*
> *Has answered light to light, and is silent, the light is still*
> *At the still point of the turning world . . .*

The same title was used by long-time fellow-traveller John Ashford, now Artistic Director of The Place, for a dance season that introduced a hundred international companies to London in the 1990s, expressing the same spirit of curiosity and desire for collaboration. The story of LIFT is the story of the entrepreneurial obsession that is a property of so many of the leaders of arts organisations in Britain and – as this book clearly demonstrates – throughout the world. For many people internationally, theatre is quite literally a matter of survival. I write this in the wake of the shattering bomb attacks in London which have led to passionate discussions about the shifting boundaries between different cultures, beliefs and concepts of freedom, subjects which have always been at the heart of the matter in many productions LIFT has brought to this increasingly multilingual capital. The debates are complex and multifaceted and often demonstrate an admirable facility to see a situation from many points of view. If LIFT has contributed just a little to opening up our minds and imaginations in the continuing quest for resolution that is implicit in all great drama, its project has been worthwhile.

**Siân Ede**
Arts Director, Calouste Gulbenkian Foundation

# Introduction

One thousand and one stories could be told about LIFT, and all could be told from many viewpoints: those of the artists who devised the shows, the audiences who crossed London to see them, the production staff who worked in unlikely places, the fire officers who came to inspect and give permissions, the sponsors who committed funds, the teachers who brought their classes, the critics who needed extra stamina – indeed, any of the individuals involved along the way.

We have chosen around thirty stories to be representative of twenty years of biennial Festivals from 1981 to 2001. Four contributors give their view of LIFT: Rustom Bharucha, writer, director and cultural critic; Lyn Gardner, theatre critic; Naseem Khan, writer and policy adviser; and Dragan Klaić, theatre scholar and cultural analyst. Between us we try to capture not only the changes in London and the world, but also the evolution of the festivals that LIFT has been a part of, and of the art form we find so endlessly fascinating.

**How It Began** describes how the Festival got started. After this, the stories are arranged under four headings: **London**, **International**, **Festival** and **Theatre**. We had to start somewhere, and, whilst most stories could clearly appear anywhere, each of the four domains has its own specific landscape, which we trust the book begins to map.

**London** recounts the ways in which LIFT has engaged with the physical, social and cultural landscape of London, and the city's connections with the world.

**International** looks at how insights into historic world events of the late twentieth century can be gained from contemporary theatre. Artists explore the place of theatre in society and tell their individual stories. LIFT experiences

Lucy Neal (left) and Rose Fenton outside the LIFT office, on the terrace of the Lyric Theatre, Hammersmith, LIFT'83. Photo: Honey Salvadori.

demonstrate how theatre visits require negotiation and cultural exchange in order to contextualise different cultural perspectives and belief systems.

**Festival** shows how we learnt to play with ideas of transgression, renewal and community, discovering what can be explored if the status quo is temporarily suspended.

**Theatre** considers experimentation in the art form when it is put in the hands of innovators, and how such risk-taking enriches the audience's experience.

The LIFT Enquiry, running from 2001–6, is introduced in the **Epilogue**, taking forward the questions that LIFT has always asked: what can theatre be? Where can it take place? Who can take part?

LIFT is more than the sum of its parts, and particular projects, such as the Business Arts Forum, the Teacher Forum and Phakama, are described towards the end of the book.

We, the founders of the Festival, tell these stories from our own perspective, their sense of breathless personal bravado contradicting at a stroke the reality of LIFT: that it belongs to many people and that there are many stories still to be told.

*But this is how it started . . .*

# How It Began

It began with a phone call from a friend. We were in the middle of a Saturday lunch amongst the sardines, baked beans and tinned tomatoes that lined the shelves of the back room of the corner shop that served as student lodgings. It was March 1978 and our friend Adrian Odell, who had gone to Portugal to teach after graduating, was ringing to say that the University of Coimbra was organising a student festival in May dedicated to 'international solidarity and friendship'; would we come? There were to be companies from Germany, Poland and what was then Czechoslovakia, and Adrian had already convinced the festival's organisers that he knew a university troupe (meaning us) from Warwick in the UK who put on the kind of radical, politicised work they were now looking for. The festival budget would cover our living expenses in Portugal, so 'all we had to do' was create a production and raise some airfares. Before the phone call ended we agreed we would do it. We had ten weeks.

Portugal had had a revolution four years earlier and a programme of collectivisation had swept the country. By 1978, the movement was faltering and the landlords who had fled the Communists were beginning to return, demanding their land back. Although at Warwick University we were very fortunate to see a wide variety of theatre presented at its Arts Centre, from Britain and overseas (performers included Mike Leigh's Hull Truck, Pip Simmons, Berliner Eckerhart Schall, and Czech mime artist Bolek Polívka, to name a few), our own experiences as theatre-makers revolved around student productions of Jacobean drama, Christmas pantomimes and occasional forays into Boris Vian, Bertolt Brecht and Luigi Pirandello. In an attempt to do justice to the revolutionary cause, we hit on what we imagined to be the perfect play – David Hare's *Fanshen*. We had just seen Joint Stock's production, directed by Max Stafford-Clark, at the Arts Centre. Describing the process of land reform in China during the Cultural Revolution, it was, we thought, appropriate and topical. A pile of vivid blue posters from the production, showing workers' arms upraised in revolutionary gestures, was still stacked in the Arts Centre's marketing office. We cut Joint Stock's name off the bottom of the poster and replaced it with our own: The 11th Hour Theatre Company. Equipped with armfuls of these, a scantily rehearsed play directed by Ben Gibson, plane tickets bought with funds raised from the University and the British Council, and a great deal of confidence and purpose, we flew to Portugal.

Despite our best efforts, which included on-the-spot improvisations and singing the *Internationale* in Portuguese as our grand finale, the play was an unmitigated failure. In contrast to the visual, robustly physical and musical shows of the other companies in the festival, our three hours of dense dialogue without translation bored the audience and got us into political trouble. Cafés buzzed with debate about whether our play was in fact a counter-revolutionary piece calculated to overthrow the revolution rather than support it. Renditions of *Scarborough Fair* and *Bandiera Rossa* on an outing to a collective farm saved us from being chased out of town. We left under a cloud.

The experience was transformative. Seeing theatre drawn from different traditions traversing music, dance and the visual arts in one confident arc was a revelation to us, and in total contrast to the text-based British theatre we knew. The vigour of the political debate and the festival's engagement with social issues inspired us. On our last night in Coimbra, we resolved to create a similar festival back in Britain. Looking down on the town from the crumbling balcony of our grand hotel we threw coins over our shoulders to bring luck to the new venture.

## 'You'll be shifting dead wood all the way'

The summer we graduated from the University of Warwick, Britain was entering a new political era. It was 1979, and Margaret Thatcher had won the election and begun her eighteen-year hold on British politics and the public realm. Declaring that 'There is no such thing as society' whilst putting the 'Great' back into Britain, her leadership heralded a culture of free-market private enterprise and union-bashing, with a war in the South Atlantic and Poll Tax riots at home. Britain was in a recession and the arts had to justify their existence in the market place, competing with hospitals and schools. International arts were off the agenda altogether and it is hard to conceive of the insularity of British theatre at that time – Peter Brook had abandoned the country in despair at its narrow-mindedness and cultural myopia to work in the more cosmopolitan Paris. On the face of it, this wasn't a great time to be launching an international festival full of 'foreign' work that hoped to challenge British theatre and open a window on the world.

Under the surface changes in the arts landscape were underway, albeit away from the establishment. Joseph Seelig founded the London International Mime Festival in 1978, Penny Francis the Puppet Festival in 1979, Val Bourne started Dance Umbrella in 1980 and Judith Knight and Seonaid Stewart began

Artsadmin in the same year. Pioneering individuals such as David Gothard at Riverside Studios, Thelma Holt at the Roundhouse and John Ashford at the ICA were opening their doors to artists such as the Rustaveli from Georgia, Tadeusz Kantor from Poland and Radeis from the Netherlands. The indefatigable Alfred Emmet at The Questors amateur theatre in Ealing was inviting companies from Eastern Europe and India. All gave encouragement and advice when we spoke of our plans for LIFT, ranging from Seelig's stoic warning, 'You'll be shifting dead wood all the way', to Emmet's invaluable knowledge of negotiating with official agencies in the Communist bloc. *British Alternative Theatre Directory,* edited by Catherine Itzin, became a point of reference. John Ashford offered us the use of the ICA. We worked as waitresses by night and researched the Festival by day.

We learnt about the late Sir Peter Daubeny and his World Theatre Seasons, which took place at the Aldwych Theatre in the 60s and 70s, from people asking us if we intended to follow in his footsteps. Until his death in 1975 he had presented, against the odds, some of Europe's established international theatre companies, such as the Berliner Ensemble and the Comédie Française, along with more unexpected productions such as *Umbatha* – a Zulu version of *Macbeth* by the Natal Theatre Workshop Zulu Company – from South Africa. The fact that he too had come up against the assumed superiority of the British theatre world was strangely reassuring to us. We contacted his widow, Lady Molly Daubeny, to ask if she would become our first patron. Inviting us to a grand champagne soirée at her town house in Wilton Square, she agreed.

We drew up lists of embassies and their cultural attachés to approach once we had worked out an itinerary of festivals to visit. The Polish Embassy produced an invitation to the Lublin Konfrontacje Teatralne festival of experimental and student theatre, and the German Embassy gave an invitation to the Erlangen International Festival. In both cases onshore costs were paid. The British Council, *Time Out* and an array of individuals were asked to assist us in buying the airfares. In *Who's Who* we found that Lord St Oswald was President of both the Anglo-Polish Society *and* Friends of Yorkshiremen in London Society. Given the explanation that Rose was a Yorkshirewoman trying to get to Poland, he agreed to see us, sending us away again almost immediately as we were wearing trousers and he didn't approve. We returned the next day resolutely in culottes to find him deliberating between buying a new lampshade for his home in Yorkshire, Nostell Priory, or giving us the cost of one airfare on condition that we find the other. In fact he wrote us a cheque there and then, and agreed to become our second patron. At *Time Out* proprietor Tony Elliott and Steve Grant, theatre editor, grilled us on our LIFT plans before giving a donation of £500 *and* the offer of editorial support. After six months of research we were making headway.

## Wisleve Moslive

The trip to Poland in April 1980 was a watershed and as rich a lesson in international theatre as we could have wished for. Powerful expressionistic shows, heavy with symbolism to avoid the censor, caught the assertive mood of the Polish public in the months leading up to the birth of Solidarity in the Gdansk shipyards. Lublin itself was renowned for its defiant spirit, home not only to the Catholic University, an institution barely tolerated by the Communist authorities, but also birthplace of Karol Wojtyla, who became Pope only two years earlier in 1978.

At the Lublin festival, new theatre forms were clearly being forged in response to the political climate and audiences were passionate to engage with the young independent companies that were raging against the system's destructive lies and propaganda in shows such as *More Than Just One Life* and *It is Not for Us to Fly to the Islands of Happiness*. As a public space for dissent and experimentation, theatre mattered. But despite the seriousness there were also jokes – our phrase book being one of them. Such gems as 'I didn't order steak, I ordered beef' provided an entire evening of bitter-sweet hilarity, as Theatre of the 8th Day improvised a script from it on food shortages and bread queues. (Their name exemplified a belief in man's right to aspire to the impossible: if God had had eight days to create the universe, he would have created the theatre in order that man could imagine all kinds of futures.)

Leaving the apartment of theatre director Leszek Madzik, we read a notice in Polish, *Wisleve Moslive*. We asked what it meant. 'Everything is possible,' he said. Our challenge to create LIFT assumed a new dimension and we returned with a sense of responsibility and urgency to communicate what was happening.

We travelled for three months around a burgeoning European festival circuit, visiting the big post-war players such as Avignon and Edinburgh (committed to building peace between nations through culture), along with the 'alternative' festivals that had sprung up in the years after the student movements of the late 60s. At Erlangen in Germany we saw the Brazilian company Grupo de Teatro Macunaíma's show two evenings running, and realised its South American sweep of sexy carnivalesque majesty could be a huge hit in London. Telling the story of Brazil's legendary folk hero Macunaíma, twenty-two performers playing

*More Than Just One Life*, Theatre of the 8th Day, Poland, LIFT'81. Photo: Christopher Pearce, Panic Pictures.

sixty parts conjured the Amazon jungle, rivers, whole cities and the clamour of street life in dizzying tableaux and rich action. Sitting in sunshine the next day by a magnolia tree, and knowing that festivals everywhere were vying for the show, we asked the show's director, Antunes Filho, if he would accept our invitation to come and play in London. Despite our lack of track record as theatre presenters, he gladly accepted our offer.

At the Festival of Fools in Amsterdam, derelict docksides, old liners, tugs and cargo boats became the setting for fifteen days of round-the-clock performance, including Hungary's Studio K, Poland's Theatre STU (Theatre of the 8th Day had been denied passports by the Polish government) and, from the UK's People Show, a peripatetic experience through interlinking warehouses, ending with a midnight feast around a campfire. We learnt that theatre could burst out of confined spaces across a whole landscape at any time and in any form. We had travelled to the Festival with a cohort from London's ICA, including John Ashford, Tim Albery and Sandy Nairne, and Jo Seelig. Whilst they stayed in a hotel on Herengracht, we were in a youth hostel around the corner – much to everyone's amusement. And we had bought our boat-train tickets with coupons from a Persil soap packet.

Returning to London we attempted to find sympathetic venues for the shows we had seen. David Gothard at Riverside Studios was already programming Tadeusz Kantor's *The Dead Class* and was not impressed by our attempts to persuade him to programme lesser-known, younger theatre companies. A bid to house *Macunaíma* took us to see Thelma Holt at the Roundhouse and John Drummond at the Edinburgh Festival. Neither wanted to collaborate, although Drummond offered to take the Brazilians off our hands 'if they got too big for us to handle'.

## Fundraising

We had selected ten visiting companies but with a budget of £120,000 to present them we needed to address fundraising very seriously. Our four Trustees (Gaie Houston, Tony Johnson, Joseph Benjamin and Denis Poll), recommended by a growing network of champions, had formally registered LIFT as a charity. They were magnanimous in their support. Houston gave hours of her time to help us plan the Festival's organisation, while Poll, an investor in communications technology, gave finance, as did Johnson from his yacht on the high seas. Benjamin, a property developer, provided us with office space in a block of service flats undergoing refurbishments at the grand address of Buckingham Gate. On an old typewriter we wrote hundreds of letters explaining our plans and seeking funding, at one point even expanding rhetorically on the power of theatre to avoid world wars. We saw Peter Ustinov on the *Michael Parkinson Show* pitching for international co-operation and immediately asked him to be a patron. He agreed: 'I'll do it. But you'll have to push me.'

We ourselves were completely broke – and exhausted. For a year we had been on a treadmill of waitressing, cycling, travelling, more waitressing, fundraising and meetings – the Chinese Cultural Attaché one minute, the Director of the Old Vic the next. We enjoyed unstinting moral support from our parents, friends and families but we were burning out. 'I don't think Rose and I can keep it up much longer,' Lucy wrote in a letter one day. 'It makes a good story but a tiring life.' Walking down Petty France on 11 September 1980, after a particularly gruelling round of rebuttals, Rose declared it to be 'the worst day of the Festival'. We thought about packing it in.

We were clear, however, about the artists we wanted to invite from Poland, Peru, Brazil, the Netherlands, Japan, Malaysia, France, Germany and the UK. The Tricycle Theatre, the Half Moon, the ICA and Max Stafford-Clark ('But how can I trust your taste?') at the Royal Court had all agreed to present shows. Our excitement about the first LIFT programme kept us at it.

## Money

*'Badges will be sold at 30p each. We need to sell 1,243 to break even.'*
Fi Godfrey Faussett, LIFT Volunteer

Despite the support we had received so far, raising money was not simple. Our plans were practical but we were seen as amateur. The budget didn't begin to break even and it was obvious we needed to move up a gear to gain credibility. Building public profile through the press seemed a possible route and a telephone call to Sue Arnold, who wrote the Upfront page in *The Observer* colour supplement, provided the breakthrough we needed. She was intrigued enough to invite us to lunch. The effect of the resulting article, published in September 1980, was astonishing. Buoyed up by Arnold's assertion that 'If the Festival is not a phenomenal success I shall eat an entire millinery collection without demur', we wrote hundreds more letters and knocked on more doors, some of which finally began to open.

In December, as swathes of cuts to the arts were announced in the press, the Visiting Arts Unit, which had just been set up by the Foreign Office to serve the principle of 'reciprocity', awarded us their largest single grant of £5,000. Both the British Tourist Authority and the London Tourist Board made grants to us. Ken Livingstone's internationalist Greater London Council welcomed LIFT as an artistic addition to the city's vibrant and culturally diverse life, and its Arts and Entertainment Unit, under the leadership of Lord Birkett and the maverick Tony Banks, gave LIFT £10,000.

A letter from the Drama Director at the Arts Council, on the other hand, dated 31 March 1981, explained why that body would not fund LIFT. 'We cannot allocate subsidy for a festival whose programme is composed predominantly of appearances by foreign theatre companies,' it said. 'Of course such a festival can have a benefit to theatre in a broad sense: the Council, however, believes that the available subsidy produces a greater continuing benefit when given to companies resident in this country.'

While other funding bodies were beginning to participate, private sponsorship was thin on the ground. As late as March 1981 minutes of a LIFT meeting record 'The situation on sponsorship is depressing and frustrating – the more the artistic side of the Festival comes together . . . the less sponsorship we seem to find.' A newsletter to volunteers reported the challenges: 'Emelia Thorold is trying to get sponsorship in kind from various large food chains – bread, milk, cereal etc. – in order to provide the groups with food to make their own breakfast with. So far she has raised £25 from Sainsbury's.'

However, with a box office budgeted at a bold 40 per cent, we were able to tell our Trustees by April 1981 that 'the financial picture looks better'. In the event the budget of £120,000 balanced, with one third of the expenditure being covered by box office, one third by public grants and one third coming through private donations.

## The Company

*'A demonstration that unemployment can be put to good use.'*
*The Times*, August 1981

An army of volunteers – forty in all, dedicated friends, family and fellow students – took over different aspects of delivering the Festival (and are now running their own festivals, television companies, theatres, law firms, literary agencies, and advisory teams to the UN). A structure was emerging, based on our Coimbra festival experience, with people delegated to find and organise student accommodation, appoint group hosts and oversee the many after-show discussions and debates, to say nothing of the Festival Bulletin and the Festival Club. Simon Evans, a Durham graduate who had spent the summer seeing international work, joined us after spotting the Sue Arnold article. 'Apart from the fact that Lucy, Simon and Rose are recognised as LIFT's organisers,' we reported to our stalwart Trustees, 'LIFT evolves daily on a sound co-operative basis. Everybody working on the Festival recognises that they are solely responsible for their own area of activity and expected to work with the level of commitment that such a responsibility demands. This proves not only to be the most satisfactory way of working together, but also the easiest way of getting as many people as possible involved in running the Festival.'

The only professionals hired and paid to work on the 1981 Festival were the press agents, Cromwell Associates (Jacquie Richardson and Helen Anderson), and Jonathan Bartlett, a production manager who impressed us on our first meeting by carrying a briefcase. Indefatigable in his professionalism and flair for making the impossible possible, Jonathan remains LIFT Production Manager twenty-five years later.

The sense of being 'professional' was indeed strange. At times it was almost as if we were playing at offices, with an endless supply of clipboards in place of desks in an increasingly packed one-room office. A press photo of LIFT's three organisers showed us gathered around an IBM golfball typewriter, of which we were obviously inordinately proud. We had one telephone – inconceivable in an age of email, mobiles and faxes. Getting 150 artists into London from South America, Malaysia, Eastern and Western Europe with one phone was a feat in itself, not to mention calls to London theatres to arrange production schedules and publicity. 'We are terrified', we wrote in our monthly update to the Trustees, 'that there are people becoming infuriated at not being able to get through to us, or simply losing initial interest in the Festival because the phone is constantly engaged . . . Important journalists have given up trying to contact us to write about the Festival because they have failed to get through all day.'

Cromwell Associates hired a photographer, Chris Pearce of Panic Pictures, to take press shots of all the companies, and set up rounds of radio, press and television interviews to promote LIFT to the media. The Lyric Hammersmith wrote to say they had received no advance bookings for *Macunaíma*: 'We're sure you have a trick up your sleeves, and if you haven't, you should have.'

On the day of Charles and Diana's wedding the streets were thronged with people making their way to Buckingham Palace – a stone's throw from our office. The LIFT team barely raised their heads from putting the finishing touches to box-office systems, brochures, contracts, carnets and freight arrangements. *LIFT OFF*, a daily bulletin which was to be commissioned, edited and printed *every* day of the two-week Festival, absorbed a team of editors, writers and cartoonists round the clock.

Lucy Neal (left), Simon Evans and Rose Fenton, press conference at the Piccadilly Hotel, LIFT'81. Photo: Catherine Shakespeare Lane.

## August 1981: LIFT-Off

A Festival Centre was given to us by Grand Metropolitan Hotels in a brilliant but unlikely location – the basement of the Piccadilly Hotel, at Piccadilly Circus. In July we held a press conference there, with Molly Daubeny heading the bill. As press and guests made for the drinks, we knew we had LIFT-off.

The Festival opened with three shows simultaneously on Monday 3 August 1981. The programme was eclectic: traditional dance dramas with a contemporary edge from Malaysia and Japan, impassioned political theatre from Poland, spectacular Brazilian music theatre, a one-man show from Peru enacting the devastation of an earthquake on a village, and a tender piece about gay relationships from Holland's Het Werkteater. Warwick colleague Ben Gibson and International Theatre Institute volunteer Debra Hauer's programme of talks at the ICA debated the role of the state and the aesthetics of theatre-making, whilst badges for Solidarity were sold in the foyer. When the elderly Count Raczyñski, President of the Polish government in exile, arrived with his entourage and made his way to the front row of the ICA to watch Teatr Provisorium's actors perform on a stark set of military beds beneath a crowned eagle, a contentious symbol of Communist oppression, we realised our London audiences had a host of international connections of their own. Out on the streets, students Gub Neal and Jonathan Young's theatre programme took to the open spaces with the Natural Theatre of Bath, the Beach Buoys (including Neil Bartlett and Simon McBurney) and others in Covent Garden, Trafalgar Square and along the South Bank.

London audiences came out in force, curious to engage with new experiences and debates. A proportionally large number of UK artists attended, along with individuals from the Polish, Brazilian and French communities. On the whole shows sold well. When *Macunaíma* opened at the Lyric on Wednesday 5 August there was a standing ovation, and as a rapturous audience moved out into the foyers they were assailed by flashing lights and TV crews clamouring for interviews. Critics' reviews, unanimous in their praise, were splashed across the papers, along with a cartoon in *The Listener* of the company drawn by the great cartoonist Feliks Topolski. LIFT had made the grade on the London scene. Though eating up a third of the Festival expenditure, this show was the box-office hit we had hoped for, contributing substantially to the balanced budget.

On a hot August afternoon you could fall into the Piccadilly Hotel's lush cool basement ballroom, eat sandwiches served by Grand Met waiters in black

The Beach Buoys at the Festival Club, Piccadilly Hotel, LIFT'81. Courtesy of Neil Bartlett.

Grupo de Teatro
Macunaíma,
Brazil, drawn by
Feliks Topolski,
*The Listener*,
13 August 1981.
Courtesy of Daniel
and Teresa
Topolski.

bow-ties, book tickets at the LIFT box office, buy a drink and listen to Lol Coxhill or Mike Westbrook playing, or watch Forkbeard Fantasy, at the LIFT Festival Club. As the Festival got under way, LIFT's artistic and social life took off. Partying late into the night, the Malaysian dancers Travolta-ed their way across the dance floor, accompanied by maverick theatre-maker Ken Campbell, who was trying to persuade them to stay to make a show with him in an abandoned quarry somewhere in the city.

A black cab lent by a friend, painted with the LIFT livery, delivered posters and bulletins around town until it was abandoned after overheating in traffic one day. And the Poles managed to bring the whole of Piccadilly Circus to a halt as they took to the wrong side of the road in their theatre truck. There was a spirit of disruption and trespass in the best sense of the words, and we caught a glimpse of a London ready to be reinvented.

Heartened by the impact of international theatre on London, we were to be surprised in some instances by the impact of London and its theatre community on our visitors. Teresa Whitfield, Group Host for Poland's Teatr Provisorium, wrote in the daily bulletin, *LIFT OFF*: 'It has been difficult for the Poles to view London with anything except blank amazement. For us, they say, it is like a Promised Land, a Welfare State. Recession? What is recession? Look at those people in the audience – I never saw such a well-fed recession.' To hear ardent supporters of Solidarity praising *The Daily Telegraph*, Ronald Reagan and Mrs Thatcher highlighted the gulf between East and West and challenged our political complacency. 'The Iron Curtain cuts across Europe as a distorting mirror,' Whitfield continued; 'the Poles may see a shining image of a Promised Land in England, but we, in the blackness that is ignorance of life in the Eastern Block, can only make romantic assumptions, seeing nothing.' Like all of us, she was grasping the opportunity LIFT afforded to engage with the world through theatre – a blueprint for a vision of LIFT that would develop in subsequent Festivals.

Outside in the wider world the press were taking note, ranging from the *Evening Standard's* Charles Spencer with his cautious, almost fearful 'LIFT-off for the foreign invaders' to *The Times's* celebratory 'End of foreign theatre famine'. *The Times Educational Supplement* was stern: 'For all its grand promises, the Festival must set [its] sights higher for next year if LIFT is to be worthy of its name – let alone survive.' Fortunately, Sheridan Morley caught the overall mood, writing on LIFT in the *International Herald Tribune*: 'Miracles do still happen. London has at last again been given a window on the dramatic world that lies beyond these shores.'

# London

Watching audiences appear at the appointed hour for a show you have spent months preparing for is thrilling – particularly when the site is an unusual one. LIFT has presented work in conventional theatres, but also in unexpected spaces across the city – in disused power stations, churches, houses and canal basins. If we simply wander along the River Thames memories of shows play themselves out again: Welfare State International's *Raising of the Titanic* in Limehouse Basin, pre-dating the rise of the commercial sector on this once derelict site; Bankside's chimney leaping with flames well before the abandoned power station became a world-class gallery; Christophe Berthonneau's *Birds of Fire*, Bow Gamelan's fiery barges, Station House Opera's breeze-block edifices outside the National Theatre, Els Comediants running with fire in Battersea Park. From the beginning, LIFT inhabited found spaces and created its own permission to re-enliven them with public events. These are stories about borders and boundaries, where LIFT projects tested the margins between public and private space. Artists are shown as explorers of the city, audaciously taking risks and changing our landscape so that we see it anew.

London's 'hybrid cosmopolitanism'[1] finds expression in many LIFT shows. With the visit of the Hanoi Water Puppets and the commission of *Flying Costumes, Floating Tombs* we explore the definition of London as a world city, mapping its evolving connections with the rest of the world, revealing a fresh perspective on what is already there, rather than creating anything 'new'. Finally, we focus on London's role as a free city which can connect countries – in this case, South Africa and Britain – highlighting London's history as a natural meeting point for those fighting for change, who in their turn inform

LIFT'93 Launch at Bankside Power Station, designed and produced by Anne Bean and Paul Burwell. Photo: Patricia Crummay.

political events here. Project Phakama's young participants show how making connections between countries can create opportunities for telling new stories about the past, sowing the seeds for theatres of the future.

## Bankside Power Station
Anne Bean and Paul Burwell, UK, LIFT'93

Artist Paul Burwell, wearing a miner's torch helmet, stops halfway up the interior of the chimney of Bankside's abandoned power station, which towers above the south bank of the River Thames opposite St Paul's Cathedral. He is clinging to a vertical metal ladder and suffers badly from vertigo. Far above his head he can see a small square of light where brick meets sky. He is recceing the 300-foot chimney that rises up from the centre of the edifice. Gilbert Scott's 1950s building has been inactive for years and is shortly to be sold off by its owners, Nuclear Electric plc. The building has not been listed so demolition remains an option for whoever takes over the site. Meanwhile, Bankside is in disrepair and no one we can find seems to know whether the interior chimney ladders are secure. Paul's solo climb is the only way to test them.

Paul Burwell and Anne Bean are founders of the Bow Gamelan Ensemble, who forge musical 'gamelans' from junkyard metal. They have won the competition to open LIFT'93 with an idea outlined briefly on one side of A4 and selected by Professor Heinz Wolff, Benjamin Zephaniah, Ken Campbell, Helen Marriage and Mark Borkowski – iconoclasts all.

Paul makes it to the top and gives the go-ahead to colleagues down below, who join the ascent, carrying up trademark Bow Gamelan paraffin pumps, paper ropes, pyrotechnics and distress flares, which are lashed securely to the chimney mouth. Thirty oil drums are strapped along the full length of the rooftop parapet. At 10.15 pm on Sunday 13 June 1993 a thunderous salute of drumming resounds across the Thames to St Paul's and back. Flames snake up the paper ropes that wind from base to chimney top and circles of fire blaze from the oil drums, now being played with deafening intensity. As the battery of drumming grows to a climax, an Olympic torch flame bursts from the top of Bankside's chimney, visible across London from north, south, east and west. Below there are shouts, cheers, impromptu dancing. Small children race wildly around. LIFT'93 has begun.

Only shortly afterwards comes the klaxon blare of eight fire-engines converging on the scene, followed by a party of serious-looking Chief Fire

Officers from adjoining London boroughs arriving to check out the event. The two LIFT Festival Directors are summoned to the night-watchman's cramped quarters on the south side of the building, which serve temporarily as a changing room for thirty-eight artists, drummers and pyrotechnicians. Bulkily clad firemen are charging through it on their way up to the roof to investigate. Dressed in our reception finery, Rose and I wait in the green-tiled shower cubicles, the only free space going. Huddled in with us, as we prepare our defence for not having alerted the Fire Brigade before the event, is sculptor and ex-Bow Gamelan member Richard Wilson. 'You have to explain that these are theatrical effects,' he stresses. 'They are less dangerous than they look. Say that you're theatre people. It's your *job* to create illusions.'

To our surprise, it hasn't been difficult to get permission from Nuclear Electric plc to stage the event, although we have had to take on the insurance of the whole building in order to indemnify the company. We haven't been able to negotiate the launch as a public event, but we are within our rights to stage it as a private party for LIFT's sponsors, artists and supporters. We have informed the police and Southwark Council. Indeed, the Mayor of Southwark is one of our guests. What we haven't reckoned on is people's public-spirited response to seeing Bankside apparently going up in flames. Londoners all over the place – including a man working late at the *Daily Express* – have dialled 999.

Fortunately, we are able to demonstrate that our fire procedures are safe and sound and that we have acted legitimately within the permissions we have been instructed to seek for a private event. Our apologies accepted, and with some acknowledgement of it all being 'more interesting than rescuing a cat', we wave goodbye to the fire-engines. We were unequivocally committed to public health and safety, yet felt space for public celebration could easily be swallowed up by risk aversion. But we know that, as with much of LIFT then and since, we have taken our own permission for creating the event in the first place.

London legend has it that Dennis Stevenson carried a photograph of the 'Olympic' flame in his pocket, using the evidence of Paul and Anne's theatrical illusion to great effect over his next few years as Chair of a Tate Gallery looking for new premises. For in 2000 the Turbine Hall we had traipsed through with our rusty oil drums was magnificently renovated and welcomed the first of millions of visitors to one of the world's most acclaimed new galleries of contemporary art.

In 2001, eight years on from the LIFT'93 launch, we chose to return to Bankside ourselves with a ceremony to mark the end of one LIFT era and the start of the new LIFT Enquiry, 2001–6. It was LIFT's twentieth anniversary, and working with John Fox, of the Cumbrian-based theatre company Welfare State International, we opted for something less overtly dramatic than transforming London's skyline. An all-night midsummer event culminated in a celebratory dawn breakfast around a kiln shaped like a double-headed chicken, in which 200 guests baked clay eggcups. Rose and I then escorted a giant egg by boat down the river to launch the new LIFT era, and at 5.03 am precisely, with a spray of fireworks jetting from our gunnels, the only dolphin in recent memory to swim upstream as far as Tower Bridge surfaced and slipped in and out of the water around us.

Taking this as a good omen we decided in 2002 to take our exploration of theatre's ceremonial roots a step further. We wanted to bring the Festival's calendar more in line with the cycle of the year and invited Anne Bean once again to create a celebration that would mark the dawn of Midsummer's Day. It was a year after September 11 and spectacular displays of fire-power were out of place. *Many Hands Make Light Work* invited members of the public to illuminate a dark glade in Battersea Park with words and poetry written with fluorescent lightsticks. When we started to plan the event we had no idea that a Buddhist monk, Reverend Nagase, lived in the Park – looking after the Peace Pagoda, which had been bequeathed to a culturally diverse London in 1985 by the Most Venerable Nichidatsu Fujii, from the Japanese Buddhist Order Nipponzan Myohoji, as a reminder of the capital's unique potential to affect world peace. When we first met Nagase he had a stiff neck from balancing high up on a Heath-Robinson scaffold of brooms and ladders in an attempt to clean the pagoda's golden Buddhas, resources to help him care for it having dwindled since the dissolution of the Greater London Council (GLC). At our subsequent invitation Nagase agreed to join us at dawn with a chant which was greeted by the waking calls of the ducks and wildlife around the lake. Staging events is often a process of simply revealing what is already there.

## Regent's Canal Dock, Limehouse Basin

Welfare State International, UK, *The Raising of the Titanic*, LIFT'83

*'Bring me a bourbon, slosh me a scotch*
*Fire off the best champagne*
*Pass the Bordeaux, let the Chablis flow*
*Let's have the champagne again.'*
Words by Adrian Mitchell, co-author with John Fox of *The Raising of the Titanic*.

The Raising
of the Titanic,
Welfare State
International, UK,
LIFT'83, Regent's
Canal Dock,
Limehouse Basin.
Photo: © Theodore
Shank.

So sang the Captain wining and dining a wealthy passenger aboard the *Titanic*, which was perched on a high stage made of freight containers beside East London's Limehouse Basin, in *The Raising of the Titanic*. This LIFT'83 commission was being undertaken by Welfare State International (WSI), experts in large-scale community celebrations and not for nothing known worldwide as 'Engineers of the Imagination' and also 'Pathological Optimists'. This was to be an outlandishly ambitious piece of open-air theatre, devised and acted out in a six-week residency with the local Limehouse community. The event was to prove memorable in capturing a moment in time, both in London's alternative theatre history and in the fast-vanishing world of traditional Docklands.

A year on from a Falklands War, in which Exocet missiles had effortlessly burnt up Britain's modern aluminium-built ships, the idea was to use the story of the 1912 *Titanic* disaster in which 1,513 people died – disproportionately more from the working classes – as a metaphor for the sinking of Western capitalist civilisation over the subsequent seventy years. In the Thatcher years of the early 80s the East End was the site of rampant market-led developments, pitching the tallest buildings of Mammon against the worst housing and poorest neighbourhoods in the country. Alongside the boarded-up houses by the Regent's Canal Dock Basin, warehouses were selling as 'yuppie' penthouse flats and the murky dock waters were shortly to be transformed into an exclusive marina to which the local population would be denied access.

*The Raising of the Titanic* was, in WSI Director John Fox's words, 'part theatre, part encampment, part community gathering, market, social dance, pageant and regatta . . . an allegorical political and mythological extravaganza.'[2] A team of sixty WSI performers, technicians, engineers, makers, designers and cooks parked their caravans and old army bell tents by the water's edge and set about recruiting 150 locals, with the help of the Limehouse-based community-arts company, the A-team, to create an event that would run for twelve nights. The climax of the show was to be a dramatic emergence out of the dock water of the great hulk of the *Titanic*. The challenge was to create a structure that would reliably perform every night. But one week before the opening, the stern of the converted iron barge succumbed to the pressure of water and the team (which included the ingenious inventor Tim Hunkin) had to work round the clock to construct a new 70-foot-long skeleton ship which could be sunk and then safely hauled up again by a massive mobile crane on the dockside, all to create the theatrical 'reveal' that Fox was looking for: a huge ship, simultaneously ghostly and solid, rising from the deep.

It was opening night and the fairground site was buzzing with a sense of survivalist adventure. To the music of the Titanic Syncopators, an open-air market of lifeboat stalls selling freshly grilled shark steaks greeted an audience milling happily about, while a cast of perambulating characters on the dockside (the Limehouse Club Players) treated them to a menu of performance entrées: the Purser, the Captain, the first-class passengers, the working class 'clichéd cleaning ladies' and 'Three Men in a Boat Versus the Ice-Queen Berg'. The allegory of the *Titanic* story was insinuated into every detail of the sideshow, down to Marcel Steiner who, in the tradition of English music-hall, had converted his Smallest Theatre in the World (a two-seater proscenium-arch theatre built on a motorcycle sidecar) into a miniature version of the *Titanic* (he checked your teeth to decide which class of passenger you were).

A call from two men in a small boat signalled the discovery of a ship's funnel emerging from the water and people moved to the dockside to watch the long arm of the motorised crane ceremoniously winch the skeleton *Titanic* up from the depths. With the light fading across Limehouse Basin, the audience took their seats in a canopied auditorium facing a stage-set of stacked shipping freight containers, manoeuvred miraculously into place by forklift trucks. Comic tableaux of *Titanic* life unfolded. On the upper deck were the Captain's Dinner Party and a Fancy Dress Ball; on the lower decks the Miraculous Farce of the Five Chinese Stowaways, the Revenge of the Lift Boys and the Routing of the Black-Faced Stokers. Finally came the Shooting of the Albatross of Hope, the Singing Icebergs and the Hand of Fate. A blind Moroccan banjo player, Hassan Erraji, accompanied the Lookout Boy's memorably plaintive song (because of a tiff between officers, the lookouts on *Titanic* did not have binoculars). The flailing blind monster of Western Civilisation was slain by a small child and a defiant upbeat tempo took over as a bobbing raft of women and children survivors appeared with their own image of the *Titanic*, a fragile lantern-lit sculpture they refused to hand over to Capitalism's clawing greed.

While the container-set was trucked away and the skeleton wreck set on fire before being lowered sizzling back down into the dark dock water, the spectators rose to their feet and took to the dance floor. Firework icebergs erupted in silver flame, the crane lowered brightly coloured bunting over their heads and, as the dance finished, a flotilla of flickering lanterns floated gently across the dock.[3]

The show made pathological optimists of us all, although its comic variety-style and political didacticism might now seem naïve. Even so, it proved prescient in terms of social change in London. Today, traffic thundering east on the A1203 from Tower Bridge to the Isle of Dogs tunnels beneath Limehouse Basin, emerging again towards Tilbury Docks and the sea. Canary Wharf has been established as the heart of London's new East End and the *A-Z* maps can barely keep pace with the rapidly developing Eastern Thames Corridor. London's pitch for the 2012 Olympic Games rested on a massive investment in Stratford East and its surroundings.

In terms of social engagement, *The Raising of the Titanic* in August 1983 set a precedent for LIFT. In his book *Eyes on Stalks* John Fox shrugs at the critics who 'refused to understand the pairing of performance and participation'. 'Had they ever experienced events in a temple, say in Bali, where the market, the priests, the shadowplays, the mythical representations and the social music are all fused together, or imagined the way things were in our own medieval cathedrals?'

By the end of the LIFT'83 Festival, we were technically bankrupt. We had overstretched ourselves and had been over-optimistic about an extra grant from the GLC that had so far failed to materialise. Our lawyers, Harbottle and Lewis, advised us to close down our fledgling business. Although the Arts Council of Great Britain had refused us financial support (on the grounds that they existed to support British, not 'foreign', work) we found ourselves owing money to several of their existing British clients – including Welfare State International. In a meeting to advise the Arts Council of our dilemma, we were frank with our options: wind LIFT up after only two Festivals or push on to fundraise post-festival, a notoriously hard thing to do. To our confusion, we were offered large gins and tonics on our arrival at 5 Piccadilly by two rather impish senior officers, Tony Field and Richard Pulford (both of whom had been seen dancing the week before down at Limehouse Basin). They withdrew to deliberate, leaving us with the gin. On their return they announced: 'Consider those creditors of yours that are clients of ours, no longer your creditors.' We thought we were drunk. In one sentence, and with no application forms, our deficit had effectively been reduced by around £20,000, signalling that there was a whisper of support for LIFT in the corridors of arts-subsidy power. Months later the GLC finally granted us an additional £70,000 and in a flurry of pre-Christmas cheque signing we paid all our debts. We did everything in our power to make sure the next Festival made a profit. Which it did. After the abolition of the GLC the Arts Council gave us full support, taking LIFT on as a revenue client.

## Bishopsgate, Spitalfields and Brick Lane

Fiona Templeton, USA/UK, *YOU – The City*, LIFT'89

Originally created in Manhattan, Fiona Templeton's *YOU – The City*, staged by LIFT in London in July 1989, was advertised as a 'city-wide play for an audience of one' and offered a depth and intensity of experience that affected many of the 250 people who saw it. Clive Fisher from *Punch* compared it to 'other difficult and unreal situations . . . like a driving test'. Robert Hewison in *The Sunday Times* wrote, 'to record that I became very angry and felt profoundly shaken is to acknowledge how successful the piece had been.'

Working with UK producers Artsadmin to commission the show with London actors, we opted for a location in the city's square mile that

YOU – The City,
Fiona Templeton,
New York, 1988.
Photo: Zoe Beloff.
LIFT staged the
show in London in
1989.

incorporated the affluence of Bishopsgate alongside the old fruit and veg
market of Spitalfields and the Bengali housing estates and Huguenot weavers'
houses around Brick Lane. Audience members, referred to throughout as
'clients' or 'YOU', made appointments for the show at ten-minute intervals and
were accompanied through scripted encounters by a series of sixteen
performers, who conducted them between indoor and outdoor locations
around the city. The script, a sustained poetic monologue in which every
sentence involved the word 'you', allowed for both interruption and
improvisation. Some clients responded to the rhetorical questions with gusto:
others more shyly wondered what was expected of them.

You arrive, at the start, at your appointed hour at a chartered accountant's
office opposite Liverpool Street Station, where you wait in reception to be seen,
along with other visitors, real – or apparently real. You complete a questionnaire
and are then summoned to the boardroom by a brusque female business
executive, who fires questions at you, regardless of your attempts to answer or
not. She seems to know all about you anyway. She ushers you out crisply ('We
will keep you on file') and takes you down by lift to the street where you have a
chance collision with a woman who greets you like a friend. She kisses you on
both cheeks, then leads you by the arm down a side alley.

And so your journey continues over two hours. Is this woman a member of
the public or a performer, a shop assistant, a prostitute or an undercover

agent? She seems to be implicating you in some kind of secret operation, the nature of which you can't quite fathom: 'You have to be careful – did they say we want you to? I said, how well do you pay? We don't know you. You don't know us.' She sidles into a peep-show doorway and disappears, leaving you with the words: 'Maybe you think you're innocent. You should talk to someone.' On the doorstep is a third performer, staring you in the eye.

From here you go on to meet a tramp who looks up from rooting in some old crates in the market to wave and sing at you, and then you're taken to sit briefly in an Indian restaurant before being delivered to the steps of a church where a priest-like man intones words of sanctuary and death. When a black cab draws up beside you, it's made clear you should climb in. As you settle in the back seat you catch the driver's eye in the rear-view mirror. He picks up the monologue and pulls away. A city narrative is unfolding, centred entirely on your involvement and presence. You feel as though you're in a film in which you've landed the main part.

You are delivered to a Georgian house in Heneage Street, where you catch a fleeting glimpse of another client. After a series of phone calls to the house, mention of a foreign spy and some split-second timing, you return to the deserted sports site you walked across earlier. The show reaches a climax when you become the object of an ingenious handover that implicates you in the conspiracy of the action. Someone is approaching from the opposite direction and you realise it is a client from an earlier stage in the play and that they believe *you* are the next performer. Initiated into the game of the show, how will you respond? Are you audience or actor?

The edge to YOU – *The City* is the chance that you might be sidetracked by a 'real' encounter at any moment – called to account by a member of the public, even stopped by the police. It's not long before you suspect that everyone on the street is a performer, as in a sense they are.

The day I (*LN*) saw the show, I found myself sitting alone for a few moments in a Tower Hamlets council estate playground surrounded by small Bangladeshi children playing noisily in coloured party clothes. It may have been a Muslim festive day. I was mesmerised by the brightness of the girls' dresses; it was as though they had all been fitted with theatre costumes. I was the play's centre, and the entire city of London buzzed with an infinite number of potential scenarios – any one of which could move into focus as I continued on the journey.

Choreographed with a precision worthy of MI5, YOU – *The City* required a production team hidden along the route with walkie-talkies to make sure no one wandered off in the wrong direction. It also demanded the complicity of local people and businesses. Actors became involved in street dramas of their own. Nevenka Koprivsek, playing the 'spy', had eggs thrown at her by residents who thought she was a prostitute collecting her clients from a black cab and escorting them, one after the other, across the park. Children, by contrast, were quick to cotton on to the theatricality and became zealous allies in guarding the actors' anonymity and moves.

*YOU – The City* taught us to be ambitious about blurring the boundaries between fiction and reality in a festival, and influenced much UK site-specific work that followed it. The entire urban landscape could be imagined as a play unfolding, allowing people to extend their sense of connection with their own city. A critic who first saw the play in New York recognised that it dissolved the conventional distance between observer and observed. 'I felt silly taking notes,' he said. 'Took a few anyway. Smiled a lot. I had become what the piece was about.'

## Battersea Park – River Thames – Brockwell Park – Victoria Park

**Theatre of Fire:** Els Comediants, Spain, *The Devils*, LIFT'85; Groupe F, France, *Birds of Fire*, LIFT'95; Groupe F, France, UK artists and pupils from Stockwell Park School, *The Factory of Dreams*, Out of LIFT'96; Group F, France, *Garden of Light*, LIFT'01

At the closing ceremony of the Barcelona Olympics in 1992, when Christophe Berthonneau's pyrotechnic finale shook the stadium with 15 tonnes of gunpowder exploding in six minutes, the Governor of Asturias turned to King Juan Carlos to ask, 'What did you give him? This year's defence budget?'

Whilst festivals in Spain fill entire village squares with fire and fireworks as a matter of course, in Britain firework events such as Bonfire Night are increasingly managed on our behalf, and in public spaces we are effectively cordoned off from any contact with danger. LIFT discovered its life-long love affair with fire through Els Comediants – a Barcelona company rooted in the traditions of popular Catalan celebration and carnival. We invited them to perform *The Devils,* in Battersea Park in July 1985, and had to learn fast about firework safety in order to secure a licence for an event billed as 'a heathen drama with demons, dragons and the heat of hell itself'. Pacing the route of the show down the wide avenues of the park with the Fire Officer, LIFT's Production Manager Jonathan Bartlett prayed he wouldn't object to the *bombetes* and *candelas* that laced the canopy of the trees above his head. Fortunately the Fire Officer was wearing a peaked cap and never thought to look above tree-trunk level. What would he have said if he'd known that a band of LIFT volunteers were being trained on the other side of the lake to *correr con el foc* (literally, to run with the fireworks)? Issued with whistles and black wool berets (so their hair would not scorch), they would create a band around the artists as they zigzagged through the crowds.

By sunset, 10,000 people were gathered in anticipation as devils drifted in boats across the lake towards the shore, then disembarked and led the way through woods now erupting with explosions and smoke. A collective demonic energy surged through the crowd. 'Man, woman and miserable mortals, we come to awaken the darkness. Do you want to dance?' the Chief Demon cried. 'Yes!' came the ecstatic response. And as capering demons threw fire-crackers at our feet and dragons emerged from the derelict pump house with nostrils flaming, we were urged forward beneath the Devil's flag. 'Fire, fire, fire!' chanted a British public, the heathen released, along with an immense good will. The revelry over, a peace descended and the crowds vanished into the night. Was this what was meant by catharsis?

Christophe Berthonneau went on to join forces with Els Comediants to close the Barcelona Olympics and anyone who witnessed his Eiffel Tower Millennium celebrations will understand the sensual, gentle grace that sets his work apart. His first visit to LIFT was in June 1995 with *Birds of Fire,* which featured two magnificent flaming birds floating like mythical phoenixes on barges down the River Thames between Westminster and Hungerford Bridges. Curtains of fire danced around County Hall and streams of gold and yellow spirals fell to earth, mirrored in the water.

On the back of such success we proposed an experiment to Christophe and his company, Groupe F. Tony Fegan had joined LIFT in 1993 and had begun to forge ideas about innovative partnerships between young people in London and international artists. It was from this work that Out of LIFT grew – a new kind of Festival between Festivals. We wanted to challenge head-on the prejudices that surrounded theatre for young people, which is often marginalised and poorly resourced. Out of LIFT was to operate like any other LIFT Festival, commissioning, producing and presenting a season of work which would be original and daring. Would Christophe consider transforming 120 Brixton 13 to 14-year-olds into fire artists?

Against a history of the Brixton riots, and further community disturbances in response to the death of Cherry Groce, the idea of wilfully combining local

*The Devils*,
Els Comediants,
Spain, LIFT'85,
Battersea Park.
Courtesy of
Els Comediants.

teenagers and fire seemed a risk too far. On a freezing day in November 1995 we climbed the hill in Brockwell Park, South London, to survey a wintry landscape and asked Christophe if the park inspired him. He liked the idea of working with young people, since he had left school himself at the age of 14, believing he could learn more that way. He said he envisaged a 'dream factory'. The next day Tony Fegan mustered his courage and asked Tony Le Mothe, the headmaster of Stockwell Park School, a man he had never met before, if he would release the whole of his Year 9 pupils for six months to work with LIFT

*The Factory of Dreams*, participants from Stockwell Park School, Out of LIFT'96. Photo: Michael J. O'Brien Photography.

artists across five curriculum disciplines: Design and Technology, Food Science, Textiles, Visual Arts and Music. Expectations of achievement for the 800 pupils of Stockwell Park – labelled disparagingly as a London 'sink' school, in a catchment area that included families from over forty different ethnic backgrounds – were low, even among its own teachers and students. The staff were at full stretch preparing for one of the new OFSTED inspections, but Tony Le Mothe recognised that LIFT's ethos was to promote intercultural cooperation in imaginative and risky ventures and was prepared to test the rhetoric. He wanted to see if an international artist of Christophe's calibre could be a catalyst for change, both for the pupils as individuals and for the school's reputation. But first he had to set about convincing a group of exhausted and disbelieving teachers that the project could be integrated into the recently introduced National Curriculum 'learning objectives' and then be transformed into a site-specific piece of fire-theatre for 5,000 spectators.

Christophe brought certain principles of 'liberty' to the project. He insisted that the ideas and vision for *The Factory of Dreams* should be created by the pupils themselves and that they should also be free *not* to perform if they didn't wish to. This particular freedom challenged even the considerable experience of Tony Fegan and the project's four London-based artists, Sofie Leyton, Ali Zaidi, Gavin O'Shea and Dominic Campbell, who throughout the project feared they might get only five performers for the final show. An initially scoffing group of 13-year-olds were asked what their dreams were. If they were prepared to sketch them on paper and give them sculptural form, Christophe promised they would finally be forged in fire. Intrigued, the pupils were drawn into the story of the eighth century Chinese cook who discovered gunpowder when he threw saltpetre on to his wood fire by mistake. Christophe talked of fire as both friend and destructive foe. He made a miniature boat to demonstrate in a classroom sink how the thrust of a firework is created through confined molecular activity transformed into energy and motion. Certain pupils not averse to throwing hammers around the classroom were encouraged to build wax patterns for delicate paper lanterns.

It was by no means an easy journey. Musician Gavin O'Shea was often left alone to work with pupils with little or no music-making equipment. But many staff went out of their way to help and week by week stories and artefacts appeared; by May Christophe was working on a fire-text for the show. The score would be sung by 13-year-old Grace, who, in declaring her dreams, said she wanted to become an architect. Her 'house' featured as one of the show's giant sculptures. If she couldn't be an architect, she said pragmatically, she would get on with her other dream – a singing career. The summer saw a frenzy of activity on the grass outside the classrooms. Beaten metal inspired by Pakistani tin art, batik lanterns and icons made of fibreglass and tissue took shape, representing dream images of footballers, brides, a flying Pegasus, houses and globes (page 150). One hundred and twenty pupils wielding chisels, welding equipment, rivets and pots of dye worked together to meet the performance deadline. Tony Fegan tirelessly drilled and choreographed sixty of the pupils in the playground, shouting through a loudhailer and watched with increasing fascination by the Head and nearly every member of the teaching staff. Brochures were out on the streets and the press were picking up on the story: 'Brixton youngsters prepare a fiery festival,' ran the ambivalent headline. Two boys sitting out on the grass in earnest discussion about the merits of their school were heard to say, 'At least after *Factory of Dreams* people won't be able to say Stockwell Park School is crap.'

A budget of £75,000 – a large sum of money for 'youth arts' – was raised, to our surprise, with relative ease, the event fitting in with the urban regeneration initiatives of the Brixton City Challenge. Capitalising on the project's educational potential, LIFT held an early Business Arts Forum seminar in a classroom. Senior managers from companies such as British Airways and SRU Group considered the connections between the global challenges of their own

*The Factory of Dreams*, Groupe F, UK artists and pupils from Stockwell Park School, France/UK, Out of LIFT'96, Brockwell Park. Photo: Michael J. O'Brien Photography.

businesses and the cohesion of a school's multilingual community. In a session that addressed the problems of building a shared vision and values in a global company, forum participants sat at school desks being taught by 13-year-olds (now experts) to beat out their dreams in tin with tiny hammers.

At the opening reception on the evening of 15 June, LIFT's Chair, Helena Kennedy QC, and Headmaster Tony Le Mothe balanced on chairs beside Brockwell Lido swimming pool to make speeches about hope and transformation, while the sixty or so performers descended on the pool's changing rooms to get ready. The theory of molecular activity in a confined space was about to be put to the test. As they trooped out carrying metal standards of flying horses, rockets and angels to face the thousands of people flooding into the park, music drifted across the evening air. They cleared the brow of the hill to a pulsating sound score that they had recorded themselves: there was no going back. A weary but elated Gavin O'Shea observed: 'I saw the group stop dead when they saw the members of the audience, then draw a deep breath and move forward as one.' As the show reached its spectacular finale, one young performer stood in awe as fireworks exploded overhead. Removing his baseball cap, he bowed his head. Another, who had steadfastly attempted to sabotage other people's work throughout the preparation, was so moved by its success that he wept openly back in the changing rooms. On the Monday morning before Christophe and his team from Groupe F left for France, every one of the 120 pupils involved came into school to give him a present of thanks.

Once described as a 'flaming French wizard', Christophe Berthonneau's pyrotechnical achievements, and those of Groupe F, have been seen in many major cities, including at the opening and closing of the 2004 Olympic Games in Athens. It still isn't easy to gain a licence in Britain for a theatre of fire, even when Christophe is lighting the fuse. Groupe F's LIFT'01 commission, *Garden of Light,* was almost derailed at the eleventh hour when a sound engineer insisted that music levels in Victoria Park be calibrated throughout the thirty-minute show with a large decibel-measuring tool. As a gathering fraternity of council officers waited for the machine to register its potential death knell on the show, I (*LN*) looked at the faces of an expectant public waiting for the event to begin and wondered why a big machine hadn't been invented to calibrate joy, so that one could wheel it into public places and denounce them, saying, 'There is not enough joy here.'

## National Maritime Museum, Greenwich Park

Hanoi Water Puppets, Vietnam; Emergency Exit Arts and Greenwich Primary
Schools, UK, *Sang Song – River Crossing*, LIFT'93

In the summer of 1993 the grounds of the National Maritime Museum in
Greenwich reverberated to the ballads, flutes and clashing cymbals of the Hanoi
Water Puppets, a 1,000-year-old tradition originally developed as a celebration
of the harvest in the paddy fields of Vietnam. Enacting the myths and history of
their ancient culture, the puppeteers, immersed waist-high in water, were
hidden behind an ornate screen from where they manipulated the richly
lacquered puppets on long rods. Dragons burst up through the surface of the
water spitting fireworks, buffaloes collided and warring armies on horseback set
fire to villages.

Later that week, within the same grounds, 250 local school children, many
of Vietnamese origin, performed *Sang Song – River Crossing*. This, by contrast,
was a contemporary tale featuring the experiences of the Vietnamese community in Greenwich and recalling their life in Vietnam, the perilous voyage across
the seas and their search for a sense of belonging in London. A local company,
Emergency Exit Arts, had been commissioned by LIFT to work closely with the
Vietnam Refugee Project in Greenwich schools to realise this ambitious re-
enactment of the memories, fears and hopes of a recently arrived community.
In geography lessons entire classrooms were given over to the exploration of
living in the two countries, with huge murals which contrasted everyday life on
the Mekong Delta and the Red River with that lived beside the River Thames.
In maths, travel shops were set up selling tickets and holidays to Vietnam. In
playgrounds the traditional handkerchief dances and music of Vietnam evolved
seamlessly into the rap dances of 1990s Britain, while in school halls the four
mythical beasts of Vietnam – the Unicorn, the Golden Turtle, the Dragon and
the Phoenix – came to life as giant papier mâché puppets.

Carnivalesque though the eventual performance was, however, the politics
were a minefield. Whilst the Vietnamese community was eager to create a high-
profile celebration of their culture within an international London-wide festival,
they expressed strong reservations about being linked with the Vietnamese
government-sanctioned Hanoi Water Puppets. This was the very government
from which they had fled in two waves of migration, the first in 1975 after the fall
of Saigon to the Communist North, the second in 1979 when the Chinese
invasion caused the exodus of many Vietnamese with Chinese family
connections. Li Vong, the Team Leader of the Vietnam Refugee Project, made

*Hanoi Water
Puppets*, Vietnam,
LIFT'93, Greenwich
Park. Photo:
Guy de Lahaye.

his case with passion to the elders, many of whom had fought in the war
against the Communists. 'We can't deny the political issues,' he argued, 'but
neither must we deny our culture. Young people need to know about this
unique form of puppetry, it is their heritage, something they can be proud of.'
After much debate, a solution was reached. A letter went out to all participants:
'We wish to make it clear to the refugee community that although the visit of the
Hanoi Water Puppets has acted as an inspiration for *Sang Song*, the Hanoi
Water Puppet company will not be involved. *Sang Song* is a self-contained
project taking place separately from the visiting puppeteers.'

In the event, though no official link existed, strong personal contacts were
naturally forged. The classical colonnades of the Queen's House officially
separating the two sites became the main gathering-point between
performances, a neutral space beyond the landmines of world politics and
historic antagonisms. Over 3,000 people from across London attended this

*Sang Song –
River Crossing,
Emergency Exit
Arts and
Greenwich
Primary Schools,
UK, LIFT'93,
Greenwich Park.
Photo: Simon
Annand.*

celebration of Vietnamese culture and many young Vietnamese who had
previously not wished to draw attention to their origins began to use their
Vietnamese names. For once, here was a positive celebratory story about their
community, far removed from the daily issues of unemployment, crime and
racism. The Maritime Museum in all its imposing British colonial splendour was
imbued with a sense of contemporary history as a recently arrived community
inhabited it to enact their story.

Shortly afterwards the Vietnam Refugee Project changed its name to the
Greenwich Vietnam Community Centre. 'The community had to move on,' Li
Vong explained. 'We are aiming to integrate, to look for equality rather than a
special separate status. Many of our young people, though still retaining
aspects of their Vietnamese culture, have no memory of the war. They are not
refugees, they are British and they feel they are Londoners.'

## Paddington Basin – Theatre Royal Stratford East

Keith Khan, UK, *Flying Costumes, Floating Tombs*, LIFT'91; Keith Khan, UK, *Moti Roti Puttli Chunni*, LIFT'93

'My work has been informed by the cultures of my native Trinidad, as well as Pakistan, India and Britain,' explained Keith Khan, director, with choreographer

*Flying Costumes, Floating Tombs*, Keith Khan, UK, LIFT'91, Paddington Basin. Photo: Michael J. O'Brien Photography.

H. Patten, of *Flying Costumes, Floating Tombs*, a large-scale outdoor commission for LIFT'91. Historically grounded in both Trinidadian carnival and the Trinidadian festival of Hosay and the Muslim festival of Muharrum, which marks the death of the two grandsons of the prophet Muhammed, Hussein and Hassan, *Flying Costumes, Floating Tombs* celebrated how cultures transform themselves as they cross continents, epitomising what the cultural thinker Homi Bhabha calls the 'hybrid cosmopolitanism' of our world cities. Embedded in the pulse of contemporary multicultural London, the performance drew in over 200 African and Asian dancers, drummers and steel-pan players, deaf signing choirs, and performers from local community groups and schools to animate the then derelict site of Paddington Basin in West London. Crane drivers, provided by prospective site developers Trafalgar House, hoisted green and red *tazias,* 70-foot-high sculptural banners, over the crowds, as a barge sailed silently by bearing white ghostlike figures. Two women – one African, the other Indian – processed along the waterway, pulling behind them two white 'colonial' children entangled in their long, braided hair. *Flying Costumes* was a key artistic moment for Keith, marking the beginning of a partnership with fellow artist Ali Zaidi and providing a template eleven years later for his Commonwealth Celebration in the Mall, commissioned on the occasion of the Queen's Golden Jubilee in 2002 and watched by millions around the world.

For the following Festival in 1993, Keith, with designer Ali Zaidi, created Britain's first Bollywood musical, *Moti Roti Puttli Chunni*, a gloriously melodramatic tale of corruption, love and intrigue, set in London's East End and involving two generations of a British Asian family (page 65). Performed in English, Hindi and Urdu and starring Bombay film star Nitish Bharadwaj as the dashing villain, the performance moved effortlessly from film to a high theatricality of revolving stages,  playback songs and elaborate dance routines, taking us from Brick Lane to downtown Bombay and back again. At the Theatre Royal Stratford East, local Asian audiences roared their appreciation. Robert Hewison writing in *The Sunday Times* said, 'The make-up of London audiences – Caribbean, Asian, Anglo-Saxon – is international, in itself. All LIFT had to do was to give it theatrical expression', acknowledging that the Festival was as much an exploration of London as of the world, and a far cry from the 'grand, rather formal events' of LIFT's predecessor, Peter Daubeny's World Theatre Seasons.

## Lyric Studio, Hammersmith – Albany Empire, Deptford – Riverside Studios, Hammersmith – Watermans Arts Centre, Brentford – Tricycle Theatre, Kilburn – Theatre Royal Stratford East

**South Africa:** Bahamutsi Theatre Company, *Dirty Work* and *Gangsters*, LIFT'85; Vusisizwe Players, *You Strike the Woman, You Strike the Rock*, LIFT'87; The Market Theatre Company, *Starbrites*, LIFT'91; The Market Theatre Company and Theatre Connections, *Jozi Jozi*, LIFT'95; The Market Theatre Company, *The Suit*, LIFT'95; William Kentridge and Handspring Puppet Company, *Ubu and the Truth Commission*, LIFT'99; Mehlo Players with the Khulumani Support Group, *The Story I'm About To Tell*, LIFT'99; Phakama, *Be Yourself*, LIFT'99

Throughout most of the 80s, until 1990 when Nelson Mandela was released from prison, the City of London Anti-Apartheid Group maintained a 24-hour picket on the pavement outside South Africa House in Trafalgar Square. In 1994 Mandela became President of South Africa and in June 1996 he stood on the balcony of South Africa House and thanked the quarter of a million cheering Londoners packed into the square for their support in dismantling apartheid.

Few of the relationships LIFT has sustained over the years have had the richness and continuity of that with South Africa. This is undoubtedly a result of the inextricable links between London and South Africa created by the presence in London, from the 1960s onwards, of the African National Congress (ANC) and the political exiles from the inhumanities of the apartheid regime. Barney Simon, co-founder and Director of the Market Theatre Johannesburg, the nerve-centre of artistic protest against apartheid, remembers his walks on Hampstead Heath – 'more essential than the Houses of Parliament' – in the 1960s with Joe Slovo and his wife Ruth First, both prominent members of the resistance movement. In August 1982 Ruth First was assassinated in Mozambique. In the same month the Market Theatre Johannesburg's seminal production of *Woza Albert*, a satire in which a black Christ returns to apartheid South Africa and signs up as an ANC supporter, was invited to London by the Riverside Studios. The play ends in a cemetery where Christ resurrects all the heroes who have given their lives to the struggle, such as Steve Biko, Albert Lutuli and Lilian Ngoyi. Barney Simon had flown to London to be with Joe Slovo. 'I remember Joe's enveloping embrace when we dedicated the opening night of *Woza Albert* to Ruth and added her name to our list of heroes,' he was later to recall at Joe Slovo's funeral in 1995.

In the early days the cultural boycott was firmly in place and every time we invited a company we would first have to seek permission from the London-based cultural spokesman for the ANC, the poet Mongane Wally Serote, an extremely stubborn man with tremendous diplomatic skills (he subsequently became Mandela's first Minister with Portfolio for Culture). Permission was always granted on the grounds that any performance offering insight into the injustices of the apartheid regime played a legitimate role in the struggle.

In 1985 we presented a double bill by Maishe Maponya. *Dirty Work* was a grimly entertaining lecture on security and surveillance; *Gangsters* charted the persecution of a militant poet, beginning with a greasily affable warning from a BOSS (Bureau of State Security) officer and ending with a brutal death in detention. In 1987 the Vusisizwe Players' production of *You Strike the Woman, You Strike the Rock*, directed by Phyllis Kloetz, drew noisily appreciative audiences in community venues across London. It took its title from a song commemorating the 1956 march in Pretoria by 20,000 women protesting against the decision to impose pass laws on black women. The play celebrated the strength of South African women struggling to feed their children and survive in a situation where black exploited black and where 'Everyone is telling you what to do – husbands, Boer, black boss . . . When are you going to say what you want?' Against a black cloth, with minimal props and using their voices as sound effects, they created a resilient image of township life shot through with grace, dignity and a sense of fun. 'Agitprop is seldom so joyful,' commented former Talawa theatre director Yvonne Brewster.

And then on 2 February 1990 President F.W. de Klerk announced the lifting of the thirty-year ban of the ANC, the Pan African Congress and the South African Communist Party. Nine days later Nelson Mandela walked out of prison. In the November of that year I (*RF*) was met at Johannesburg airport by Mannie Manim, co-founder with Barney Simon of the Market Theatre, and the actor John Kani, who was assuming a more active role in the running of the theatre. On the way back into town, driving through the purple-blue jacaranda trees of early summer, Mannie stopped alongside a public swimming pool, visibly moved. 'This is the first time I have seen black kids and white kids swimming together in a public space,' he said.

Later that week the Market Theatre hosted an evening to welcome back artists and cultural activists returning from exile. The lawyer, writer and veteran ANC campaigner Albie Sachs was there, as was the poet Vernon February and Wally Serote. The feeling in the theatre as the audience roared their joy was one of tremendous energy and euphoria. A new era had dawned. Albie Sachs triggered a debate by suggesting that the phrase 'culture as a weapon of struggle' should be banned for five years, that the arts should be released from

*You Strike the Woman, You Strike the Rock*, Vusisizwe Players, South Africa, LIFT'87. Photo: © Ruphin Coudyzer FPPSA.

the stranglehold of apartheid. But, as John Kani of the Market Theatre replied, 'It is understandable that black work is full of pain and anger and has even assumed the title of protest theatre. Actually, it is not protest; it is simply a record of what is happening to people in their everyday lives.'

That month *Starbrites*, a tragicomedy about a down-and-out musician who pulls himself out of the gutter and finds redemption through friendship, had opened at the Market Theatre. Created in collaboration with Handspring Puppet

*The Suit*, The
Market Theatre
Company, South
Africa, LIFT'95.
Photo: © Ruphin
Coudyzer FPPSA.

Company, who filled the stage with shebeen queens, gossiping shadow
puppets and traditional Japanese Bunraku figures, *Starbrites* was hailed as 'a
beginning of the theatre of the new South Africa with its humour and message
of hope, and a departure from the protest, agitprop theatre which has dominated
our stages for so long' (*The Star*, Johannesburg). In London, however, at the
Tricycle Theatre as part of LIFT'91, the production was heavily criticised for its
'reckless optimism'. As one commentator in *The Guardian* noted, 'the violence
that has followed the release of Mandela, especially the violence of blacks
against blacks, now makes the show's euphoric, upbeat message seem
alarmingly facile.' Barney's response was clear. In an interview in *The Guardian*
with the writer and campaigning journalist Mary Benson, one-time secretary to
the young Mandela and key figure in the London anti-apartheid movement, he
defended his choice: 'At all times we live the dichotomy of what we expect and
what we hope. What can we do but find the courage and energy to remember
that human beings cannot live in anticipation of disaster.'

In the spring of 1994 Barney Simon was in London staying in Mary
Benson's tiny, immaculate mansion flat. It was definitely a no-smoking zone
so like a naughty schoolboy Barney climbed on to the windowsill to light up.
He told me about two new productions at the Market, *Jozi Jozi*, a satirical a
cappella musical about the 'not so new' South Africa, where a harsh post-
apartheid reality was beginning to bite, and *The Suit*, which he had directed, a

tragic love story based on a short story by Can Temba, master chronicler of 50s township life. 'Reclaiming the stories and classics from our past, classics which were lost to us through the machinations of apartheid,' was how Barney described the impetus behind *The Suit*. Both productions came to LIFT the following year. Tragically, Barney did not. On the eve of leaving for London, he went into hospital for an unexpected major bypass operation and died several days later, though not without hearing on the phone from his bed the rapturous applause that greeted the opening night of *The Suit* at the Tricycle Theatre. That adaptation has now become a classic in its own right; five years on Peter Brook created his own production (presented by LIFT and the Young Vic in 2001), openly acknowledging his debt to township theatre and the work of Barney Simon and the Market Theatre.

'God created men because he liked to hear stories,' Barney used to say, quoting his favourite Hasidic saying. For him, story-telling and listening to stories was 'as organic to our survival as oxygen'. A few weeks before his death, in an interview in Stockholm, he talked about the role of the theatre in a post-apartheid era:

> *'We live at a time desperately in need of understanding, repentance and reconciliation . . . we are still living with the toxins of apartheid . . . in South Africa there has been a change in legislation, not a change in human hearts . . . And I know that theatre is a great educator of the human heart because true theatre moves human beings into empathy when witnessing the lives of others.'*[4]

In 1999 LIFT presented a trilogy of productions, which in their very different ways dealt with the 'toxins of apartheid'. *Ubu and the Truth Commission*, conceived by the artist William Kentridge with Handspring Puppet Company, and *The Story I'm About To Tell*, by the Mehlo Players, both highlighted the contradictions of the Truth and Reconciliation Commission (TRC). The TRC had been set up with the mandate to create an environment for national reconciliation, through retrieving the lost histories of the victims of apartheid, making reparation to those who suffered and providing amnesty to the perpetrators for acts which were demonstrably political in purpose. The ironies were legion: amnesty as incentive for full disclosure, the public airing of private loss and grief as a road to healing, and reconciliation for a nation that had kept a generous distance from its own truths wherever possible. 'The TRC raises the question of truth versus justice,' Kentridge explained. 'Ideally you would have both. This way you try to find out all the truth at the price of prosecution . . . As people give more and more evidence of the things they have done, they get closer to amnesty and it gets more and more intolerable that these people be given amnesty.' In his multimedia production of *Ubu and the Truth Commission*, with its evidence-guzzling crocodiles and animations of violent metamorphoses intercut by news footage, the medieval Polish dictator of Alfred Jarry's absurdist play *Ubu Roi* becomes a government torturer in apartheid South Africa. The quiet, hesitant testimonies of the gnarled, roughly hewn puppets are in moving contrast to the brutal, underpanted Ubu who bellows ominously before setting off to win his amnesty at the TRC, 'Our reign of terror was no reign of error!'

Put together by cultural activist and journalist Bobby Rodwell, *The Story I'm About To Tell* was a very different event, featuring six performers on a bare stage – three professional actors, together with three members of the Khulumani Support Group for survivors of human-rights abuses. One mother tells us how she was witness to her son's assassination by a bomb, another activist describes how she was repeatedly raped in police detention. At the end of each performance the audience entered into a discussion with the company. The desire to exchange experiences, to know more, was intense, the quality of the exchanges raw and honest. 'How can there be grand cartharsis when you are sifting through remnants of the brutality the people have suffered?' asked one member of the audience with incredulity.

The third production, *Be Yourself*, was created by Phakama, an arts-exchange programme to build creative skills amongst young people, artists and educationalists from South Africa and Britain. Initiated by LIFT following a visit by Lucy Neal to the Grahamstown Festival in the days after South Africa's first democratic elections in 1994, Phakama – whose name has its origin in a Xhosa word meaning 'lift yourself up' – set out to explore new models for artistic process rooted in personal encounters and stories.

In July 1996, at the invitation of Phyllis Kloetz, Tony Fegan, LIFT's Education Director, led a team of four artist practitioners to Benoni, Johannesburg, to run a theatre-making process with thirty teachers and sixty young people representing each of South Africa's cultural communities. The cultural diversity of the London team (Ali Zaidi was Pakistani British, Beverley Randall Black British, Andrew Siddal English and Tony himself Irish) was critical in signalling to the South African participants the positive reality of working across cultural divides at a time when South Africa was building the 'rainbow nation'. This early encounter between artist tutors and young people laid the groundwork for a pioneering exchange of skills and ideas that would flourish in the years that followed.

*Ubu and the Truth Commission*, William Kentridge and Handspring Puppet Company, South Africa, LIFT'99.
Photo: © Federico Pedrotti, Munich.

*Be Yourself*,
Phakama,
UK/South Africa,
LIFT'99. Photo:
Michael J. O'Brien
Photography.

In 1999, after a series of further exchange visits, *Be Yourself* was created. The starting point was a guided tour of London for the fifteen South African participants by their hosts, Lewisham Youth Theatre. Along with trips to Big Ben, the Tower of London and Notting Hill, they also visited the site of the black teenager Stephen Lawrence's murder in Eltham, South London. It was a shock to the South Africans to realise that their London peer group lived with similar realities of racial hatred and violence. The group set to work creating a performance about the city. London's landscape was presented as a meandering village of brightly lit tin-foil buildings along the River Thames, interconnecting with the rivers of South Africa and setting the scene for an evening in which the Cockney chimes of *Maybe It's Because I'm a Londoner* sung from the upper balconies of the theatre were offset by *Shosholoza*, a popular rugby song derived from a Zulu song about migrating people travelling by steam train. The story of Stephen Lawrence was movingly recounted through the eyes of the South Africans, witnessed on the opening night by his father, Neville Lawrence. When the cast came into the audience with bowls of water offering to wash our hands we felt as if we were present at some kind of ritual atonement.

'We can't help what happened in the past. But we, as a new generation, can make the future,' declared 17-year-old Chevonne Nel, at a reception at South Africa House for all three productions, held by Cheryl Carolus, the first female black High Commissioner for South Africa in London. At the end of Cheryl Carolus's welcoming speech, in which she acknowledged the pain of the past, another Phakama member, Pogosi Mogwera, began to sing *Shosholoza*. Within a few seconds it was taken up by the rest of the group who then formed a human train joined by the other guests, adding yet another dimension to the rooms still displaying the tribal ethnological Boer paintings of a colonial age.

Phakama UK continues to develop its work across Southern Africa, in London and, more recently, in India and Mauritius, as part of a network of self-organised groups whose central philosophy is that everyone, irrespective of age, experience or culture, has equally something to give and gain from each other. After LIFT'99, South African Phakama members were invited to stage the first cultural event on Robben Island to celebrate Freedom Day, to mark the island's transition from being a place of commemoration to one of participatory celebration. In London Phakama is now working with recently arrived young unaccompanied refugees from places of conflict across the world – the Balkans, Iraq, Sierra Leone, Liberia and Somalia – developing skills and creating performances across the city, rooted in the experiences and dreams of the participants as they navigate their way through a new life.

Equating a sense of art with a sense of community is nothing new, but in a world of exile and of conflict perhaps Phakama, pioneering a theatre rooted in participation, holds some critical answers for a theatre of the future.

1.  Homi K. Bhabha, 'Re-inventing Britain: A Manifesto', in *British Studies Now*, 9, April 1997.
2.  John Fox, *Eyes on Stalks* (London, Methuen, 2002).
3.  For further details see Baz Kershaw and Tony Coult, *Engineers of the Imagination* (London, Methuen, 1983; revised 1990).
4.  Mary Benson, *Athol Fugard and Barney Simon: Bare Stage, A Few Props, Great Theatre* (Johannesburg, Ravan Press, 1997).

# London

# BUILDING FROM BELOW

## Naseem Khan

On the face of it, you might think that there was not much call for LIFT in London. After all, the city has long been acknowledged as one of the theatre capitals of the world. It has not been a stranger to incoming overseas productions, from Peter Daubeny's years of the World Theatre Season to Jerome Savary's Grand Magic Circus, from La Mama to the Comédie Française. Nor has it been a stranger to theatrical experiment either. The avant-garde movement that burst over London from the later 1960s on, breaking free of text-based constraints, had spawned a wealth of physical-based and radical theatre – Lumière and Son, Pip Simmons, Naftali Yavin's The Other Theatre, even Steven Berkoff's own experiments with his London Theatre Company.

Like LIFT, this movement had also on occasion explored unusual venues. I remember watching events unfurl in a damp wood in Suffolk, and in a quarry amongst large ice blocks lit by small candles in Burnley; and I have memories of huddling on the pavement in a steady drizzle (the organisers, Artangel, kindly handed out black plastic bin bags) to view shadowy activities taking place inside a bland house in a backstreet in Spitalfields. In the cause of art, I have been ritually insulted, blindfolded, fêted and treated. On one occasion I was even asked to put my hand down Ken Campbell's trousers to see if there was a ferret in them.

So why LIFT? Rose Fenton and Lucy Neal's accounts in this volume of

*Journeys from Jourouvert*, The Costume Designers Club, UK/Europe/ Caribbean, LIFT'93 (page 70). Photo: Richard Ellis

how they lit up London are inspiring, but they need contextualising. The immediate impression is of a determined and somewhat anarchic passion, bolstered by an attractive joyfulness. Why isn't there a machine to calibrate joy, Lucy Neal wonders as they watch – with bated breath – the faceless minions of the council measuring the decibel level of one event to determine whether it is too noisy to go on. If there were indeed such a machine, Fenton and Neal would undoubtedly break it, because their joy clearly goes above the standard decibel level.

But in the midst of all the turmoil and triumph a small question remains. Did LIFT ultimately matter? Or, to be more precise: given that London was not starved of theatre, did LIFT bring something special – added value – to the mix? I believe it has done, for three main reasons. Two of them are seeded throughout Fenton and Neal's texts. The third – to my mind the most important – curiously, is not.

Firstly, it provided an anchor. It is true that London had seen its fair share of international work previously, here and there, off and on. But it had been sporadic and for the most part unpredictable. Events had erupted on the London stage almost without a context. Consider, for instance, the first season of New York's famous La Mama Theatre Club in 1967. Brought over on a shoestring by Ed Berman, they took over and transformed a tiny theatre in Notting Hill (now home to the Ballet Rambert). Going to see their repertoire had an air of a daring discovery, like finding an exotic plant in your mundane backyard. LIFT – to carry on the metaphor – naturalised the plant. The shows they brought over have been determinedly set in London soil. Sometimes that has been a literal and earthy planting – in the churned-up mud of Battersea Park to watch Berthonneau's firework extravaganzas, for one. The location has always mattered. La Mama's siting, by contrast, was almost accidental. Its advantages were that it was cheap and it was available. Other early visitors, like New York's Paper Bag Players, found themselves in traditional spaces of convenience, like the Royal Court and the Young Vic. Admittedly there was an air of subversion to the productions in the Roundhouse – Mnouchkine's Théâtre du Soleil, Savary's Grand Magic Circus – but this was unusual and due to the Roundhouse's nonconformist history.

On the whole, foreign work has sat like a magpie in whatever nest it could find, and that anonymity has essentially affected the experience. Those who attended seasons of Daubeny's World Theatre Season at the Aldwych will doubtless recall the conservatism of the venue, in contrast often to the radicalism of the shows.

*Roman – Photo Tournage*, Royal de Luxe, France, LIFT'89, Broadgate Arena, Liverpool Street. Photo: Michael J. O'Brien Photography. The filming of a photo-romance comic-strip story becomes a nightmare of revenge, burning cars and blood. An early show by the company, who are renowned for their ingenious and epic outdoor performances.

Almost from the start, LIFT married productions and settings. Indeed, it was the vital first step of the process, as these chapters make clear. While that was not the first time, the consistency of the venture in which London has been explored year after year has given it a particular coherence and character. The city has become a major player in the events. The effect has been to change – ever so subtly – our view of familiar places: they present themselves in a new light. I cannot now pass the rather sterile space of Limehouse Basin without having an image of dragon boats skimming across its surface from the far side as twilight deepened on its mauve and shiny water (*Gor Hoi – Crossing the Water,* 1987). King's Cross carries memories of crawling through strange mazes in a disused coach station (*Oráculos,* 1997). And a run-of-the-mill Victorian Gothic church in Vauxhall still contains ghosts of a Gothic performance that took place in it many years back (*Visions of Earthly Paradise,* 1996).

It seems amazing now that London has not had a large-scale arts festival before, on the level of Edinburgh, Singapore or Sydney. Maybe it has not felt it needed it. LIFT has shown what the impact can be – its second major strength. Festivals are a useful format: they provide a heightening of effect and context. The work acquires a sense of occasion and a dynamic that the various parts separately would be hard put to achieve. The format has been useful for several British groups which had established themselves before LIFT arrived – Welfare State International, Bow Gamelan, Pip Simmons and others. They had been staples of the young *Time Out's* Theatre Fringe pages in the early 70s when I was working on its theatre staff and they had already firmed up their artistic vision well before LIFT was devised. But inclusion gave them a platform and a prominence that they had not generally had, and that they totally merited. Ironically, all had appeared and been greatly praised overseas and been invited to perform in many major international festivals – Adelaide, Singapore, Wellington, Sydney. Perhaps a sense of natural hierarchy – a British tendency – had been to blame, with the division of theatre into 'mainstream' or 'West End' and 'fringe'. LIFT started to shift the balance, blur the distinction and open out the divisions.

Good in itself, it also meant that LIFT did not fall prey to the danger that can beset festivals – a type of artistic ghettoisation: the syndrome whereby the caravan hits town and all is carnival; but then it moves on and life reverts. The question of legacy can't be avoided. For a festival to operate at its maximum it needs to create reverberations that in their turn create change. On a certain level, this can simply be a change in individual attitudes, the ending of certain stereotypes. But for it to really work, change needs to be institutionalised. And for that to happen, you need a receptive seedbed – producers who have vision and capability, funding schemes that respond to new work, critics who can recognise it and editors who have the nous to embrace the new. You could argue that this has come about in the case of

*Moti Roti Puttli Chunni*, Keith Khan, UK, LIFT'93 (page 49). Courtesy of Moti Roti.

LIFT – witness the Barbican's BITE seasons, Sadler's Wells, the ICA and an enhanced presence of international work in the capital. Complicite at the National Theatre, let alone the prospect of Mike Leigh with his uncompromising way of working, would have been unthinkable in earlier times.

But there is a third reason – more intangible than the previous arguments about breadth, groundedness and focus. This relates to that vague entity called Zeitgeist. LIFT belonged quintessentially to a particular moment in time and has helped, in its turn, to reinforce its trends, part of an overall opening out of attitudes, forms and theatrical conventions. However, there is one very specific aspect that has particular relevance to London, and this is LIFT's role in the unfolding of cultural diversity and social change.

There is hardly a more crucial and central issue for London than diversity. Even more than a theatrical city, it is a diverse one – every fifth person originally came from somewhere else in the world and 307 languages are reportedly spoken in London's schools. It is historically diverse, going back in time, but it is also a city of more recent settlements and enclaves, from the Italians of Clerkenwell to the Turks of Green Lanes, the Punjabis of Southall to the West Indians of Brixton. The layering this creates is unique. To reach my house in East London, I pass through five distinct worlds on the way back from Liverpool Street Station – the gloss of the city fringes (cappuccino carts on the corner and smart bars), former Huguenot weavers' streets containing the atmospheric old synagogue of Princelet Street, Bengali Brick Lane with its razzmatazz, the small galleries and workshops of young artists and then, finally, as I reach my front door, white working-class Shoreditch with echoes still of Michael Young's classic study, *Family and Kinship in East London*.

LIFT has nudged itself into these nooks and crannies, but not in the manner of wide-eyed explorers or Victorian exploiters and prospectors. It has taken in the demography of the city not as a special category but on an equal footing with all the other work it has commissioned. There is no hint of the exotic about it, and more than a hint of a sharp contemporary perspective. Take the work of Keith Khan, for example. His large processional piece, *Flying Costumes, Floating Tombs,* in 1991, created a vast metaphor for colonialism, combining it with the flamboyance of carnival alongside Paddington Basin. Mischievousness surfaced in his feisty take-off of Bollywood, *Moti Roti Puttli Chunni*. The title of the theatre piece itself pokes fun at convention – the received wisdom of community elders who claim that wives who make thick rotis will also wear scandalously thin veils, and clearly be making eyes at other men through them. Virtuous wives make elegantly slim rotis and keep their eyes decorously down. But the point of it was not fun alone. Moti Roti – as Khan and Ali Zaidi's company came to be called – played with a particular mix. It tossed in whatever influences were in the air as they worked, in the spirit of what Homi Bhabha would recognise as 'vernacular cosmopolitanism': Trinidadian carnival, pop culture, transvestism and gay culture, Bollywood. It echoes the high praise given by Anthony Burgess in his 1970 introduction to that extraordinary book *All About H. Hatterr* by G.V. Desani, an early example of magic realism: 'It is not pure English; it is like the English of Shakespeare, Joyce and Kipling, gloriously impure.' The ease and confidence of the endeavour contrast sharply with earlier attempts by other artists to find cultural marriages. These often ended up as wooden collaborations that shackled both sides of the partnership. Khan, Zaidi and others like them in increasing numbers have created a brand of work that is, as Burgess saw in that early example, distinctively British.

But we could see LIFT's relationship with diversity in a wider perspective still. LIFT arrived on the scene at a very particular point in time. An extraordinary shift was in the process of taking place. The policy of the Arts Council in 1983, as relayed to Rose Fenton and Lucy Neal, was that it could not support 'foreign' work. The general feeling about theatre that came in from outside seemed to typify a cautious and respectful distance. For instance, when you entered the Aldwych for the World Theatre Season in the 1960s, you were handed a set of headphones so that you could hear the simultaneous translation, for all the world as if you were at a UNESCO international conference straining to understand 'the other'. Attitudes towards home-grown diversity or difference – when it was seen at all – were not dissimilar. Compare the responses to the LIFT events. Passionate, opinionated, exploratory, they provided opportunities for audiences to engage in a very different way. And they arguably helped to bring about a change in the way that 'foreign' work and 'foreign' people too were looked at. They started to unpick the old ideas of 'authentic' culture and expose it for the fallacy it really was. The Push festivals in 2001 and 2004 demonstrated this particularly well. Push effectively threw down a gauntlet. Devised by actress Josette Bushell-Mingo and producer Ruth Nutter (ex-administrator of the People Show), it was designed to challenge prevailing stereotypes about black culture, often subscribed to, the pair felt, by black people themselves. Push deliberately took down the barriers by commissioning or discovering work that ran counter to the stereotypes. So it staged both high quality and the unexpected – a circus, for instance, a new opera, a surreal street event outside the Young Vic – and had almost every denizen of black theatre contributing to a long dramatic reading of *The Odyssey*. Why, Bushell-Mingo and Nutter asked determinedly, should black people and black culture accept any limitations?

Behind that question lies a long and pertinent history. It had been building in the wings for several years before LIFT came on the scene, and loosened the rivets that held together the old iron-clad ideas of what is British culture. Immigration had brought Britain many gifts, amongst them work made by artists whose origins were elsewhere but whose living and imagination were based in Britain. At first, in the 1960s, the work was often strongly rooted in, and confined to, distinct communities – Gloria Cameron's popular Caribbean folk group in Brixton; the Polish Club in Kensington, with their plays for both adults and children; Indian festivals like Navratri and Holi that were celebrated in style in various Indian communities, rarely seen by the population outside; and, away from London, round the docks of Liverpool and Cardiff, African seamen had left their mark on old institutions like the Ibo and Yoruba Clubs.

Although these worlds were closed and private, they provided the security and rootedness that nurtured later artists and from which they drew a sense of ballast. From this base came events like the annual Black Book Fairs, the painters and theatre groups, dancers like Akram Khan, who originally had planned a traditional future along the lines of his revered Kathak guru, Pratap Pawar. Multiculturalism has come to have a bad press and been seen as a fragmenting device that keeps communities apart. There is a temptation to see the achievement of high-flyers like Chris Ofili, Anish Kapoor and Yinka Shonibare and to believe that all is well in multiracial Britain: all that is needed for equality is time. But that fails to take into account the way that the 'interculturalism' of Ofili *et al.* evolves, or the speed at which communities themselves integrate and adapt. Multiple identities allow flexibility, but the ease with which they are manipulated differs considerably from case to case.

Multiculturalism in fact means the empowerment of communities, leading to the growth of choice. It can build strengths and perpetuate a healthy sense of heritage, however much its later forms have been adapted and mutated in Britain. It gives the launch pad for change because it develops confidence. As *Guardian* journalist Gary Younge once said, 'Identity . . . is a great place to start and an awful place to finish.' Without an awareness of the importance of identity – multiculturalism – interculturalism would not exist.

The gear shift from communities to mainstream was underway as LIFT emerged. You could say that they were both playing on the same side. While

*QPH*, Sistren Theatre Collective, Jamaica, LIFT'83. Courtesy of Sistren Theatre Collective. The Collective was formed in 1977 by women with a common interest in drama and its use for social change. *QPH* is based on the lives of three real women, Queenie, Pearlie and Hopie, who met at the Kingston Alms House.

London-based groups like Tara Arts, Talawa and Carib Theatre were challenging the convention from within, LIFT brought in work that subverted the old sense of separateness and views on authenticity. Side by side went a renaissance of black visual arts and major shows like *The Other Story* at the Hayward Gallery (1989).

Inevitably it was not an easy gear shift. Britain was in the throes of a radical cultural change and it brought up sharp questions about identity and culture that are still unanswered. A number of them directly affected LIFT. How far could essentialism go? Rose Fenton and Lucy Neal were appreciative of the special qualities that London's black audiences gave to companies like Jamaica's Sistren Theatre Collective. But that needs to be considered carefully, for there is a controversial history. The case of Frank Cousins sticks in the mind. The doughty founder-director of the Dark and Light Theatre in the 1960s, he attributed his theatre company's closure to 'ethnic thinking', if not downright racism. He had been strongly directed by the Arts Council of the day to tour the company to black areas and audiences. It was misguided, to say the least. There was little or no audience base in those areas, the available venues were unequipped community halls and the company's evenings in them – often just one-night stands – needed to have lights and sound brought in and laboriously rigged up in order to turn such functional spaces into semblances of theatres. The Dark and Light might anyhow have run out of steam – who knows? – but the simple equation of race = taste was too easy and unconsidered. If LIFT was to escape that trap, they needed to be alert to it.

In fact, their basic philosophy directed them away from it. Participation was written into their basic brief to themselves. LIFT achieved this by working with communities and artists and taking direction from them. A lot of the time this was invisible work and involved partnerships and collaborations. In 1991, for instance, they were approached by a grouping of London's carnivalists who were distressed that carnival was regarded so often as an excuse for a mammoth party or jump-up and its basic skill and artistry ignored. It was an art form, they argued, and it deserved a platform that would make that plain. LIFT was sympathetic and in LIFT'93 organised a large stage in the middle of Spitalfields Market. But they also brokered a partnership for the Costume Designers Club with the Ghana Dance Ensemble, so the huge and elaborate costumes of *Journeys from Jourouvert* acquired an added dimension (page 60). The strong production of Biyi Bandele's dramatisation of Chinua Achebe's classic novel *Things Fall Apart,* in 1997, had been preceded by two years of discussion, workshops and visits to Nigeria. The director they brought in – Chuck Mike, an African-American who had lived in Nigeria for twenty years – worked with local black British actors to find an idiom that would speak for both cultures. Translation has always been an issue with work of whatever sort that sprang from other cultures and conditions. How can it be assessed and understood? How can meaning be transferred from one language to another? LIFT's regularity meant that it could begin to develop a methodology or series of methodologies to address this long-standing issue.

But one of the most significant areas of LIFT did not fully emerge until 1992. Its education work had always been present, but under the campaigning leadership of Tony Fegan it became a year-round activity, eradicating the sense of marginality that so often clings to education work. One of its initiatives graduated into a separate entity, Phakama. It functions internationally and consistently and is at the heart of LIFT's philosophy, with its stress on freshness, participation, reinvention and ownership. LIFT's aims and outlook connect naturally with young people, whether they are from Weekend Arts College, Stockwell Park School, Battersea Arts Centre's Youth Theatre or South Africa's Sibikwa Community Theatre. They are embodied in Phakama events like its 1997 show, *Ka Mor Walo Ka Seatleng* (*With a Suitcase in My Hand*). Based in Seshego, it grew out of a week-long workshop in which British and South African teams worked with seventy young South Africans. The show they built came from stories out of suitcases carried by migrating people. It was performed in a vast disused warehouse and led to the establishment afterwards of an arts centre in Seshego.

LIFT sits in the highly contested arena of race and identity. Culture is breaking up and being reformed. Identity is being questioned. The boundaries between British and 'other' are becoming thinner and more porous. The old binaries – national and international, indigenous and foreign, mainstream and grassroots – are looking less clear. Alongside the work that LIFT brings in, lies the work of Britain's diaspora communities, who have a long history of maintaining cultural links across boundaries. At the 2002 conference Connecting Flights: New Cultures of the Diaspora, Stuart Hall talked inspiringly about the growth of 'globalisation from below'. A counter to the MacCulture that imposes homogenising globalisation from above, it operates at the grassroots, along the channels that artists themselves set up, and through alliances across boundaries between like-minded people. When the history of globalisation from below comes to be written, LIFT will undoubtedly have a place in it.

# International

LIFT stories run parallel with historic world events: the break-up of Yugoslavia, the fall of the Berlin Wall, the 'handover' of Hong Kong, the conflict in the Middle East. From our first trips to Poland to our more recent engagement with artists in Beirut, we have gained an understanding of world events through the prism of theatre created during these times. The paradox is that often the more personal or intimate the story, the more universally it is understood. The artists we have worked with recognise theatre as a medium for creating a shared language of the imagination that can cross cultural barriers. 'We were not Hindus, Muslims and Sikhs,' said Indian theatre director Habib Tanvir, 'but all artists subscribing to only one religion: the theatre of commitment.'

While LIFT was creating new spaces for theatre-making in London, theatre-makers in other countries – some of which were in a state of war – had to fight defiantly for any space for public performance, often taking great risks in the process. As Palestinian director George Ibrahim remarked in 2000: 'We will live and dance in spite of everything.'

We have learnt that humility is an essential starting-point for exchanging different ways of seeing the world, requiring subtle negotiation in order to contextualise different cultural perspectives and belief systems, as will be seen in the case of the visit of the Balinese Seka Barong. The most difficult experiences we have had to deal with have turned out to be the most salutary. Sensitive negotiations often need to happen at a one-to-one level and in the most successful examples this sows the seeds of international solidarity, though there may still be a painful potential for misunderstanding along the way. What Rustom Bharucha calls the 'embrace of difference' is not always easy: it involves generosity, vulnerability, personal risk and respect.

*A Midsummer Night's Dream*, Comedy Theatre, Bucharest, Romania, LIFT'91. Courtesy of LIFT archive. Theseus photographed in front of Ceausescu's megalomaniac project the People's Palace.

## China

The 4th Beijing Opera Troupe, *The Three Beatings of Tao San Chun*, LIFT'85; Chengdu Theatre Company, *Ripples Across Stagnant Water*, LIFT'93; Beijing Jing Ju Opera Troupe, *The Little Phoenix*, LIFT'93; Geremie Barmé and He Yong, *Red Noise: Bringing the Streets of Beijing to London*, LIFT'93; Xi Ju Che Jian Theatre, *File O*, LIFT'95

*The Three Beatings of Tao San Chun* tells the story of a plucky water-melon grower who takes the world to task. With baton-wielding leaps she conquers a series of overbearing men: her melon-thief husband-to-be, an emperor and several armies. Set in the ninth century during the Sung Dynasty, this comic Peking opera was written in 1962 by the distinguished playwright and fierce defender of women's rights Wu Zuguang. A Chinese *Taming of the Shrew,* the play is a satirical portrayal of the pressures on Chinese women, even 'warrior

*The Three Beatings of Tao San Chun*, The 4th Beijing Opera Troupe, China, LIFT'85. Courtesy of LIFT archive.

women', to marry. It was the first Chinese play to be brought to Britain after the Cultural Revolution and possibly even since the establishment of the People's Republic in 1949. In 1985 it proved an unlikely theatrical coup for LIFT, giving the Festival a reputation for 'pluck' in ways we could never have expected.

From inauspicious beginnings, the visit must have had several monkey gods watching over it. Mao Tsetung's Dictatorship of the Proletariat and the Cultural Revolution had not only put intellectuals into forced labour camps but had outlawed green grass and bird song as 'bourgeois' – birds were shot down from the trees. Mao's wife and the Gang of Four had found only eight traditional operas to their liking. They had re-written them as 'revolutionary operas' and tannoys at Chinese workplaces up and down the land would summon citizens to watch them by way of instruction for the socialist revolution.

Eight years after Chairman Mao Tsetung's death in 1976, we were attempting to instigate an independent invitation to a Chinese theatre company, inspired with no more than a curiosity to 'see what theatre was happening in China'. A new Anglo-Sino cultural agreement had been signed by the respective governments in 1984 and I (LN) was lucky to be included on a ten-day visit to China, sponsored by Visiting Arts and the British Council. We were hoping that the government of the People's Republic of China, through their monolithic Ministry of Culture, would consider paying the travel costs for any Chinese artists we chose to invite to the UK. We weren't then aware that the same government was still arresting 'counter-revolutionaries' from the Democracy Movement of 1978–9. In 1984 leaders of the Movement such as Wei Jingsheng, along with the country's most enlightened and creative spirits, were being imprisoned, often in solitary confinement, and were frequently tortured in Beijing's infamous No. 1 Qincheng gaol. Western films were smuggled into the country and Western students were required to leave university buildings five minutes after the Chinese so that their friends would not be picked out by the authorities for fraternising with foreigners.

All 'foreign experts' visiting China were allocated a chatty government minder and mine stuck to me like glue throughout the official visitors' programme, which included the Forbidden City, the Great Wall, pagodas, forlorn circus acts in which acrobats combined cycling upside down with balancing bowls of water on their feet, Western-style Chinese ballet and long, long evenings of the *Jade Bracelet* Peking Opera – all followed by banquets of delicious Peking duck and less appealing monkeys' brains and sea slugs. I was determined to make the most of my time in China and had hoped to be able to talk to practising independent artists. My UK travelling companions had more realistic expectations of what could be achieved on a monitored visit. There were repeated instructions to take three-hour 'rests' in hotel rooms far from anywhere and, to cap it all, a day-long visit to a lovely but not at all living-artist-related bonsai tree nursery. To add to my frustration, any conversation about 'modern drama' or suggestion about making contact with the address book of people who had been recommended to me met with a stone wall and offers of more sea slugs.

Luckily I had two days to myself after the 'official' tour had finished and could explore Beijing under my own steam. Exhilarated at being free, I cycled around the city following up the contacts given in Britain, meeting theatre director Lin Zhaohua and playwright Gao Xinjian (who later received the Nobel Prize for Literature), both of whom we invited to London as visitors to LIFT'85. With just a few hours to go before my flight home and led by Australian sinologist Geremie Barmé, I found myself climbing the four flights of stairs to the apartment home of Wu Zuguang, one of China's best-known playwrights. Wu had served his time doing hard labour in the countryside and, unusually, managed to balance membership of the Communist Party with criticism of it until he was expelled in 1987. Equally unusually, he was respected throughout China in the literary, theatre, opera and film worlds.

The actress Tsai Chin (of the 1959 play *The World of Suzie Wong* fame) had recommended that I ask Wu about his play, *The Three Beatings of Tao San Chun*. Her father, Zhou Xinfang, a great opera star killed during the Cultural Revolution, had known the Wu family well. I listened as Wu explained how he had dedicated the play to his wife of thirty-three years, Xin Fengxia, sitting beside him, who had also been a much-loved celebrity of Peking opera before she was permanently disabled by the severe beatings she received during the Cultural Revolution. He wanted people to recognise the indomitable but little-credited strength of Chinese women. With time running out, I succeeded in watching only three-quarters of the play on video. Gripped by its energy and joie de vivre, I asked Wu if he would consider bringing a troupe to London to present *The Three Beatings of Tao San Chun* at LIFT. I rushed to catch my plane, knowing that the trip had initiated a dialogue that could continue from London.

It was December 1984 and we had £65 in our bank account with nothing raised towards a July Festival budget of £260,000, and we failed to find any UK public arts funder to cover the costs of the Chinese visit. The friendship between Tsai Chin and the Wu family provided an invaluable link that enabled LIFT to make what felt like a hopelessly over-ambitious assault on the Chinese

*Ripples Across Stagnant Water*, Chengdu Theatre Company, China, LIFT'93. Photo: Shen Yantai.

government to try and persuade them to cover the costs of the thirty-five artists assembled to travel to London. Wu Zuguang was proved to have just enough of the essential *guanxi* (connections) to plead his case and in July 1985 a resplendent 4th Beijing Opera Troupe arrived in Sloane Square to play at the Royal Court Theatre, with every coloured bauble, prop, drape and costume shining new. Each return airfare had been paid for by the government of the People's Republic of China – an astonishing turnaround after the British Council's gloomy predictions that 'the Chinese will never pay for anything'.

Anglo-Sino relations were on the verge of stepping up a gear and His Excellency Zhu Muzhi, the Chinese Minister of Culture, had recently made his own first visit to Britain. The Chinese were taking the *Tao San Chun* visit very seriously and considerable razzmatazz surrounded it, with official gatherings at the Chinese Embassy and the somewhat maverick Wu now being fêted as a cultural hero. It was therefore confounding for the Chinese artists and Embassy alike to learn that the visit was hosted by a small independent organisation unable to produce lengths of red carpet, but which nevertheless could provide enthusiastic hospitality and weekly passes for London Underground.

In the hours before the opening night we came perilously close to a cultural stand-off when the acrobats, not wanting to perform their somersaults, complained of severe headaches from being forced to ride on the tube. We phoned the office of Mrs Thatcher's Minister for the Arts, Lord Gowrie, to explain that as he would be sitting next to the Chinese Ambassador, Hu Dingyi, and Lord Maclehose, former Governor of Hong Kong, at the Royal Court that evening, he might like to consider paying for the Chinese artists to travel around London in the comfort of a coach. It took his office two minutes to agree to our proposal, signalling how quickly diplomatic somersaults could be performed when expedient for saving face. Observing that a significant precedent had been set, Penny Brooke, Director of the Great Britain China Centre, was later to report to the diplomatic world that 'LIFT had made a considerable contribution to Anglo-Chinese cultural relations.'

When Wang Yuzheng, the show's indomitable leading lady, took to the stage later that evening, members of the audience in the intimate auditorium of the Royal Court Theatre were so close to the action that they were nearly able to touch each quivering feather and bobbing pink pompom on her splendid head-dress. With a wink in their direction, she fluttered her flowing white sleeves, arched her eyebrows high and to the taut, clashing music of cymbal, gong and Chinese violin (*hu qin*) she hurled herself singing into another acrobatic spin, fielding an arrow in mid-air. With the flick of a tasselled whip, she spurned the offer of the king's escort and rode off on her imaginary donkey. The public and press response was unanimously upbeat, acknowledging that, by using traditional Peking opera to create a modern Chinese contemporary classic, the play broke new ground. The show had queues around the block. Grey Gowrie was very taken by the heroine, 'She's a little like my leader,' he said, and also by LIFT – he went on to become Chair of our Board.

After the events of Tiananmen Square in June 1989, China was much more in the world's gaze but although cultural exchanges with the UK were more common they were still diplomatically testing. For LIFT'93 we invited three productions from China: a play called *Ripples Across Stagnant Water* from the southern Sichuan city of Chengdu (the first city to respond to the events in Tiananmen Square with protests of their own); a Chinese *Madame Bovary* set on the eve of the 1911 revolution, directed by a woman, Zha Lifang; another Peking opera, *The Little Phoenix*, directed by the *Tao San Chun* heroine Wang Yuzheng; and *Red Noise*, a risky new commission which captured the energy of a growing younger counter-culture.

This latter had involved me (*LN*) in moonlit bike rides around the lake and Hutong back alley-ways on the eastern outskirts of Beijing to track down, via word of mouth, what was going on in the growing new underground movement of the experimental arts. This impoverished district was home to several artists who were creating one-off performances around the area. There had been reports of punk-like happenings, pictures painted in pig's blood, people stitching things into their skin, and disturbing private acts made public. Many involved stoic feats of endurance and overt displays of individualistic behaviour that challenged head-on the Confucian concept that the individual is constructed from a set of social relationships. The artist Zhang Huan, in a piece entitled *Twelve Square Metres,* had coated his body with honey and sat naked in a public toilet covered in flies for three hours.[1] Pop musicians were also emerging as a force for an anarchic, public rebelliousness. The search ended with a Beijing rocksinger He Yong, whom we commissioned to co-devise with Geremie Barmé the satirical double bill *Red Noise.* This was to consist of a collage of He Yong's blaring punk songs ('We chomp on conscience and shit out thoughts') with TV adverts, government propaganda, poetry, videos and the patter of streetwise black marketeers, reflecting the cacophony of Beijing's burgeoning urban capitalism. The Chinese authorities tolerated the angry protests of young pop stars up to a point. With a market economy invading every corner of private and public life, decisions to clamp down were sudden and arbitrary. Perhaps it was because He Yong had his hair in a pony tail and carried a guitar, or maybe because at the last minute the authorities feared the impact he'd make in London, but just as he was boarding his flight his passport was removed and he was temporarily refused permission to travel. The passport was not returned for a week, at which point the British Council's Joanna Burke took the matter into her own hands and walked He Yong on to the plane brazenly waving a pretend ticket (since we couldn't afford a replacement), carrying his guitar for him lest it attract attention. He appeared on stage at the last moment, unrehearsed, and chose to mime his songs. A notable Chinese economist living in exile in New York saw the show and described it as 'the bravest thing I've ever seen outside China'.

We learnt from European colleagues that commissioning *Red Noise* had set an example. Later that year, Frie Leysen at the Kunsten Festival des Arts in Brussels commissioned Mou Sen, an artist in his early thirties from the independent theatre company Xi Ju Che Jian, to create *File O,* based on the 1994 avant-garde poem *File Zero* by Yu Jian, which took its inspiration from the notorious Dang'an – the official state files which contained the personal details of every Chinese citizen. *File O* was programmed by LIFT in 1995. Visual images from the piece still burn in the memory: an actor, using an acetylene flame, welds a forest of metal spikes from bits of iron to disturbing footage of a baby having a heart transplant projected on to the back wall at the ICA; a woman carts a crate of apples on stage and sticks them matter-of-factly on to rods. Lyrical and beautiful by turns, the show ends on a shocking image of fury and carnage as huge ripe tomatoes are hurled into the turning propellers of a giant fan, their red flesh splashing out across the stage. '*File O* depicts private life in China,' said the performer Wu Wenguang in debate. 'It is violent because our reality is violent.' Although it was hotly questioned on the festival circuit as to whether the piece was as outspoken as it claimed, it nevertheless gave audiences outside China an experience of a new theatre language from that country. In truth the really outspoken Chinese were doubtless either in exile in Paris or New York, or in prison in solitary confinement.

On 29 June, the final day of LIFT'97, Chris Patten, the last Governor of Hong Kong, amid a theatrical display of boats, umbrellas, bands and sad faces, handed over the keys of Hong Kong to China, ending 156 years of British colonial rule. The Sino-British treaty that returned Hong Kong to Chinese rule was meant to ensure that Hong Kong moved towards free direct elections, but seven years on Beijing claimed its right to veto electoral change, formally shutting the door on hopes for Hong Kong's democratic self-governance.

Heavy prison sentences were meted out to the editors of a Guangzhou newspaper responsible for exposing the cover-up of the Sars virus, and, according to Amnesty International, in 2004 China was one of four countries, along with the US, Iran and Vietnam, that are responsible for the overwhelming majority of executions worldwide (Justin Huggler, *The Independent*, 7 April 2004). With Beijing hosting the Olympic Games in 2008 and the country becoming the undisputed new economic force in the world, it will be for artists both within China and beyond to grapple with these contradictions.

## Former Yugoslavia

Mladinsko Theatre, *Mass in A Minor – Matters of State and Revolution*; LIFT'85; NSK (Neue Slowenische Kunst)/Kosmokinetical Theatre Red Pilot, *Fiat*, LIFT'87; Intercult Sarajevo Company, *Sarajevo – Tales of a City*, from an original idea by Haris Pašović, LIFT'93

In June 1991 Slovenia declared its independence from Yugoslavia, thus setting in train a whole series of secessions, first of Croatia, and then Bosnia and Herzegovina and spilling over into Macedonia and Kosova. For ten years the region entered a period of brutality and ethnic cleansing on a scale not seen in Europe for half a century. More than quarter of a million people died and seeds of hatred were sown that continue to flourish today.

Back in 1985 we had presented Mladinsko's Theatre from Lubljana, at that time one of Yugoslavia's leading companies for experimental, radical theatre. Much of their work engaged with the tensions and contradictions inherent in Tito's vision for a non-aligned socialist state, uniting Serbs, Croats, Slovenians, Macedonians, Montenegrins and Bosnians as one nation. *Mass in A Minor – Matters of State and Revolution,* based on the novel *A Tomb for Boris Davidovich* by Danilo Kiš, told the story of Novsky, a scientist and professional revolutionary who was a victim of the Stalinist purges. Audiences sat on cushions in the middle of the theatre as the action erupted in anarchic tableaux around them. Tracts from Trotsky and Bakunin were chanted, Lenin sat impassively in his library whilst gartered girls in black tights strutted their stuff in a Teutonic cabaret and the company sang Yiddish folk songs. Directed by the maverick visionary Ljubiša Ristić, this provocative piece went beyond a mythology of revolution as framed by ideology to explore the role of the dissenting individual in history. The critic Michael Coveney, a keen observer of Yugoslav theatre at that time, welcomed the production in the *Financial Times* as an 'outcry of anguish and defiance from a country that knows the price of freedom and the value of independence.'

Towards the late 1980s, nationalist frenzies across Yugoslavia were escalating. The provocatively named artistic movement Neue Slowenische Kunst (NSK) was examining the forces of European nationalism and totalitarianism through the prism of Slovenia's history: as part of the Austro-Hungarian Empire; as the Kingdom of Serbs, Croats and Slovenes; under occupation by Nazi Germany; and finally incorporated into Tito's socialist Yugoslavia. Borrowing freely and ironically from the iconographies of totalitarianism, NSK artists, whose work spanned music, visual arts and theatre, were accused in turn of being neo-Nazis, Communist subversives, revolutionaries, reactionaries, media manipulators and spiritual terrorists.

I (*RF*) visited Lubljana in May 1987 at a time when NSK was causing a furore. It had won a competition for designing the poster for Yugoslavia's Day of Youth, a relay race that ended on 25 May, the anniversary of Tito's birthday. Just days before NSK was to be awarded the prize, a retired engineer in Belgrade spotted that the image was almost identical to a Richard Klein fascist poster of the 1930s. This was no postmodern playful prank but, in those ideological times, a dangerous political provocation. Members of NSK were

*Fiat*, NSK/ Kosmokinetical Theatre Red Pilot, Yugoslavia, LIFT'87. Photo: David Corio.

summoned before an investigating magistrate and put under police surveillance. Theatre director Dragan Živadinov, who had just directed a new production, *Fiat*, by NSK's theatre wing, Kosmokinetical Theatre Red Pilot, was called up for military service. Undeterred, NSK continued with their plans to première this show. They had let it be known that for the past few days they had spent the hours between 1.00 and 4.00 am on the phone to 400 leading figures across the political, religious, artistic and media establishment, including Madame Jovanka Broz, Tito's widow, announcing the opening of *Fiat*. In the event no member of the establishment joined the huge youth cult audience, all dressed in black, who made their way through a fur-lined grotto into a performance area of burnished steel dominated by a circular fiery furnace. There, to an ear-splitting score of grinding industrial rock music spliced with nineteenth-century Romanticism, we witnessed a reworking of the Medea and Jason myth, performed as a humiliating ritual of alienation between the sexes. Humanity seemed doomed. Three openings – a cross, a circle and a triangle – were guarded by men with cropped haircuts and military uniforms. The soldiers danced a can-can, a live rabbit was produced from a hat and three Medeas (played by well-known divas) cat-walked their way across the stage.

Down at Riverside Studios as part of LIFT'87, NSK announced the arrival of its artists in Western Europe as 'smarting intruders in the decaying entrails of a greedy animal'. Alternatively viewed as totalitarian chic, surreal anarchy or simply pretentious provocation, *Fiat* delighted NSK London devotees and baffled the wider public. But the essence of their work was chillingly prophetic, as throughout the 90s Yugoslavia was ripped asunder by the forces of nationalism. An event by NSK, the *Zenit Drama Observatory* – in the spring of 1990 at the Informal European Theatre Meeting (IETM) in Zagreb – imagined with deadly accuracy the horror that was about to erupt. As we arrived for the performance in a remote rail depot on the outskirts of Zagreb, our passports and identity papers were taken away. Then with much aggressive shouting we were herded down the track and crammed into two abandoned freight wagons spruced up to look like rockets. There we endured repeated banging on the outside walls before being shunted into a large warehouse. Just over a year later, following the declaration of independence of Croatia from Yugoslavia, the historic Croatian port of Dubrovnik was under siege. The Yugoslav People's Army imprisoned hundreds of Croatians in large metal containers, subjecting them to constant banging during the weeks of a late summer heat wave.

As the conflict escalated, Ljubiša Ristić, desperate to hold on to Tito's vision of a Yugoslavia in which nationalism supposedly played no part, became

President of the JUL (Yugoslavian United Left) Party, led by Mira Marković, wife of President Milošević, the man responsible for some of the most heinous war crimes in the latter half of the twentieth century.

In July 1993 the Bosnian capital of Sarajevo was on the verge of collapse as the Serbs closed in from the surrounding hills. That same week at Riverside Studios, as part of LIFT'93, a European cast, including actors from Bosnia, Slovenia and Croatia, performed *Sarajevo*, a haunting lament for the ideals of a multicultural city that had been crushed as ethnic hatred inflamed its inhabitants. Though fuelled by grief, *Sarajevo* was not a violent portrayal of war. 'How can one write a play about Sarajevo today? How does one touch an open wound?' asked its Macedonian playwright Goran Stefanovski. 'One thing I knew was that I didn't want a play about the massacred "body" of the city as portrayed daily in the media. Instead I was interested in the soul of the city. What is the inner reality of this tragedy? What are the human tangents of this black hole?'

In the play, Sara, a wounded young girl, emerges from her cellar to wander through the ruins and meet people from past and present. Bosnian fools from earlier centuries, performing Sufi dances and musical laments, mingle with athletes from the 1984 Winter Olympics. A smuggler makes a plea for normality: 'Can't we go back to the small times please, and watch a match on Sunday like everyone else?' A cellist is raped by her neighbour and a housewife howls at her departing husband: 'I didn't know I had a nation, I married you, not your past.' Another Sarajevan recites a recipe for a good Bosnian casserole, but breaks down when he reaches the ingredient 'water'. At that moment, as we in the audience knew, there was no clean water in Sarajevo. The drains and pipes had been destroyed by Serbian shells.

The following week we joined a coalition of London activists from Amnesty International, the Refugee Council and Charter 88 and marched on Downing Street to plead for international intervention, brandishing urine-filled milk bottles, symbols of the city's polluted water supplies.

## Tunisia and Palestine

Familia Productions, *Familia*, LIFT'95; al-Kasaba Theatre, *Ramzy Abul Majd*, LIFT'97; al-Kasaba Theatre, *Alive from Palestine*, LIFT'01

In the full theatres, busy cafés and bright streets of a North African autumn there is an outward air of ease and a freedom of discourse as the biennial Carthage Festival, the Edinburgh or Avignon of the Arab world, rolls out its programme across the city of Tunis. Underneath the surface, however, an unease lingers. President Ben Ali rules with an iron fist, debate is smothered as the economy falters and unemployment rises, and there is a growing possibility of Islamic fundamentalism spilling over from neighbouring Algeria and taking hold in the disenfranchised districts on the edge of Tunis. We are fortunate that our Lebanese friend Pierre Abi Saab, Arts Editor of *al-Wasat*, the cultural imprint of the London based pan-Arab newspaper *al-Hayat*, accompanies us through the Festival, introducing us as we walk down the main boulevard to every cultural mandarin and theatre experimenter of the region. Pierre is an original character who since the early 1980s has made Paris and then London his home. Resplendent in his silk dressing gown, he receives us on the terrace of his spacious hotel room for a champagne breakfast 'seminar' on our first morning. His view is that 'the majority of Arab artists, in their search for originality, have nothing but urgency and crisis as their discourse but when they try to escape the imposition of Western European theatre they often venture on to the slippery ground of folklore.' Tunisian director Fadhel Jaibi's work, he believes, hits another register. In trying to exorcise the traumas of a society on the brink of collapse, Jaibi concentrates on the actor's physical presence and on the visual and the aesthetic. In his black comedy *Familia*, which we have just presented in London as part of LIFT'95, three ageing sisters, trapped by their mutual hatred and jealousy, live out frustrated lives in half-lit, shadow-filled rooms. Outside a mysterious and menacing enemy lies in wait. The water and electricity have been cut off, the ancient trees in the garden have been burnt down and the cat has been killed. The toad-like eldest sister, Bahja, reveals the tragedy of her youth when as an aspiring singer she was forbidden by her lover to appear in public. 'All I wanted was to perform just once, but he said, "If you sing, you will only sing for me."' And then, in an extraordinary moment, Bahja begins to shudder until her whole body twists and contorts. In an agony of metamorphosis, raging and struggling, she escapes the bent decrepitude of an embittered old age and before our eyes transforms into the beautiful, erotic woman of her younger self. But Bahja's regained youth is brief; she has not the energy or will to sustain it and eventually she slumps back into old age.

Following the success of *Familia* we were eager to know more about contemporary theatre from the Arab world. At Carthage, companies from Egypt, Palestine, Iraq, Kuwait and Tunisia were gathered to present performances ranging from folk tales to Brechtian fables to stories that grappled with current politics. And it was here that LIFT first encountered al-Kasaba from

East Jerusalem in a production of *Ramzy Abul Majd*, initiating a relationship with Palestinian theatre that was to grow over the years.

*Ramzy Abul Majd* is an adaptation of Athol Fugard's classic *Siswe Bansi Is Dead*, transposed from the building sites and prisons of apartheid South Africa to the situation of impoverished Palestinan workers from Gaza and the West Bank looking for work in Israel. 'It's about identity,' said George Ibrahim, Director of al-Kasaba. 'It's about the way Palestinians say, "I'm here, this is my country. I'm entitled to be here."'

George is a youthful white-haired, former children's TV star, a celebrated figure in the Middle East, a flamboyant personality and the driving force behind Palestinian theatre for more than thirty years. In September 1996 I (*RF*) was sitting in his small dark office in East Jerusalem, a television flickering in the corner giving out the latest news from the tension-filled West Bank. We were planning to invite *Ramzy Abul Majd* to LIFT and I was there to find out more about al-Kasaba's work. George lit up his shisha and the sweet smell of apple-scented tobacco filled the air. He had a cherished project to create a cultural centre from a disused cinema in Ramallah. Despite the recent Oslo Peace Process (hopes for which even then were fast disappearing), Palestinians only a few miles away in Ramallah or Beit Jala with no permit to cross the Israeli cordon around the city were finding access to Jerusalem increasingly difficult. So, he explained, he was relocating the theatre to the heart of the community. Two performance spaces, an art gallery and a restaurant were planned. It would be, he said with pride, the only professional, fully equipped multipurpose venue in the entire Palestinian territories. It would also provide a much-needed meeting place, a spiritual home for artists and audiences, and a place of connection to local, pan-Arab and international cultures.

The previous year George had worked on a UN-funded Israeli/Arab production of *Romeo and Juliet* that had toured widely in Europe, supposedly heralding the dawn of a new era of relations between the two nations following the Oslo Peace Process. Now he was feeling very disillusioned and regarded the venture as a false symbol, cynically engineered by the authorities for foreign consumption of a peace that did not exist back home. For George the need for cultural practice to be in the hands of the Palestinian artistic community was paramount.

George achieved his ambition. In June 2000 al-Kasaba opened their new space. Then, in September, Ariel Sharon provocatively visited the Haram al-Sharif, or Temple Mount, sparking dormant Palestinian anger into the Second Intifada against the Israelis. The theatre became a focus for Ramallah residents to meet and talk about their experiences of the Israeli occupation. Two years later, in April 2002, during the re-invasion of Ramallah, the Israeli army attacked and ransacked the theatre.

As the Intifada gathered momentum, back in London we began to hear from other Palestinian artists we had encountered on our travels. Marina Barham, the Manager of INAD, a theatre company based in Beit Jala, whose name means 'stubborn', wrote emails daily: 'I feel there is no use in telling anyone what has been happening here tonight. Since 4.30 we have been under heavy shelling from the Israelis. We tried to hide our nieces behind a cupboard, but they are babies and cannot be still. Guess what – we could see our houses being shelled on TV.'

Despite the situation, INAD continued to present their shows to children. Marina wrote: 'We thought that after a week of violence it would be impossible to perform, since in our culture we cannot have any entertainment while people are in mourning, but the headmaster said that his students are suffering from traumas and are stunned [and] . . . felt we could do something to help. After the performance the children were able to smile and laugh and discussions after the show helped them to share their fears.'

In Feburary 2001 the Royal Court and LIFT organised a special benefit performance of Caryl Churchill's *Far Away,* directed by Stephen Daldry at the Albery Theatre, to raise money for al-Kasaba and INAD to continue their work during the Intifada. Vanessa Redgrave and David Hare (whose monologue *Via Dolorosa* about the tragedy of the Holy Land had just finished a hugely successful run in New York) were amongst those from Britain's theatre community who rallied to support the cause.

The Intifada was the spur for a new kind of devised theatre for al-Kasaba. With Palestinian cities under siege and with blockades, bombings and gunfire in the streets, actors could not get to rehearsals on a regular basis and it was almost impossible to conduct normal rehearsals for straight plays. 'It's like trying to walk through drops of rain without getting wet,' George said to me in despair on the phone, 'yet we will live and dance in spite of everything.' (George is an indefatigable dancer – his very presence in a room is guaranteed to get a party going.) So the idea of a quick-fire response to the changing situation took root and became a series of evolving monologues created by the actors – as and when they could make rehearsals – with the intention of 'de-itemising' and humanising the Palestinian experience.

Together with Elyse Dodgson at the Royal Court, with whom we had presented *Ramzy Abul Majd* in 1997, we felt it was important to show the

*Alive from Palestine*, al-Kasaba Theatre, Palestine, LIFT'01. Photo: Michael J. O'Brien Photography.

monologues in London in LIFT'01, even though it was not possible to see the pieces before issuing an invitation. They were evolving daily. Every week a new sketch arrived for us to translate. 'God knows what our situation will be like in June. As you can see, events on the ground change dramatically from day to day!' wrote al-Kasaba's Artistic Director, Abed al-Jubeh. 'However, I realise you need something for your programme and I have therefore drafted something which only details those sketches that we are sure we are including.'

There was a correspondence about the title. An original suggestion from London, *West Bank Stories,* was rejected. 'The West Bank is something that has become synonymous for us with the occupation itself and others' definition of us,' argued Abed; 'I would like rather to suggest *Alive from Palestine.* It plays on the word 'live' and our main linking theme is media representation and our survival!' Our initial reaction to the sketches was surprise. They were upbeat, at times flippant, their tone humorous, even farcical. Amidst mountains of shredded Palestinian newspapers actors emerge to tell their stories. A father phones his son in Britain and cheerily reels off a catalogue of deaths, imprisonments and maimings that have befallen the family, reassuring him at the end of every piece of news, 'But we're fine, praise God, don't worry.' At that point a missile rips its way through the window. 'It's all right,' the father says, 'it went out through the other window. We're fine, thank God.' Lovers meet for dinner and exchange rubber bullets as love tokens. An eager young fan of American movies rushes off to be an extra in what he believes to be an action-packed film shoot with Sharon Stone, only to find himself in the midst of a demonstration against Ariel Sharon with real bullets. His friend Yusuf is fatally shot.

How, we wondered, would a London audience relate to the sketches? How would the changed context from Ramallah to Sloane Square affect the power and impact of the monologues? Six weeks before the London opening we wrote to the company: 'We can appreciate how the upbeat nature and ironic tone of the monologues would really lift the spirits in Ramallah. But for the London context we would prefer to see these mixed with more serious pieces that offer a direct, immediate response to the situation . . . including more details of individual experiences and giving audiences here a chance to understand the hardship and difficulty of everyday life in the present Intifada.' The company patiently wrote back. *Alive From Palestine,* they said, was not documentation of a situation, more an artistic response. 'And we are not planning to bomb London to get the right sound effects,' remarked the director, Nizar, drily.

The company's instincts were right and the show spoke directly to its audiences. In an after-show discussion George Ibrahim explained, 'Life in this region is very complex. It is not simple. It has lots of levels. It can be sad and dark, but sometimes it can be really funny. People are throwing stones at soldiers and one metre away others are selling vegetables. If you look at it from the side it is funny. As a whole it is very sad, but our possibility to smile and laugh is a big victory. We are losing everything. Laughter is our only weapon. We joke because we want to survive.'

## Indonesia

*The Seka Barong of Singapadu*, LIFT'95

I defy anyone to land in Bali and not have their breath taken away by its astonishing natural beauty (*LN*). There are beaches covered in discarded plastic bottles, but on first arrival these are not what you see. Driving into the hills of Central Bali, around Ubud, I travelled past banyan trees and bamboo arches waving in the wind. Greeted by brightly coloured umbrellas and fluttering flags, I couldn't quite believe my senses – and this was the road from the airport? As we climbed higher, buffaloes plodded through muddy, green terraced paddy-fields, mountains rose in the distance and temples and frangipani trees, it seemed, went on for ever . . .

Since my trip there in 1994, Bali has suffered two massive traumas: the rioting that led to the overthrow of President Suharto in 1998, when angry, fire-bombing protesters took to the streets against corruption and food shortages, and the post-September 11 terrorist bombing of a hotel in Kuta in October 2002. But before these violent events hit our television screens, Bali's hold on its 'paradise' status was already fragile.

In contrast to the mythical lotus-blossom haze enjoyed by so many tourists in Bali, I had a tense time there. I had set myself an impossible LIFT mission: to travel rather vaguely in Indonesia on the off chance that something LIFT-like might crop up that could fill the Queen Elizabeth Hall for a week in July 1995. Brochure deadlines meant that we had committed to a booking at the QEH before I set off. We wanted to extend our virtually non-existent knowledge of Indonesia by making an exploratory trip. Britain has no colonial links to Indonesia and it was sobering to realise that one's knowledge of a country and culture is informed by such histories.

With 13,000 islands in Indonesia and a total of 300 languages spoken, the range of options at the outset was bewildering. Scaling the ambition down, I opted for the two most 'obvious' islands: Java and Bali. In all humility I confess I knew little about either. I had twelve days.

Java was tantalising. I rushed through it, gathering enough knowledge from dance expert Sal Murgiyanto and publisher John McGlynn to realise that my understanding of 'contemporary' and 'traditional' was to be challenged by the more integrated connection for artists in Indonesia between their politics, ecology, art, everyday lives, religious beliefs and often their survival. Sal was about to host a festival, on the beautiful small island of Flores, of traditional village music, dance and song from the outlying islands of the archipelago. He

explained that many of these 'traditional' arts had taken on an urgent contemporary significance as a consequence of their extended relationship with
the natural world on which islanders depend for their survival. The damage
done by government and multinationals to forests and rivers made a dance
performed for hundreds of years an act of outspoken political protest. The
right to perform and to preserve island cultural heritage had become an issue
of life and death.

I had an appointment in the city of Solo, Surakarta, with Princess 'No. 28'
(twenty-eighth descendant of King Pakubuwono) at the great court, Karaton
Surakarta, where her court company put on a chartered performance just for
me. To the celestial sounds of an eighteenth-century gamelan, and seated on a
large throne, I watched an exquisite evening's entertainment of stately Javanese
court dance. Accompanied by bats swooping low through the rafters and cats
creeping across the palace floor, it left me bewitched and deeply moved. This, I
realised, was graceful classical art preserved beautifully – but not the more
'immediate' stuff we were looking for. The clangorous and comic antics of the
Balinese were to come as a big surprise.

Bali crawls with visiting musicologists, dancers, teachers and mask-makers
from every continent who have travelled there to study, research and contribute
to dialogues about Bali's complex cultural life. It is impossible to separate
religion in Bali from arts and culture, which are informed by the island's own
distinct Hinduism and indigenous animist and ancestor-worship traditions. In a
Balinese village everybody really does make 'art' – children, parents, and
grandparents. The simplest activities are carried out with precision and flair.
There is no word for artist. Dressing up in gold brocade, playing the gamelan
and making temple offerings to honour the ancestors are normal everyday
things. The performing arts have developed out of daily acts of worship and
traditional ceremonies: temple offerings, weddings, cremations, tooth-filing
ceremonies, mask dances and trance dances to exorcise evil spirits. Each day
has a festival of its own.

I spent five days in Bali and I was never going to be an expert on anything.
Hurling myself back and forth, contributing to the increasing volume of traffic on
the Ubud–Denpasar road, I caught up with as much of the island's performing
arts as I could – the riveting Kecak monkey dance, the elegant Legong, the
endless telling and retelling of the love of Rama and Sita, the jewel-like fifteenth-
or sixteenth-century Gambuh, the improvised comic operatic form of Ardja, and
a Sanghyang trance dance in the hills near Lake Batur where a pre-pubescent
girl walked over burning coconut shells.

By good fortune, I had arrived in the
middle of the all-important Balinese festivities
of Galungan and Kuningan, a ten-day holiday
period in which the gods and ancestors come
down to earth and are made welcome with
untold quantities of beautifully prepared temple
offerings and religious celebrations. It suddenly
became possible to find music and dancing
*everywhere*, spilling out from every temple. In
the compound where I was staying, the whole
family's fast fingers worked each evening to
make intricate decorations out of banana
leaves, using the corners of plastic bags to
push rice into pointy-shaped cones. I had not
met a single person on my travels around the
island who seemed to question the central
idea that spirits are everywhere to be either
honoured or placated. The black and white
checked cloth that drapes every temple
symbolises these extremes: Balinese Hinduism
sees the world through the constantly
changing relationship with the benign right and
the malign left. The aim is to accept positive
and negative as part of a whole and occupy
the centre position, maintaining equilibrium
between order and disorder, good and evil,
rather than simply aiming to wipe out evil
forces and promote good. People live between
these opposites and their rituals strive to
maintain a middle ground. If you follow the rules, you don't offend the gods.

As I sat under a large banyan tree to ponder on my Queen Elizabeth Hall
options, with a sacred Topeng mask dance being played out in the packed
village square of Batuan, I wondered how on earth to connect all this to a multi-
faith or secular London audience. Shouldn't one just say, 'Catch the plane, see
for yourself'? The Balinese themselves were adept at translating their arts for
tourists and at any hotel anywhere on the island you could see Rama and Sita
piling off the village truck to earn a secular living, holding their spiritual fire for
their own ceremonies back home. The first answer came as I was driving back

*The Seka Barong of Singapadu, Bali, LIFT'95. Courtesy of LIFT archive.*

late one evening through a village. I caught a runaway Barong led by some small boys who had succeeded in whipping up into wild excitement a whole crowd of children who were running away in terror whilst screaming with delight.

The Barong is a ritual drama used, like the Sanghyang, to exorcise evil spirits. It is fun and, predictably, very popular, incorporating slapstick and seriousness, misadventure, abduction and black magic. I had recognised something of this in the screams of the children. A battle between good and evil, the Barong (half lion, half shaggy dog, played like a pantomime horse by two dancers) represents good, whose opponent, Rangda, is the evil widow witch, spirit of a medieval Balinese queen. The Barong, both village protector and clown, flounces mischievously around the stage until required to do real battle, with the help of dagger-wielding men at his side. Rangda enters, tongue lolling, breasts wobbling, human entrails draped around her neck, fangs protruding from her mouth. Battle ensues. Rangda casts her magic spells over the warriors who turn their knives on themselves in an agonising suicide dance. In a thrilling theatrical showdown, good triumphs over bad and holy water revives the faint-hearted. In its original form Barong summons powerful forces and can be played, even today, in cemeteries.

The second part of my answer came from Dr I. Wayan Dibia, then Deputy Director of the STSI (Sekolah Tinggi Seni Indonesia) in Denpasar, the most experienced teacher and 'gatekeeper' to Balinese culture that I could have hoped for. Dibia was both in charge of the instruction of all of Bali's young performing arts students and himself a practising artist and innovator. He trod the difficult ground of maintaining Bali's traditional arts (a mainstay of the island's commercial success) and of keeping these traditions alive and relevant.

The plan was that Dibia would bring his village of Singapadu (winners of the 1993 Bali Barong) to London with a Calonarang Barong drama. To represent the spirit of the village it would be necessary, he said, to bring children, grandparents, a priest, the best gamelan players and mask-makers, dancers, Barong players and so on ... I decided to postpone a discussion about numbers until after I got home. *The Seka Barong of Singapadu* was engaged to play the Queen Elizabeth Hall in June 1995. The photographer Gavin Evans was sent to Bali to take colour shots immediately.

In the six months that followed, Dibia gave us up-to-date news on the decision-making process about which forty villagers would come. Balinese villages have a strong religious and social organisation. They are divided into *banjars* and villagers are summoned to the *banjar* hall by the sound of the *kulkul,* a hollow wooden bell, to reach a community consensus on issues and decisions of the day. In this slow consensual way, the LIFT invitation was processed by the *banjar* political system and full accord was reached from the youngest (14) to the eldest (81). It was therefore possible to say truthfully that the *whole* village of Singapadu visited LIFT.

Throughout the 1980s we had often been asked somewhat disparagingly by other festival programmers if we still presented 'folk theatre', by which they generally meant theatre from the Third World, despite LIFT's intention to look at innovative theatre in different forms – irrespective of the country of origin. Prior to the villagers' arrival, betraying a lapse in my own faith, I asked a great expert on South-East Asian culture, Rachel Cooper at the Asia Society in New York, whether or not we had invited a 'top' troupe – by which I meant a company that would be rated in the competitive world of international trading cultures, where the élitist stakes are high for 'premièring' work of excellence. There was a pause on the telephone line. 'If you're asking me tip top, I can't answer,' she said, 'but if you're asking me spirit, I say, yes, you've invited a troupe with spirit.'

We planned to build a beautiful decorative temple festooned with fruit and flowers in the foyer of the QEH and Singapadu's own priest would consecrate the stage to the Hindu deities before each performance. But beyond this, how do you programme something that is so much part of another culture that it is almost untranslatable? Would we be able to avoid what Homi Bhabha, the writer on cultural difference, calls 'fixity'– the stereotyping of 'the other', the exoticising of forms that can only be observed from the outside, rather than understood in human terms from within? Could we communicate anything of the delight and power of the Barong?

Dibia made a serious proposal to stage the Barong in a London graveyard at night. With hindsight we're sorry we missed this opportunity, but we had 4,000 tickets to sell and we also balked at the task of negotiating with the keepers and controllers of multiple religious faiths in London, let alone the dead. Instead, we decided to create an artistic welcome to the Balinese from a community of London participants. Tony Fegan was then pioneering a schools programme more akin to an artistic laboratory than any existing model of 'education work'. For the Bali visit, ninety 8-year-olds from Charlton Manor Primary School, Greenwich, were trained in the Kecak chant and made a giant puppet show to enact the Monkey King Hanuman's story from the *Ramayana*. The Kecak vocal chant is fiendishly complex and the children were not to know that Dibia was an expert in this ritual form, which is performed in temples alongside Sanghyang trance dances to exorcise spirits. The *cak* of the Kecak is thought to derive from the sound of, and therefore attract, the house lizard, the gecko, bringer of good fortune.

Of his own accord, Dibia proposed that the children would perform on a Saturday matinée as part of the Barong, as though presenting the same seamless show on the stage of the QEH. This was to be done without rehearsal. Spirit and faith indeed! When the day came a crowd of London children and their families processed across the walkways of the concrete South Bank, bearing gifts for the temple with a gamelan clash of cymbal and gong (page 109). Clement Crisp, reviewing for the *Financial Times,* was not remotely amused: 'I was less than enthusiastic to learn that Wednesday's matinée was chiefly intended for London school children, that it was to be somewhat abbreviated and that local tots would take part in a Kejak,' he wrote. But added, 'Events proved me hugely wrong.'

The floppy lion-figure of the Barong rollicked along, followed by dancers with frangipani behind their ears. The children placed their 'offerings' at the temple, as the audience, children (tightly bound in black and white check cloth) and Balinese (in red, gold and yellow) processed together into the hall. The afternoon's performance became charged by the exchange of performance 'gifts'. It was thrilling to see the Balinese performers' delight at watching the children perform their Kecak on stage. The gamelan players played the children out, before the Barong ran amok in the auditorium, leaving everyone in stitches, whether they understood Balinese or not. 'It was a memorably good afternoon, thanks both to the tremendous Balinese visitors and to the Charlton Manor juniors,' wrote Clement Crisp as though reporting in the local parish magazine rather than the pages of the world's leading financial paper. We're left to imagine what he might have written had the show been performed in Nunhead Cemetery, but for one Saturday afternoon spirit and faith in the theatre's power to make intimates from strangers were found. 'Community spoke to community and not unworthily,' Crisp concluded.

## India

Naya Theatre, *Bahadur Kalarin*, LIFT'83

Habib Tanvir is widely acknowledged as the most influential Indian theatre director of the last fifty years, beginning his work as a cultural activist at a time of radical social and political change in a recently independent, secular Indian democracy. I (*RF*) had first spent time with Habib in India when preparing for the LIFT'83 Festival. He had flouted convention at every stage, not least as a Muslim by marrying a Bengali Christian, Moneeka Misra, a fellow visionary and a generous, practical, strong woman. Together they founded Naya Theatre in 1959. Talking about those early days, he says, 'We were not Hindus, Muslims and Sikhs, but all artists subscribing to only one religion: the theatre of commitment.'

In the mid-50s, Habib had studied at RADA and the Bristol Old Vic. 'Britain made me even more Indian and I realised that those who are trying to behave like the English actor or producer will only produce pale copies. It made me acutely conscious of the fact that India needs to fall back on its own resources and traditions in order to evolve a new type of theatre which will be both authentic and contemporary.'

On his return to India Habib began working with the Chattisgarh folk actors and musicians: farmers, washermen, nomadic tribal women, tailors, pan- and cycle-shop owners from his native Madhya Pradesh in Central India. Workshops in lighting, make-up, martial arts and improvisation were held alongside classes on youth leadership and sanitation. Drawing on ballads, classical Sanskrit texts, traditional dances and music, the company became a pioneering force of the indigenous theatre movement in India, establishing folk dramatics as an acceptable form on city stages. In 1982, while looking for inspiration for the *Mahabharata*, Peter Brook was astonished by the company: 'They are born actors. They produce stories that they tell compulsively on their own terms . . . It's pop art using the vocabulary of natural fun.'

In the spring of 1983, Habib and Moneeka had established a temporary base with forty members of the extended Naya Theatre company and their families in a large dilapidated house on the outskirts of Delhi. Children ran around, women cooked squatting over open fires, preparing endless cups of refreshing sweet cardamom *chai*, while in the courtyard rehearsals went on late into the night. *Bahadur Kalarin* was a tale of incest, greed and corruption. It was based on a story Habib had heard from the elders of a small village about a winemaker and her son, who marries 126 women before realising that the only woman he desires is his mother. Appalled, the mother murders her son before killing herself.

Habib had been an MP. He was also something of a celebrity and was invited to all the official government cultural evenings, something he did not relish, but which, he admitted, could prove useful. One evening we buzzed into Delhi in a motor rickshaw, precariously making our way through the chaotic jumble of bicycles, dented Ambassador cars, ambling cows and hooting buses, to attend a cocktail party on the lawns of the grand Lutyens house belonging to Minister of Culture Pupul Jayaka, right next door to Mrs Gandhi's residence. Across the sea of waiters and gossiping matriarchs resplendent in their silk saris, I was sent on a mission to persuade the Director of the Indian Council for Cultural Relations to cover the costs of Naya Theatre's international travel to London. I failed. He had, he said, committed all his budget to the official Festival of India to be held in Britain the following year. But I had better luck on my return to London. A fortunate encounter with the Maharaja of Kashmir and the Director of Drama at the British Council, Robert Sykes, in the actor Roshan Seth's dressing room at the National

Theatre after a perfomance of David Hare's *A Map of the World*, produced a cheque for £3,000 from the British Council.

Every evening before their performance of *Bahadur Kalarin* at the Lyric Theatre, Hammersmith, the company would make a ritualistic offering of a coconut to the gods, an acknowledgement of the inherently sacred act they were about to engage in. Londoners relished the Oedipal tragedy with its parallel commentary on land expropriation and appreciated the plaintive quality of the live music, the haunting songs of the chorus and the tribal dances. However, I felt something had been lost in the transition from the courtyard where I had seen the company rehearse. Encased within the fourth wall of the ornate and formal proscenium, a distance was created, a separation between audience and performers which militated against the improvised play and spontaneity built into the texture and spirit of the performance. For LIFT this was an important lesson in recognising how space and context profoundly affect the meaning and reception of any live performance.

Habib continues to be a pioneering force. Almost twenty years later, in 2002, from his base in Bhopal, amidst a rising tide of religious fundamentalism and communalist violence in India, he made a brave speech about the natural process of exchange and influence between cultures, decrying the forces currently ranged against this dialogue. 'Diverse fabrics are interwoven into the tapestry called the culture of this subcontinent and they have given it perfect harmony and unity. Yet some sections of fundamentalists, both Hindu and Muslim, would have us believe that the Hindu and Muslim cultures are two diametrically opposed phenomena . . . the fact is that our great and flexible Hindu culture has through the centuries influenced and been influenced in its own turn by the various Islamic strains

*Bahadur Kalarin*,
Naya Theatre,
India, LIFT'83.
Courtesy of LIFT
archive.

that flowed into the country from Uzbekistan, Turkey, Iran and Arabia . . . As
Gandhiji once said, he wanted his hut to be rooted in native soil, yet its
windows to be thrown open to the buffetings of the winds of the world. No
one understands this better than artists.'

Habib's views made him very unpopular with the then ruling Bharaitya
Janata Party activists and in 2003 he was given security guards to protect him
in the theatre where his company was performing. 'Security cover for

beleaguered Tanvir,' announced the headlines. Habib was only too conscious of the dangers. On New Year's Day 1989, his friend the visionary poet and playwright Safdar Hashmi was brutally murdered at the age of 34 on the streets of Sahibabad, just outside Delhi, during an outdoor performance to factory workers and local residents. Tensions in the community were running high in the wake of recent strikes and in the run-up to local elections. The sitting candidate having failed to prevent the play from taking place returned with a gang of *goondas* or hired thugs, brandishing arms to terrorise the spectators. Their attack left one member of the audience dead and Hashmi beaten on the head with iron rods, dying in a ditch.

## Chile, Argentina, UK

Ariel Dorfman, *Death and the Maiden*, LIFT'91

1991 was an auspicious year. All over the world a tenuous democracy seemed to be winning out over dictatorship as communities in Eastern and Central Europe, Latin America and South Africa were learning to take the political reins and endeavouring to come to terms with their one-time oppressors. LIFT, in partnership with the National Theatre Studio and the Royal Court, was planning *Cross References,* a set of commissioned short plays that created a dramatic snapshot of the times, giving writers from different continents a chance to air the issues about which they felt most passionately.

Over a drink one evening, we were alerted by the lawyer and writer Albie Sachs, who was in London developing the new Constitution for South Africa, to a play he had heard that week at a reading at the ICA. He explained that it was a kind of psychological thriller which dealt with the near-impossibility of reconciliation without retribution in a post-totalitarian state.

Set in a fragile new democracy in South America, *Death and the Maiden* by Ariel Dorfman truly caught the mood of the times, exploring the nececessity of redeeming the guilt of the past in order to build a more hopeful future. The story – about a young woman, Paulina, who recognises that the man whom her lawyer husband brings home one evening is her former torturer – was recognisable in Eastern Europe and South Africa and in all recently liberated regimes. What price justice? Is the personal cost to be paid in the purchase of democracy too high when it comes to having to forgive your former oppressors? And how do you build a civil society after dictatorship?

Max Stafford-Clark, Director of the Royal Court, was not convinced but

*Death and the
Maiden*, Ariel
Dorfman, Chile/
Argentina/UK,
LIFT'91. Photo:
Mark Douet.

agreed a production could go ahead as it was in the context of the LIFT
season. He had a bet with the director Lindsay Posner that Juliet Stevenson
would not agree to play the part of Paulina. In the event Max paid up his £100
and the play was a huge success, transferring to the West End. The following
year it became the most performed contemporary play across the world, and
was later to be made into a film by Roman Polanski.

*The Government Inspector*, Katona József Theatre, Hungary, LIFT'89. Photo: Marie Laure de Decker.

# Hungary

Katona József Theatre, *The Government Inspector*, LIFT'89

In December 1989 the Berlin Wall fell and with it almost half a century of a Communist-dominated Eastern Europe. From Solidarity in Poland through to *Perestroika* and *Glasnost* in Gorbachev's Soviet Union, changes had been underway for some time. An increasingly strong independent theatre movement had been gaining momentum across the Eastern Block and for LIFT'89 we invited four pioneering companies from Moscow and Leningrad in the Soviet Union and from Budapest in Hungary.

In April 1989, Hungarian soldiers equipped with secateurs and protective gloves began to cut down their country's iron curtain, a 165-mile electric fence on the border between Hungary and Austria. This laborious dismantling was a powerful symbolic and practical act, a sign of the new times in a country on the verge of breaking away from the rule of one-party communism. Four months later, at the Old Vic, the Katona József Theatre, a company who had themselves broken away from the state National Theatre of Hungary, performed *The Government Inspector,* Gogol's comedy of mistaken identity, hypocrisy and corruption. Gabor Zsambeki's ensemble production was an excavation of a contemporary Hungary, panic-stricken at the prospect of the arrival of a new broom sweeping clean existing political cobwebs. It was brilliantly rendered in an expressionistic gloom with leaking roofs, creaking fans and terrified clerks in ill-fitting clothes, desperately shredding incriminating papers amongst banks of rusty clapped-out lockers. An exuberant athleticism and furious comic energy shot through the action as the opportunistic dandy Khlestakov, gaudily dressed and with canary-colour loafers, swung in a drunken delirium from a clothes-horse and postured his way through the ingratiating villagers, liberally partaking of their hospitality, money and women.

On the opening night Lawrence Olivier died. Hundreds of bouquets were delivered to the theatre, television crews and arts reporters descended. Before the show the entire company and audience stood in silent tribute, paying homage to a man whose career was so inextricably linked to the Old Vic. Gabor Zsambeki spoke movingly about how theatre can transcend political barriers through the example set by Olivier who had profoundly influenced a whole generation of theatre in Hungary. The company then bowed their heads towards the box that bears his name.

1. Carla Kirkwood, 'Chinese performing Artists: Redrawing the Map of Chinese Culture', in *Theatre Forum*, no. 25, summer/fall 2004.

# International

## REINVENTING THE INTERNATIONAL

### Rustom Bharucha

LIFT's history has been so vividly encapsulated by its Directors in this *Festschrift* of a book that one runs the risk either of succumbing to the sheer seduction of its rich description, or of coming out like the proverbial spoilsport by interrupting its flow. Taking my cue from Bertolt Brecht, who had warned us not to be seduced in the theatre, I would say that there could be some value in 'interruption', so long as it unpacks some of the illusions of the narrative. What follows, therefore, is a cryptic series of reflections, in which I will try to contextualise LIFT's intervention within a broader framework of ideas relating to the 'international', which could be the most devious term in its nomenclature and self-representation.

By the early 1990s, when I first came into contact with LIFT, it was becoming clearer to me that interculturalism, far from being an autonomous, liberal pursuit of 'cultures of choice' freely 'exchanged' across the globe, was actually mediated by the mechanisms of the nation-state and the global market. Countering the dominant academic views on the subject, I realised that interculturalism was not the antonym of internationalism, but rather its unacknowledged, politically correct, surrogate. But I still didn't have the guts to actually claim the term 'international', because it was so thoroughly discredited for its official and sterile management of anachronistic state-approved national cultures. Today I am beginning to realise that not only do we need to claim the international, but we urgently need to reinvent it, if only

*Gaudeamus (19 Improvisations)*, Maly Drama Theatre, USSR, LIFT'91. Photo: Victor Vassiliev. A brilliantly funny look at the lives of military recruits in the Russian Army, exposing the moral decay of Soviet autocracy. Performed as an historic double bill with *Brothers and Sisters*.

to counter political unilateralism and the defunct institutionalisation of 'world culture' created by agencies like the UN.

A somewhat lone voice in the field of interculturalism in the early 1990s, marked 'Third World' for my dissenting views, I tried to puncture the apparent ease of border-crossing by pointing out the disparities and differences in the actual practice of intercultural projects. To the best of my knowledge, most of these projects, based and funded for the most part in Euro-American locations, were confined conceptually within Eurocentric frameworks, with non-Western cultures providing some exotic material or technical expertise. More disturbingly, as a result of the politics of my location in India, the theatre of interculturalism began with the onerous task of obtaining a visa, followed by interrogation by immigration officers. While in some parts of the world, as in Europe, borders were disappearing for its citizens, in other parts, they were proliferating. And indeed, nationalisms were seethingly alive and well.

It is not insignificant, I think, that I first met Lucy Neal in my home city of Calcutta at the old British Council office on Shakespeare Sarani (previously called Theatre Road). This was the most appropriate meeting place, even though it was not the most congenial place for forgetting the colonial past. In reflecting on Indonesia's possibilities for LIFT, there is a telling remark in Rose Fenton and Lucy Neal's narrative: 'Britain has no colonial links to Indonesia and it was sobering to realise that one's knowledge of a country and culture is informed by such histories.' I appreciate the contradictory truth of this statement even as it appears to counter the post-colonial celebration of hybridity, new ethnicities, and diasporic public spheres. For all the ecological priorities of interculturalism affirming 'the basis for survival of the species', as the director Peter Sellars puts forth in one of his messianic messages, one should not forget that it has also been fuelled by colonialism, imperialism and dominant modes of cultural globalisation.

Following my meeting with Lucy Neal in Calcutta, I was invited by LIFT to give a lecture on 'Somebody's Other', my first public articulation on the sectarian politics of 'othering' in cultural practice. It was to take place at the Royal National Theatre in London. How the 'royal' could coexist with the 'national' remains a conundrum for me, but it was obvious that here again, as with the British Council, one was 'entering the lion's den', as Rose Fenton put it to me with some trepidation. I was more than ready to eat the lion in that lecture, but in the event I charmed the National's formidable chief supervisor of talks with my time-keeping professionalism. 'We will simply down the lights after forty-five minutes,' she had announced rather officiously before the lecture, asserting her authority with very definite signals of territory and ownership. *This is our space, and we're giving it to you for a set amount of time*. I performed within those limits.

As I look back on this officiousness, so typical of national institutions, I am compelled to ask where the limits of institutional civility lie. What has struck me strongly about LIFT's reportage in this book are the numerous indications of its capacity to transgress protocol, even as this transgression is handled in an eminently English way, with perfect manners, concealing a thoroughly irreverent agenda. Call it sly civility, or civil incivility, Rose Fenton and Lucy Neal have clearly mastered the art of Englishness in order to transgress its implicitly conservative, stuffy, regimented, if not implicitly racist, codes and rules. Whether they are dealing with the Police Force, the Fire Brigade, sound engineers or religious bigots, they ultimately manage to disarm the establishment, even while breaking all the rules in mounting their risky, site-specific productions. Not without some chutzpah do co-conspirators Neal and Fenton claim after one of their early coups: 'We have taken our own permission for creating the event in the first place.'

I applaud this irreverence, but I am compelled to question the privilege that facilitates its articulation. I am struck, for instance, by the ability of LIFT to have its debts written off by the Arts Council after their 1983 Festival when they faced near bankruptcy. Likewise, I am awed by the confidence with which they acknowledge how 'a budget of £75,000 was raised with relative ease' for *The Factory of Dreams,* a collaboration between internationally renowned fire-artist Christophe Berthonneau and the students of Stockwell Park School, branded a 'sink' school, representing families from over forty ethnic groups.

In both cases, it becomes obvious that the support for LIFT's economics has been facilitated through the politics of *multiculturalism* – a troubled term that is never once invoked in the book, but which underlies the considerable patronage that LIFT has received from political and commercial establishments. If the Arts Council could write off the debts of LIFT, it is not merely because its officers were entertained by the iconoclastic aesthetic of the Festival. More precisely, this iconoclasm had the potential to feed the tenuous multicultural priorities of the state. Likewise, if *The Factory of Dreams* could be sponsored by urban regeneration initiatives in Brixton and used as a learning programme for the Business Arts Forum, it was because corporations like British Airways had imagined a cosy nexus between 'the global challenges of their own businesses and the cohesion of a school's [multi-ethnic] community.'

The subtext of multiculturalism, which could be described in the British context as the management of diverse cultures within an ethos of integrating differences, becomes all the more evident through its erosion in the story of the Hanoi Water Puppets project. Here there is a clear rift between the advocates of multiculturalism, as represented by the members of the Vietnam Refugee Project based in London, and the state-sponsored Hanoi Water Puppets group from Vietnam itself. Cultural affinities notwithstanding, there is total distrust among the former refugee community of this 'international' intervention, which cannot be separated from memories of violence, Communist aggression and the trauma of migration. The only solution is for the local production of *Sang Song* to dissociate itself from the Vietnamese puppet group and to assert its 'self-contained' autonomy. So much for internationalism.

Not surprisingly, the production turns out to be a euphoric experience in which young Vietnamese can reclaim their cultural identities, without living in denial of their origins or names. 'For once, here was a positive celebratory story about their community, far removed from the daily issues of unemployment, crime and racism,' as the LIFT narrative affirms. This, I fear, is the language of feel-good multiculturalism, which the British state has consciously promoted over the years, despite numerous setbacks. To what extent it has contributed to racism, as the Slovenian critic Slavoj Žižek has suggested provocatively,[1] is a complex matter, but it comes as no surprise that the Vietnam Refugee Project should rename itself as the Greenwich Vietnam Community Centre. The 'refugee' is dropped in favour of 'community', thereby playing into the seemingly harmonious ghettoisation of ethnic communities on which multiculturalism thrives, despite – or perhaps because of – its over-emphatic rhetoric of inclusion.

The point that I would like to make here is that LIFT's internationalism, at least in its early years, corresponds with the state's advocacy of multiculturalism in an integrative mode. To elide the international with the multicultural is to miss out on the tensions that separate their agendas. At all costs one has to avoid the kind of naïvety conveyed by the critic Robert Hewison in response to 'Britain's first Bollywood musical', *Moti Roti Puttli Chunni*, when he asserts that, 'The make-up of London audiences – Caribbean, Asian, Anglo-Saxon – is international in itself. All LIFT had to do was to give it theatrical expression.'

Two critical inflections are needed here: first, the make-up of the London audience is better described as potentially multicultural rather than intrinsically

Pupils from Charlton Manor Primary School process on the South Bank before performing in the Queen Elizabeth Hall with the Balinese Seka Barong, UK, LIFT'95 (page 95). Courtesy of LIFT archive.

international; and, second, it is presumptuous to assume that any 'theatrical expression' can automatically evolve through the mere existence of a heterogeneous population. There are mediations and specific interventions at work, which shape the transition of the energies in the public sphere into the articulation of particular theatrical forms. In contrast to Hewison's assumptions of the international, the critic Clement Crisp is more on the mark when he grudgingly praises the improvisatory Kecak and processional drama of the 'local tots' from Charlton Manor Primary School, Greenwich, during a matinée

performance of the Indonesian Barong: 'Community spoke to community and not unworthily.' This is a very English, Sunday-school endorsement of 'community', almost homiletic in its genteel patronisation of different cultures, divested of multicultural-international tensions.

The critical point is that LIFT's internationalism has been grounded through its close interaction with local communities in London. Even when it has invited foreign productions with no local participation whatsoever, the city has served to catalyse its connections, as, for instance, in its initiation of the Chinese opera *The Three Beatings of Tao San Chun*, which was 'the first Chinese play to be brought to Britain after the Cultural Revolution and possibly even since the establishment of the People's Republic in 1949.' This, indeed, is a *coup de théâtre*. But how was it made possible on a lightning trip to China when one of LIFT's Directors managed to see the director Wu Zuguang for merely a couple of hours before catching her flight back home? This would seem to be an exemplary case of what has been branded as Instant Interculturalism, a last-minute purchase on a festival shopping spree.

And yet, when one reads the documentation more closely, one realises the simmering action behind the scenes, inspired partially by the London-based star Tsai Chin of *Suzie Wong* fame. In this context, a sentence in the LIFT narrative is well worth quoting at length for its sheer audacity: 'The friendship between Tsai Chin and the Wu family provided an invaluable link that enabled LIFT to make what felt like a hopelessly over-ambitious assault on the Chinese government to try and persuade them to cover the costs of the thirty-five artists assembled to travel to London.' On the one hand, the international is facilitated through old family connections between a diasporic star and a great master back home, who uses his own *guanxi* (connections) to bargain with the very government that has been responsible for disabling his wife, an erstwhile star, through repeated beatings. LIFT capitalises on these connections to make an 'assault on the Chinese government'. An outrageous hyperbole, if one considers whether the Taiwanese government would ever dare to 'assault' its Chinese counterpart. But what are the stakes of this particular 'assault'? Thirty-five round-trip air tickets.

'The Chinese will never pay for anything,' LIFT is warned by the British Council. Not only do they pay, LIFT calls up Lord Gowrie, Mrs Thatcher's Conservative Minister for the Arts, and suggests very tactfully that he might consider paying for a coach in which the Chinese company could travel around London in relative comfort, instead of using the tube and getting headaches in the process. Once again, this is an instance of LIFT's chutzpah, but would I go to the extent of saying that such gestures contribute towards 'Anglo-Chinese cultural relations'? I am not so sure.

What I would like to insert into the discussion here is the keyword 'complicity', without which cultural exchanges across borders cannot be facilitated. In this regard, the Lebanese theatre-maker Rabih Mroué, who makes a brief appearance in this book, hits the nail on the head with his acute observation: 'All authority and power is ultimately created by us. No one is innocent and somehow we are all complicit in whatever happens around us.' I wish that there could be more evidence of this reflection in LIFT's history, and a little less bravado, as, for instance, in its description of the Beijing punk rock singer He Yong, whose passport is detained just before he attempts to depart for London. In this post-Tiananmen period, he is held up for a week, until the British Council officer takes control and whisks him on to the plane, guitar in hand, 'brazenly waving a pretend ticket'. He Yong makes a last-minute appearance on the London stage, but he 'chose to mime his songs', which would seem to me that he feared the possibility of persecution. At one level, it could be argued the performance appears to be an assertion of freedom, but, at another level, it merely capitulates to the terror of censorship. LIFT can merely facilitate and observe this phenomenon; it can do nothing to change it.

But perhaps, it is unfair to ask theatre to change anything beyond a few perceptions of the world. LIFT is duly taken to task when its political illusions are called into question by al-Kasaba theatre from Ramallah, Palestine. Shrewdly, the group turns down LIFT's suggestion to create a production entitled *West Bank Stories*, on the grounds that 'the West Bank . . . has become synonymous for us with the occupation itself and others' definition of us.' Countering the deadening impact of Palestine's media image, al-Kasaba prefers to de-itemise and humanise its struggle through the more deftly worded *Alive from Palestine*. When the initial sketches of this play-in-the-making appear a little too humorous and ironic for the political expectations of LIFT's Directors, they are reassured that the play is not mere documentation of what is actually happening in Palestine, but an artistic response to its state of siege. 'We are not planning to bomb London to get the right sound effects' – a devastating comment by the director that debunks political correctness in favour of creative immediacy and common sense.

One of the joys of the LIFT history is that it embraces such self-critique in an ironic mode. But I would like to push the point further by emphasising that LIFT has demonstrated an extraordinary hospitality and generosity in opening its Festival to groups like al-Kasaba that are struggling to survive in a state of war. This is an instance of international solidarity without which there can be no hope for civility in theatre. Having acknowledged this point, I am also compelled to question the limits of such civil gestures. Indeed, do they not run the risk of appearing tokenistic in the lack of a follow-up to their incorporation in the Festival?

At a broader level, there are more critical questions that need to be asked. How can the civil meet the challenge of the political, instead of retreating into the shell of its imagined security? How can an international theatre festival make itself more vulnerable to misunderstanding and attack, especially when it presumes to represent groups like al-Kasaba, whose theatre has been physically targeted by the Israeli forces? Is it sufficient merely to showcase their work and highlight its 'humanism', or can one cross the existing structures of civil society to ignite a more politically charged theatrical discourse and practice?

Through these questions, we are compelled to imagine other forums of interaction and dialogue that need to exist outside the boundaries of theatre, in which representatives of civil society and the state can be made more accountable for their lack of sufficient support for particular struggles, as in Palestine. Here, there can be no reassurance of civility, because the dialogue could break down through accusations of partisanship and divided loyalties. I believe that an internationally oriented theatre today has no other option but to take on the discomfort of such accusations through an embrace of difference.

Certainly, I welcome the critical doubts of George Ibrahim, the indefatigable Director of al-Kasaba, when he looks back on a UN-funded Israeli/Arab production of *Romeo and Juliet* that had toured widely in Europe, in the wake of the euphoria hoped for in the Oslo Peace Process. The LIFT history documents Ibrahim's doubts with empathy: 'Now he was feeling disillusioned and regarded the venture as a false symbol, cynically engineered by the authorities for foreign consumption of a peace that did not exist back home.' Instead of the theatrically mediated peace process of the UN, Ibrahim is compelled to endorse a more grounded, if volatile, cultural practice in Palestine itself.

But then, one could ask, would this theatre not cease to be international? LIFT does not sufficiently probe this question in its failure to investigate what constitutes the 'national' in the first place, in different locations. In Britain, at least one important agency in re-imagining the national would have to be attributed to multiculturalism, which the book completely elides. In the case of Palestine, however, to which al-Kasaba is inextricably linked, the national has not yet petrified in the form of a recognised state. Turbulently, it is in the making, through the mutations of an intense struggle. But this doesn't mean that the international cannot be envisioned in places like Ramallah, even though the so-called world community has yet to respond to Palestine in a sufficiently cohesive way.

I am reminded of the philosopher Frantz Fanon's important injunction that in a state of struggle, 'National consciousness, which is not nationalism, is the only thing that will give us an international dimension . . . It is at the heart of national consciousness that international consciousness lives and grows. And this two-fold emerging is ultimately the source of all culture.'[2] While this complex statement cannot be unpacked here, it challenges the liberal premises of internationalism that exist independently of national struggle and redefinition. Fanon's statement also compels one to question more fundamental issues relating to the location of international cultural practice. One task that lies ahead in this context is to stop thinking of the international as the prerogative of the cosmopolitan global city, which has been far too valorised in contemporary postmodern discourse. The international, I would insist, has the potential to exist anywhere. In London, but also in Ramallah.

Secondly, for the new international to exist, we need to work towards not merely an exchange of 'who we are' and 'where we're coming from', but how and where we *differ* from each other. This is the real test. We need to be prepared to work towards an exchange of differences, while keeping in mind that there is every possibility of misunderstanding and more intensified hurt in the transaction. But, without this risk, I fear that the international can go nowhere in its search for a more peaceful and harmonious world. It will become yet another dinosaur, rather like the International Theatre Institute, which has long lost its *raison d'être,* but refuses to die.

In this context of negotiating differences, we can learn from Pascale Feghali, who single-handedly ran the Ayloul Festival in Beirut. The LIFT narrative informs us how she had to face the dismay of the European Union officers, who could not understand why the new Lebanese productions, which they had funded, should be so obsessed with the past, instead of celebrating a more optimistic future. Feghali was compelled to point out the critical truism that differences need to be acknowledged and exposed, instead of festering through erasures of their imagined resolution or extinction. She could also have added that the smallest differences are also the ones that tend to be most virulent, if not explosive. How does an international festival inscribe – and transform – this bitter truth through the alchemy of its vision, and its playful ability to detoxify the evil forces of our times?

That great soul of the theatre of freedom, Barney Simon of the Market Theatre in Johannesburg, is reported in this book as saying, 'We are still living with the toxins of apartheid . . . in South Africa there has been a change in legislation, not a change in human hearts.' I think he would be very moved by

*Met'n Sak Onner die Blad*, Phakama, South Africa/UK, Cape Town 1998. Courtesy of Phakama archive. A hundred young people from across South Africa and London joined Western Cape participants in exploring stories and responses to a series of cultural visits to Robben Island, District Six and Cape Point (page 207).

LIFT's interventions in the New South Africa through groups like Phakama, who have not merely narrated their own history with exuberance and song, but who have dramatised the stories of black teenagers like Stephen Lawrence in London, another victim of a different kind of racist apartheid.

In this production dedicated to Lawrence, the young cast of Phakama came forward with bowls of water offering to wash the hands of the audience. I have mixed feelings about this 'ritual atonement', because it seems to play to the myth of forgiveness and cleansing the sins of the past. Indeed, this gesture would seem to contradict the more politically valid observation made by

William Kentridge, among many other critics of the Truth and Reconciliation process, that truth without justice, facilitated through the amnesty given to former perpetrators of violence, cannot result in reconciliation. Indeed, such truth becomes 'intolerable', and to watch its ritual re-enactment in the theatre becomes all the more offensive precisely because it can move you to tears.

With South Africa on my mind, I remember visiting Robben Island with two of the LIFT/Phakama organisers in preparation for the celebration of Freedom Day, in which Phakama had been given the honour of marking 'the island's transition from being a place of commemoration to one of participatory celebration'. I was not around to see the celebration, but what I did observe very closely was the negotiation of the LIFT/Phakama team with the Robben Island authorities. This was very different from any production meeting that I had attended in my life. Would it be possible to use Mandela's cell for an installation? What could we do in the lime quarry where the white of the lime was so stark that it had dried up the tear-ducts of the prisoners? How could we bus the visitors on Freedom Day from one end of the island to another? Practical questions, involving the nitty-gritty of mounting yet another site-specific show.

However, it was different. In the forthright answers of the Robben Island authorities, some of whom had been prisoners in the past, and the down-to-earth questions of theatre workers linked to an international festival based in London, I saw the beginnings of a 'new international' emerging through an altogether unprecedented dialogue: outside the boundaries of theatre, but also outside the borders of an erstwhile prison. Neither entirely civil nor political, this interstitial space was where the new international was being reinvented in concrete terms, albeit for a specific project. In this reinvention, there was no memorandum, no treaty, no re-mapping of borders, no song, no production, just the beginnings of a dialogue facilitating a new kind of cultural practice.

Significantly, I felt these beginnings not in cosmopolitan, multi-ethnic, multicultural London, but on a bleak island with a fragile ecosystem on the point of collapse, which had served as a prison-house for the numerous fighters of apartheid, most of them dead, but a few alive: Robben Island. This resurgence can serve as a sign of what remains to be reinvented in our understanding of the international in the theatre today.

1. For more elaboration on Žižek's position on multiculturalism as 'a disavowed, inverted, self-referential form of racism,' read my book *The Politics of Cultural Practice: Thinking through Theatre in an Age of Globalization* (London, Continuum Books, 2000; Hanover, Wesleyan University Press, 2000), pp. 34–41.
2. Fanon's concluding statement to his seminal essay 'On National Culture' has been discussed *vis-à-vis* the intercultural in *The Politics of Cultural Practice*, op.cit., pp. 26–30.

# Festival

Over the past twenty-five years we have been welcomed by festivals all over the world – from PanaFest in Ghana to the Golden Mask in Moscow, from Ayloul in Beirut and Grahamstown in South Africa to Los Angeles, Bogotá, Tehran and Adelaide. Life-long friendships have been forged and insights gained that have inspired and fuelled our work.

What has struck us repeatedly is that these gatherings, while all rooted in the political, social or cultural specificities of particular times and places, have an essential commonality: they play at the edges of what is real and what is not, disrupting borders and questioning the status quo. In the process – in the true tradition of festivals throughout the ages – people can fall out of their normal patterns of behaviour, creating what Dragan Klaić calls 'experimental zones of sociability'.

The stories in this chapter also recount some of the challenges we have grappled with at LIFT over the years, and how we have attempted to generate a sense of festival in a city as large as London. A festival's social interactions and the shifts of perception these engender prove time and again ultimately to become its real subject matter. Mischief can be made, hierarchies can be inverted and social boundaries pushed. In the words of Welfare State International's Director John Fox: 'The Lords of Misrule have a sacred duty to rock the boat.' Driven by artistic experimentation, festivals are ultimately ephemeral utopian spaces. Yet, we believe, their legacies live on in the imperceptible shifts that occur in our everyday realities, once the revels are over.

**LIFT'83 Launch in Covent Garden, Urban Sax, France (page 142). Photo: Irmgard Pozorski.**

## LIFT'87

La Cubana, Spain, *La Tempestad*; Circus Oz, Australia; Vusisizwe Players, South Africa, *You Strike the Woman, You Strike the Rock*

It began to go horribly wrong when a man with a decibel-counter was to be found stumbling around in the rose bushes opposite Sadler's Wells, where an assembled company of LIFT staff, Catalan artists and theatre personnel held their breath while they waited for him to deliver his verdict on the sound levels of a show that was threatened with having its entertainment licence withdrawn. The company in question, La Cubana, from Barcelona, was to stage an inventive version of *La Tempestad,* which was to involve a *real* tempest. On the opening night of the show, the first act of a cod version of Shakespeare's play was interrupted with the news that London was being engulfed by tempestuous floods. The audience was instructed to don the plastic macs which they would find stowed beneath their seats and then to abandon the auditorium. Bundling into the foyer they were to discover that the theatre had been turned into the fairground of surprises promised in the brochure. To a

*La Tempestad*,
La Cubana, Spain,
LIFT'87. Courtesy
of LIFT archive.

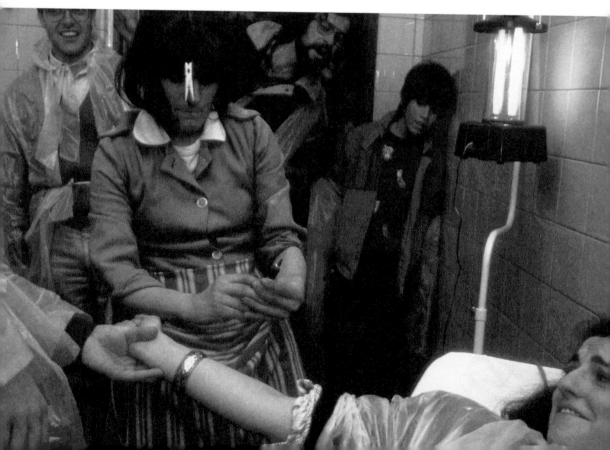

rough theme of 'Enjoy-yourself-before-you-die' they could make a last confession in the stalls bar, join life-enhancing initiation ceremonies, sip vitamin juices, buy raffle tickets or join increasingly manic Catalan singalongs while waiting for Prospero and his colleagues to mount a promised rescue operation. Swimming lessons were underway throughout the building and the foyers and corridors swirled with people rustling in their coloured plastic macs as ever more surreal scenes unfolded around them. Who could forget the sight of Guardian critic Michael Billington learning to swim on a lilo in the Circle Bar, as naked-buttocked frogmen proceeded to lead us towards an awaiting yellow submarine? Finally ushered out into the street, we had to brave blowing leaves, wind machines and a cascade of water running down the front of Sadler's Wells. A thunderstorm boomed out over Rosebery Avenue and people passing on the Number 19 bus stared in puzzlement as a damp and chuckling audience gathered on the pavement.

The show was a sell-out before it opened, but in the event we had to refund every ticket for the remaining performances. After the abolition of the GLC, licensing powers had recently been devolved to local boroughs and Islington Borough Council proved nervous of anything that attracted an unusual amount of comment from the public. It was reported that local residents had complained about the thunderstorm noise and at the waste of water, especially 'as there were droughts in Essex'. The next day, the man with the decibel-counter in the rose bushes declared that the noise of the thunderclaps exceeded the agreed sound levels and the show was cancelled.

This production was the first (and only, so far) to be cancelled in twenty-five years of LIFT. And, as if on cue, the following day the real skies opened and London was drenched in rivers of rain for a solid three weeks at the wettest Festival on record. As the devastated Catalans returned home, we moved on to the next crisis. Production staff at the Circus Oz tent at Coin Street, on the South Bank, were developing trench foot because the site was flooded; and the Australian circus artists were refusing to go on because damp duckboards made the soles of their acrobat pumps dangerously slippery. From LWT next door, fellow Australian Barry Humphries came to liven the gloom, promising to heap on the gladioli glitz and, with the acrobats finally back on board, he waltzed into their Big Top to open a hugely successful show. Meanwhile, at Riverside Studios, the Russian director Anatoli Vasiliev's leading actress had locked herself in her hotel room, refusing to perform unless we upgraded her accommodation. As her fellow actors paced their dressing rooms convinced she would hold to her threat we were

forced to call her bluff – we had no spare budget. She appeared on stage
one minute before the curtain went up.

Most dramatically, a new theatre space had to be found for each of the
three weeks of the LIFT run of *You Strike the Woman, You Strike the Rock* by
South Africa's Vusisizwe Players, because London's Tricycle Theatre, where
they had been booked, burnt down a few weeks before the Festival
(coincidentally the show running at the time was John Cooper's *Burning Point*).
With a total of nineteen productions, LIFT'87 featured first-time invitations to
companies from Mexico, Australia, Spain, Argentina, Nigeria and the Soviet
Union, with new productions by Anatoli Vasiliev, Robert Lepage and George C.
Wolfe, a big-top circus and no less than three Festival commissions. When we
look back at that programme now, we are quite simply astonished any of us
survived it.

## LIFT'99

Festival Club, HMS *President*; Forced Entertainment, UK, *Who Can Sing A Song
To Unfrighten Me?*

People often ask us how we create a sense of festival in a city the size of
London. It helps to have a physical space to call home, where the experiences
of art, dancing and socialising can overlap for artists and audiences – a
metaphoric base camp from which to explore. With festival-goers travelling in
from theatres all over London and tubes and licensed bars closing down
around midnight, finding the right kind of space has always proved difficult.
Over the years our solutions have been many: we have taken up residence in
the basement of the Piccadilly Hotel in the West End; we have built a 1920s
Dutch *Spiegeltent*, an elaborate hexagonal wooden structure with beautifully
carved pillars and lined with mirrors, in Camden Lock; we have recreated the
Almeida Theatre as a dance hall; and held party nights at the Diorama, the
original Regent's Park venue for Daguerre's illusionist experiments in the 1820s.
For LIFT'99, the former First World War minesweeper HMS *President*, moored
on the River Thames at Victoria Embankment next to Blackfriars Bridge, was an
ideal space. Its prime London spot, poetic nautical feel and open-air decks
more than compensated for the rusting portholes, leaking roofs, clanking
gangways and other idiosyncratic dilapidations. The ship was theatrical in itself.
A beautiful large ballroom (the old drill hall) opened into bars with varnished
wood and polished brass handrails. Time was marked not by the clock, but by

**HMS *President*,
Victoria
Embankment,
Festival Club
LIFT'99 and '01.
Photo: Michael J.
O'Brien
Photography.**

the rising and falling of the ship on the river's tidal water. By day there were Daily Dialogues[1] with the visiting artists, chaired by passionate arts advocate, writer and broadcaster Professor Lisa Jardine. By night London-based music promoter Max Reinhart and the Vauxhall Tavern's gay punk cabaret team of artists, Duckie, joined performers from across the world, including the inimitable drag diva Stayfree from Venezuela. Throughout, the up-and-coming celebrity chef Allegra McEvedy produced miraculous banquets from a galley kitchen with a broken-down cooker.

HMS *President* was also the temporary home of Maurice O'Connell. Commissioned to be the LIFT Cartographer, he called himself 'the Stowaway' and slept in a small cabin below deck. Maurice was to map LIFT, moving between Festival events and sites, taking audiences on improvised tours across the city. We asked him to reflect the Festival back to us and like a lightning conductor of Festival interactions he did just that, hosting impromptu

*Who Can Sing
A Song To
Unfrighten Me?*,
Forced
Entertainment,
UK, LIFT'99.
Photo: Hugo
Glendinning.

conversations and connecting people and places. Like Flann O'Brien's Third
Policeman, who lived between two walls, he took up residence inside the
Festival, exploring its spaces and telling its stories.

   During the four weeks of LIFT, Maurice infiltrated every corner of the Festival,
from Arding and Hobbs department store in Clapham Junction to the top of
Euston Tower office block and on northwards to the Tricycle Theatre in Kilburn.
On Friday 18 June, an expedition involved crossing to the South Bank where
fourteen artists were about to launch into a 24-hour performance described as
a 'journey from night to day and back again'. It was a show about staying up all
night as a protection against the demons that hide in the dark. Seven hundred
people had gathered at the Queen Elizabeth Hall to see Forced Entertainment's
*Who Can Sing A Song To Unfrighten Me?* (the question asked by director Tim

Etchells's small son Miles as they had travelled by car one night in the dark across Snake Pass in the Pennines).

Audiences settled in for a vigil as the actors improvised a version of the world they inhabited, telling bedtime stories about love, hate, fear, monsters and death. Rituals, games of enchantment, transformations and the act of dying were constantly repeated. The actors shuffled on as forest trees or dressed as animals, then went behind a bed-sheet to re-emerge as humans. One performer wrote on the blackboard the word 'live' just as another performer fell down dead. When the word 'dead' was written, the performer stood up.

During the 24 hours, we felt tired, got bored, went out for coffee, talked to friends, returned to the auditorium. Some went home for the night and came back at breakfast. Others stayed for the long haul. The auditorium was filled with sleeping people strung out across the seats, alongside those tuning in for a further burst of fairy stories, jokes, fantasies or confessional tales. Forced Entertainment's work has been described as 'spiritual theatre for atheists'. In the context of an urban international festival, we liked to see *Who Can Sing A Song To Unfrighten Me?* as a kind of secular equivalent to the great religious festival epics such as the *Ramayana*, *Mahabharata* or Medieval Mystery Plays, where communities would come together over several days to witness – or challenge – stories that gave meaning to their lives.

Extraordinarily, a similar process of questioning – also theatrical – was unfolding in London that very day outside the theatre. The dramas of the Festival became, in the minds of the audience, interspersed with the dramas on the streets, as London, along with other cities, experienced its first major protest against a globalised world order. Ten thousand revellers and rioters took to the streets for a day of action and carnival aimed at the heart of capitalism and the global economy. Oxfam had a run on second-hand suits, as rioters masqueraded as city workers. But city workers had been reminded that it was 'dress-down Friday' so that they should not stand out. Maurice took off towards Big Ben, camera in hand to film the historic moment, joining militant eco-warriors and nude unicyclists in a riot of theatre that threatened to overwhelm London.

Throughout the day violence increased as protesters attacked city institutions, turned over cars and defaced statues. The police responded with tear gas and force. As we walked over Waterloo Bridge on our way to the South Bank, we passed a cordon of police in riot gear holding back an angry crowd. Someone had been shot, we heard, and the ambulance was about to arrive. Pushing our way through, we arrived at the Queen Elizabeth Hall to catch just the last moments of Forced Entertainment's rehearsals. 'So here we are making theatre,' remarked Tim wryly, when he heard what was erupting in the city all around, 'whilst outside the real revolution is happening.'

## LIFT'87

Free Street Theater, USA, *Project! The Cabrini Green Musical*

Cabrini Green in the heart of Chicago, whose construction began in 1940 on the day Pearl Harbour was bombed, was the first ever high-rise, high-density housing development in the world. With 14,000 people living in an area of one square mile, this 'little hell' was acknowledged in 1987 to be one of the poorest and most violent communities in America, run by armed gangs and filled with fear and social despair.

From out of this community came the Free Street Theater with *Project!,* a defiant musical documentary, created by Patrick Henry and the inhabitants of Cabrini Green, describing oppressed lives, lived against great odds. Stacks of TV screens, recreating the tower blocks, flickered into life as residents told their tales of anger and family disintegration, and of their dreams and hopes. On the ground below, encased by wire meshing, the cast, aged 7 to 50, performed a cabaret of rock, rap, gospel and blues, celebrating the energy and humanity of the estate.

*Project!* was performed during LIFT'87 at Philip Hedley's Theatre Royal Stratford East, in Newham, a London borough with its own high-rise blocks, poverty and social deprivation. Philip, after considerable lobbying, had secured an invitation for the company to a lunch-time reception at the American Embassy, hosted by the Ambassador. The Ambassador's office realised only the day before the reception that the Free Street Theater artists were from the infamous Cabrini Green estate. An embarrassed Social Secretary rang the Theatre Royal Stratford East to cancel the lunch, claiming they were double-booked. This raised a storm of protest from LIFT, the theatre and the company. The Embassy backed down, nervously seeking assurance that the company would behave themselves in the presence of the Ambassador. In Grosvenor Square the next day, two of the younger members of the cast stepped dramatically up to the Ambassador, startling him as he came out to greet the company. In a moment of panic, two bodyguards almost threw themselves at the boys who, ignoring the commotion around them, broke into a specially composed rap of welcome directly addressed to 'His Ex-cell-ency Mister Am-bass-ador'.

Since the days of Joan Littlewood in the 50s and 60s, the Theatre Royal Stratford East has always presented shows that draw on, and resonate with, the stories and lives of its community. It would be said of Joan Littlewood's work that: 'Good theatre takes the energy from a place and hands it back as *joie de vivre*.' And Free Street Theater struck a chord at Stratford East. Newham audiences heard their own stories through the stories of Cabrini Green and the company became stars overnight, with local children and teenagers queuing at the stage door for their autographs. In London, the Cabrini Green residents had become ambassadors for their own country, with a greater impact than many officially sanctioned holders of that post.

At the US Embassy, Ambassador and actors joined together around a table of sandwiches, Kit-Kats and soft drinks. On leaving, we sneaked a peep over some partition walls into an adjoining larger reception room to see a bigger table groaning with lobster, strawberries and champagne. Who did you have to be to get that deal?

## LIFT'99

Neil Thomas, Andrew Morrish, David Wells, Nick Papas and Richard Jeziorny, Australia, *Urban Dream Capsule*

*Urban Dream Capsule* was commissioned originally for Myers Melbourne, the fifth-largest department store in the world. Four men create a living breathing 'Urban Dream Capsule' in the store's windows, which are transformed into serviceable living spaces where the performers eat, sleep, cook and bath under 24-hour non-stop public gaze for fourteen days. At no point are the blinds lowered and shoppers can watch the daily rituals of the four men as they act out their lives in full view, never leaving the capsule. The performance is wired electronically with telephone, fax and internet, creating an inter-active performance that builds over the performance period.

Could we find a store in London? Despite the fact that the show had a track-record of increasing a store's income by 14 per cent, we could not. These were the days before Reality TV and *Big Brother* and we were viewed with incomprehension. Selfridges flinched at the idea of a plumbed lavatory in their shop window, Harrods stuck at displays of tilting Range Rovers, and at Whiteleys the idea was ruled out in case the men were fried alive in their 360 degree greenhouse if the summer proved hot. Dickens and Jones said No, John Lewis said No, Top Shop, Debenhams: No No No. Up and down Oxford Street we traipsed.

The answer lay where we least expected. Clapham Junction is an area better known for its railway station and its grand, but slightly battered, corner department store, Arding and Hobbs (Allders), than for its avant-garde art. The ten-minute encounter with the store director Richard Cooney was brusque. 'Nice idea, my dear, but how would I ever persuade my boss?' He stopped in his tracks when we proposed, out of desperation, to speak to his boss on his behalf via someone we knew. We were putting into action the first law of the parallel universe: the licensed circumnavigation of existing hierarchies. Meanwhile, way down on the corporate ladder, Colin the maintenance man was measuring for sewage pipes, as the Clapham Junction Town Centre Manager persuaded the Wandsworth Economic Development Office that the regeneration of the area needed more buzz than mere redesigned street furniture. Where plumbing led, policy could follow.

How did four men in a shop window for fourteen days do this? Other cities had placed the four men – Andrew, Dave, Neil and Nick – in ritzy retail malls and thoroughfares. But Clapham Junction offered them their first taste of a rooted local community. By day part of a busy local shopping area, Arding and Hobbs sits on a border-line between the gentrified houses around the Northcote Road and the tough housing estates of Battersea. As the local police discussed with Richard Cooney ways of reducing the risks of possible violent attacks by night, the show's creator and director Neil Thomas calmly observed that: 'This project is about human relationships. Believe me, it weaves a ring of safety around the shop. It creates its own magic.'

Once we had the green light, with Allders not just giving permission but also financing £12,000 of the show's costs (matched by an equal award from Arts and Business), an obligatory three-way marriage began between a department store, an international festival and a group of shaven-headed experimental artists. In a matter of weeks we had to build a bright yellow 'submarine capsule' in the menswear window (referred to in production meetings as 'the intrusion into menswear'), plumb in showers and a toilet (for the curious, the dry chemical toilet could not be seen, and was emptied daily by LIFT technical staff), choose bed linen, pots and pans, build bunk beds, fit computer terminals and, critically, ensure the safety of the men. They needed fresh air, oxygen, ventilation by day, heating by night, along with a 24-hour guard. The windows were reinforced with bullet-proof glass and the Battersea police and their 'rapid-response teams' were on

*Urban Dream Capsule*, Nick Papas, Andrew Morrish, David Wells and Neil Thomas, designer Richard Jeziorny, Australia, LIFT'99, Arding & Hobbs, Clapham Junction. Photo: Michael J. O'Brien Photography.

high alert. At no point were customers to be held up in their daily rounds of ironing-board- or carpet-buying.

On a sunny day in June, the willing captives were 'sealed' into the capsule for their two-week 'artstronaut' journey. The clock started to tick and everyone started to play. Schoolchildren came to watch them, pressing their cheeks up against the glass, the store staff took their cigarette breaks out on the pavement, and increasing numbers of the public slowed down beside the window, first in curious amazement (Is it for charity?) and increasingly in familiar connection, miming questions: How's it going in there? OK Dave? How's your knee? Better? As Neil himself said, 'We just presented our lives and people flocked to see. No one would have thought that life could be so interesting.'

Over the weeks, the men performed, bathed, cooked, knitted, washed up, danced, wore kilts one minute, pyjamas the next, spoke to people on their mobiles, and (as they could not be heard) answered questions by writing on small notice boards. Pupils from a school for the deaf revelled in their superior abilities to communicate gesturally through the glass barrier. People donated potted plants, teddy bears and recipes for Jamaican stews. Ladies from the bakery brought them buns, others carried over a table and sat outside on the pavement joining the men for a dinner party, tables inside and out buttressed up against the pane. A teacher brought her whole primary school class, a secondary school brought their drumming group to play to the men, and sometimes at night people returned disbelievingly to see if the men 'really were' asleep and then gazed silently at them lying there like babies. 'Experts' were suddenly those who established an immediate rapport with the show's existential sense of alienation and isolation. New dialogues became possible outside the window. Shy adults relied on children and well-healed Claphamites on their way to dinner parties turned to the homeless youth for an explanation of what was happening. One correspondent wrote:

> 'It filled me with sadness to encounter you, and that's not at all a criticism, for some of the sadness is my own. I think it's about separation and loss and mourning and how to make reparation for broken-down relationships when it's suddenly the eleventh minute of the eleventh hour and you realise that what was really important was exactly the thing that you dismissed or denigrated all the time ...'

The customary LIFT Daily Dialogue, held in conjunction with each Festival show, had to be staged in the store canteen, with the men connected via a TV link. Honorary guests Elaine Showalter from the US and Mary Portas from retail design consultant Yellow Door duly discussed shop windows as portals of desire and longings, dreams and aspirations. High cultural theory gave way to dramatic practicalities as the Clapham drains decided that day to show their age. Out of view to those of us in the canteen but much to the hilarity of a growing crowd on the pavement outside, the men's shower was overflowing with copious quantities of a noxious looking fluid and, judging from the men's reactions, with accompanying stink-bomb smells. Neil, Nick, Dave and Andrew made valiant but increasingly hopeless attempts to stay in the virtual screened dialogue being conducted for their benefit up in the canteen, while at the same time attending to the more pressing matters of rolling up their trousers and wielding mops and buckets. The dialogue had to continue without the men's involvement. The empty TV screen beside the panellists upstairs however offered a tantalising reminder that what the public down in the street were witnessing was far more interesting than any theoretical discourse at one remove could ever be.

The four security guards were initially the least keen on being involved. Art was sissy stuff and they were having no part of it. They were required to stand watch over the men, particularly as they slept. As the nights passed they encountered drunks barrelling down the street who stopped in their tracks out of curiosity. Night after night one young girl returned to stand in tears at the window to watch the men sleep. When finally asked by one of the security guards why she was so sad, she explained that she was three months pregnant and her boyfriend had just 'done a runner'.

On the day the men came out, they could have been space-travellers returning from Mars. The 'release' hour – moved back several hours after days of successful lobbying by local schoolchildren who wished to be present – was preceded by the men grooming themselves in their best capsule suits of candlewick pink, green, yellow and blue. They stepped out of the submarine hatch to roars from waiting crowds packing the pavements. The normally surly security guards puffed up their chests as they held back the crowds, while Richard Cooney and the ladies from the bakery looked visibly moved. The men leapt on to a passing Clapham omnibus, followed in hot pursuit by their biggest fans, the deaf schoolgirl groupies. The Mayor, Councillor Chief Mrs Lola Ayonrinde, in full regalia, received the returning heroes in her mayoral chambers. In role-play, she toasted 'her boys' before offering her hand in marriage to the director. The four security guards, chosen as the men's guests of honour, rubbed shoulders with the dignitaries of the council, the store director and men from Urban Regeneration. For a giddy moment the customary rules of status and hierarchy were all inverted. An enormous cake was presented and an eight-door white limousine whisked the men back to the Holiday Inn for their first night of 'freedom'. For some the play continues to this day. Neil and his three 'artstronauts' receive letters from people in Clapham Junction still.

## Ayloul Festival, Beirut, 1997

The civil war in Lebanon is a story of betrayal, internal corruption and illusion, of Western ambition and arrogance. It was a war that left more that 150,000 dead, a shattered economy, massive social upheaval and a country in ruins. In 1997, after surviving fifteen years of war, which officially ended in 1990, the heart of Beirut was being erased to create a superimposed view of what a city ought to be. The bulldozers were demolishing the last of the old souk, the cranes were poised to build a gleaming new commercial district financed by the private investment company, Solidere, whose members were also leading figures in the Lebanese government. The distinction between public and private was blurred and it felt, said Pascale Feghali, founder of the Ayloul Festival, as if the city no longer belonged to the people.

The Ayloul Festival was in one sense an attempt to reclaim the city. A one-woman operation, Pascale ran the Festival from her car. Contracts were scattered on the back seat, programmes and leaflets filled the boot and the entire Festival administration was conducted on a mobile phone. The Festival Club where everyone congregated to talk, eat and party, was her parents' house, situated just next to the Green Line that had divided East and West Beirut in the civil war, with buildings all round pockmarked with mortar fire and bullet holes. During the war, Pascale told us, families had crammed together in cellars for days on end, seeing no light, emerging only at the all-clear, at which point they would rush down to the sea to swim until the sirens sounded again to herald another dash for safety. Later on in the war, however, people would tarry in weary defiance and complete their day on the Corniche, sirens notwithstanding.

The European Union agreed to support the Ayloul Festival as a gesture towards restoring an international dimension to this once thriving cultural capital of the Arab world. But how, asked Pascale, could a city still so divided between Muslim and Christian factions play host to international visitors? In the first year she decided to focus on the city's own talents and bring together the artists who lived there, so they could begin to forge their own community. Six new Lebanese works commissioned from young artists were to be shown in theatres, galleries and 'found' spaces in both East and West Beirut. But the EU cultural commissars were dismayed. Why does each artist rake over the past, concentrating on the fractured city of the civil war, when they could be celebrating an optimistic future? they wondered. 'There have been three civil

*Wonderful Beirut* postcard designed by Joana Hadjithomas and Khalil Joreige for *Homeworks*, Beirut, 2003, and LIFT 04: Enquiry. Courtesy of the designers.

wars,' Pascale explained, 'and each time that we have swept our differences under the carpet they have festered and re-emerged more virulent than before.' 'We are living a lie and if we don't confront what happened we'll have another war,' insisted theatre-maker Rabih Mroué, whose predominantly wordless show *Extension 19* took its title from a column in the newspaper *Annahar*, where readers would lodge complaints against the government and their fellow citizens. Four characters sit in a claustrophobic white space, shifting uneasily, avoiding eye contact as they wait in vain for the police commissioner. Spotting what they believe to be a surveillance camera on the ceiling and continuing to ignore each other they begin a litany of mean-spirited, petty complaints: the diminishing quality of their daily bread, the detrimental effect of beggars on the country's image and their suspicions about a group of young people meeting to plan terrorist activities. They even complain about people who like to complain. As they leave they light up cigarettes and the 'camera' which they have invested with so much authority is exposed as a fire alarm. Violence breaks out, fuelled by a mutual mistrust and the disappointment of not being heard. 'All authority and power is ultimately created by us,' said Rabih; 'no one is innocent and somehow we are all complicit in whatever happens around us.'

Pascale was also in trouble with the older established-theatre generation who objected to a programme which seemed excessively marginal and challenged everything they cherished about theatre. Far removed from the conventional productions of the largely francophone-dominated theatre tradition came experimental multimedia performances, non-narrative texts, films, video screenings, installations.

Walid Sadek, who had been commissioned by Pascale, has described his role as an artist in a city emerging from a 'collective nervous breakdown': 'One of the debts incurred by a society plunged into a long and complex war is that of rewriting those wars, of re-presenting them as tangible proof and witness of a society desperately trying to find its way back to the "home of humanity" and its consensual and binding laws.'[2] His multimedia piece *The Last Days of Summer* was dominated by a large screen. Walid was to be seen blacking up, cleaning off and blacking up again, in a kind of endless ritual atonement, but also as an expression of the impossibility of ever retrieving a lost innocence. Alongside the screen, a battery-operated monkey constantly banged its cymbals and music occasionally burst forth from a series of small video monitors featuring an image of an empty room. This music was from Fayrouz, Lebanon's most popular singer, appropriated during the civil war by the right-wing Phalangist militia as the symbol of a 'pure' pre-war Lebanon whose nostalgically remembered 'idyll' was to be shattered by 'strangers'. The strangers were Palestinians exiled in 1948 and expelled from Jordan by King Hussein in 1970 and 71.

Despite opposition from the establishment, the Ayloul Festival flourished, touching a nerve with a young public and giving an important platform to an emerging generation of artists who are developing a potent and playful language with which to navigate the ever-present trauma of the civil war. So when Pascale left Beirut to pursue a PhD in Paris, it was very natural for the independent curator Christine Tohme to step into the Ayloul space with *Homeworks,* which she described as 'a forum on cultural practices in the region', one which attempts to create a secular, citizen-based public sphere away from a city dominated by religion. I (*RF*) returned to Beirut to attend the 2003 edition. It was my first visit since 1997. The city had changed. New buildings had gone up everywhere and highways cut through revamped districts. But the war was also still very much in evidence. Partially destroyed buildings remained and elegant houses overgrown with vegetation were open to the elements, their battered balconies hanging at rakish angles, precariously close to passing pedestrians. Over towards Martyrs' Square and its surrounding area, the destruction and reconstruction were complete. What had been the symbolic centre of the country's civic and political life, was now dominated by a Virgin Megastore, and had become a sanitised commercial centre for the privileged, governed by private interests, with banks, security guards, expensive cafés and exclusive boutiques. It was, indeed, an attempt to reproduce through a pastiche of old architectural styles the original look and feel of a central Beirut as seen through the eyes of city planners beguiled by a nostalgic vision of the city that had never really existed.

The writer and architect Tony Chakar cites the observation by the then Prime Minister Rafik Hariri that 'Lebanon is not a country at all, but an idea.' 'But how', he asks, 'is one supposed to live in an idea?'[3] It seems that this

generation of Lebanese artists with their insistent and wry questioning might
offer some clues to us all; by focussing on apparently peripheral and
inconsequential details of daily life, they reveal symbolically what is in truth at the
very heart of the matter.

## Fadjr Theatre Festival, Tehran, 2002

'To make theatre in Iran is a form of resistance. We are part of a generation who
did not participate in the Revolution of 1979 because we were too young or not
even born. The Fadjr Theatre Festival offers us a greater freedom to express our
thoughts.' Thus spoke a young artist in the basement café of the shabby City
Theatre, a large circular building in the centre of Tehran housing some eight
sparsely equipped performance spaces.

It is on the smog-filled streets of Tehran, surrounded by snowy mountains,
that one sees the contradictions inherent in a changing society. Here, in a
country in which 70 per cent of the population are under 30, the archaic laws of
the mullahs are challenged by desire for personal freedom. Painted billboards or
notices everywhere proclaim 'The Hijab [the headdress] is Dignity' even while
boutiques in the affluent parts of town display sexy, strappy evening dresses
and city buses play pirate tapes of the latest Western pop music.

The Fadjr Theatre Festival signals the changes. *Fadjr* means dawn and the
Festival was launched in 1982 soon after the Islamic Revolution in 1979 to
herald a new start after the imperial regime of the Shah. Twenty years on,
galleries and cinemas were open and women allowed to perform on stage,
though no physical contact between the sexes was allowed. By 2002 the
Festival was becoming international, a clear indication of President Khatami's
cautious liberalisation and his desire to engage in a new dialogue with the
West. More than a hundred Iranian companies from all over the country, along
with others from Greece, Germany, Canada, Afghanistan and Italy, performed
to overflowing theatres. In a country where opportunities for young men and
women to socialise are often restricted to family gatherings or the university
campus, the theatre offers a possibility of real exchange. Hours before a
show begins queues form, young people mingle freely – the women wearing
the obligatory Hijab – talking animatedly and calling each other on mobile
phones. They come with serious intent, eager for information and discussion.
Waiting in the impatient crowd pressing forward to enter the theatre, I (*RF*)
spoke to a group of students. 'I come above all to seek what I cannot read in

the press,' said one. 'The theatre offers me a barometer of the situation in my country.' This view was reiterated by Delphine Minoui, a young Iranian-French woman working for Radio France, who like many young intellectuals and artists are beginning to return to Iran. 'For the young directors the theatre is not the only means of self-expression beyond the official discourse, but it is above all a tool to explore one's individuality, to reinvent an identity. So in a country that has been culturally suffocated for twenty years they search, they experiment, trying out all manner of theatrical expression – a kind of do-it-yourself theatre, drawn from everything they seize upon.'[4]

The Festival presented a surprisingly eclectic mix of local shows from Iran's thriving, largely amateur theatre constituency, which ran the whole theatrical gamut from melodramatic soaps to expressionistic, multimedia productions through to contemporary versions of the Persian classical text *The Conference of the Birds* and a traditional *ta' zieh,* Iran's form of passion play about the massacre of the Prophet Mohammed's grandson, Iman Hossein, performed in a temple antechamber at the heart of a community on the outskirts of Tehran.

On our first evening we attended *Love on the Ridge,* a light-hearted comedy set in an old people's home which explored issues around the strict segregation of the sexes in Iranian society, as well as the dismissive treatment of the elderly. It was directed and performed like a TV sitcom, ending with the triumphant get-away of a supposedly dead octogenarian couple in an ambulance destined for the morgue.

Other shows tackled the big questions: religion versus dogma, morality versus ethics. *The Mission,* performed in a highly mannered declamatory style, brimming over with obscure symbolism, was set in Second World War France. The show opens with a monk in crisis with his faith: 'If God exists why does he allow war and so much suffering?' On a raised platform a young man drinks, reads the newspaper and listens to the radio. It was later explained to us that he is a German spy. Another man sits on a broken lavatory bowl drinking beer and from time to time staggers around to pull on an imaginary bell, or gather piles of shoes – representing, we were told, the strong footholds of stability and faith.

The boldest show, both in form and content, was *Dance on Glasses,* by the young director and writer Amir Reza Koohestani. The first ten minutes were in complete darkness, as Foroud, a deeply disturbed dance teacher, talks on the phone to a psychologist about his girlfriend, Shiva, who, we subsequently learn, has committed suicide. It is a very different Iran that we encounter in this play, a world of drugs, sexual desire and homelessness. The sparse style of the production makes it deeply affecting in its simplicity and directness, with the

*Dance on Glasses*, Amir Reza Koohestani, Fadjr Theatre Festival, Tehran, 2002. Photo: Thilo Beu. Koohestani's subsequent production, *Amid the Clouds*, came to LIFT in 2005.

audience at each side of a long table, witnessing at close quarters the pain of Foroud and Shiva's failing relationship, which is partially fuelled by their inability to deal with a deeply repressive society.

The presence of the Fadjr Theatre Festival, with its international visitors, challenges the censors to take a tolerant attitude with shows that grapple with taboo subjects – the restrictions imposed by religious dogma, the desire for freer male-female relations, the alienation of youth in a traditional, often repressive society. But the Mullahs still hold sway and the Minister for Culture is simultaneously responsible for Islamic Guidance. In the imposing marbled foyer of the Vadhat Opera House built by the Shah, I came across a member of the Festival jury. His task was not to spot the best actor, new play or director but to identify the performances which most eloquently demonstrated the moral and spiritual guidelines prescribed by President Khatami for Iranian society. Our group of visitors were being very carefully shepherded around by our minders, our every move monitored, our every desire to go off on our own for a meeting questioned – and rarely allowed. It felt like being back in Communist Eastern Europe during the 70s and early 80s. One morning I had been in the hotel lobby testing out a tape recorder lent to me by Jim Muir, the BBC correspondent in Tehran. On returning to my room I received a phone call from someone who announced himself as a good friend of the reporter John Simpson. In urgent broken English he said he had something important to show me and insisted that I accompany him in a car waiting outside. I declined, explaining he was mistaken, that I was here as a Festival Director and not as an investigative journalist.

Later the editor of the *Festival Daily Bulletin* asked me, 'Why did you in the West abandon us for all those years? Why did nobody come to Iran and speak to us until now?' Rather feebly all I could say was that it had appeared to us that Iran had been firmly closed to the outside world, that it had not been possible. 'Please', she said, 'don't lose contact again, keep in touch with us.' She was right to insist. The week after my return from Iran, US President George Bush made his famous declaration about the Axis of Evil that threatened the world's security, the main culprits being North Korea, Iraq and Iran. And Iran now is top of United State's list of countries suspected of harbouring international al-Quaeda terrorists. Meanwhile, inside Iran, young people, impatient with the pace of reform, are taking to the streets to demand greater liberalisation.

## LIFT'89

Station House Opera, UK, *The Bastille Dances*

In the summer of 1989 LIFT formed an unlikely but affectionate relationship with the light-weight concrete breezeblock. A hand-width wide and a staple of the building trade, it was also the key ingredient of Station House Opera's *Bastille Dances,* performed continuously over five days and nights on the South Bank's river walkway outside the National Theatre. Led by its architect-trained director, Julian Maynard Smith, Station House Opera was one of a select band of UK performance-arts companies (including Hesitate and Demonstrate, Pip Simmons and Impact Theatre, amongst others) whose reputation abroad far exceeded that at home. Indeed, *The Bastille Dances* was already booked to play with other co-producers in Cherbourg, Amsterdam, Salzburg, Barcelona and Paris before we had even secured a site in London.

*The Bastille Dances* was an ingenious piece of 'sculptural theatre' created to dramatise the chaotic events of the 1789 French Revolution on the occasion of its bicentenary celebrations. Composed like a musical fugue, it involved eighteen performers and five musicians and 8,000 breezeblocks, which were to be kept in constant motion for 120 hours to form a shifting landscape of prison walls, sweeping staircases, delicate arches and towering pillars. Marie Antoinette's magnificent 3,000-block crinoline dress would slide and crumble into a blank wall to re-merge as a doorway or a small house. Where at 8.00 am there had been ornate gardens with hedges and paths, at 5.00 pm there would be a grand colonnade, Robespierre's tower and a court of law, and at 9.00 pm each evening, the rising and falling of *The Bastille Dances* would erupt dramatically into performance.

The production was co-produced by LIFT with Artsadmin and provided a surreal foray into collaboration with the National Theatre. At an alarmingly large production meeting, representatives of every one of the National's theatre-making departments sat more or less silently around a very large table as Julian explained the creative dynamics of his 8,000-breezeblock show. Having outlined the needs for forklift trucks, cherry pickers and keys to the dock doors, Julian was asked solemnly by the Head of Wigs if the play would involve any new wigs or not. This would have been a reasonable question if we had been discussing a piece of Restoration drama, but at the same meeting we were also trying to convince Lambeth Council that even very high wind speeds were incapable of blowing breezeblocks off into the trees.

A last-minute crisis deficit of £8,000 propelled LIFT's Development Director Julia Rowntree into devising a cash-raising scheme that took its inspiration from the history of the Bastille itself. After the storming of the Bastille in 1789, an entrepreneurial local demolition man, one Citoyen Palloy, had sold the Bastille stone by stone, encouraging people to invest personally in the Revolution. Julia's 'Be a Brick Buy a Block' scheme invited supporters to pay to take home an inscribed breezeblock, choosing their status in society in return: £10 for sansculottes, £100 for members of the bourgeoisie, £1,000 for aristocrats. Key players in the building of London's physical and cultural world, including Richard Rogers, Stuart Lipton and Melvyn Bragg, were to be seen staggering off down the river walkway carrying their breezeblocks, while Peter Palumbo, then Chairman of the Arts Council – and an ambitious building developer – had to be persuaded to buy two £1,000 aristocratic blocks, rather than the 200 £10 sansculotte blocks he had asked for.

The rapid expansion of London's financial services in the late 80s meant that London's skyline was dominated in every direction by the rise and fall of cranes and buildings. On the last evening of the production, as a soft rain descended and the performers came to the end of the most gruelling of physical tests, I (*LN*) walked out on to the National Theatre's balconies to look

down. One of the performers lay on his back high up on one of the temporary structures. As he started to sing, the other players placed breezeblocks on his stomach – first one, then two, until he was supporting a trembling tower. He continued to sing and with each block the sound became more and more resonant. An exquisite unearthly song produced under severe endurance soared into the night.

During the labour-intensive operation to clear the breezeblocks away, I rescued a small piece of crumpled paper. On it were Julian's notes to the actors:

> *Bruce, Mole: Finish bottom of wheel and add choppy water*
> > *Try sailing, try drowning.*
> *Jane, Pascal: Try saving Bruce, Mole from drowning. Build top of wheel.*
> > *Build things on top of wheel.*
> *Steve, James: Build a house from the chaos on the main platform. Build*
> > *hovels on stilts in the water under the wheel. If you bring them*
> > *crashing down, use already broken blocks, please.*

The show was prescient. On the night of 9 November 1989, the Berlin Wall started to come down. Berliners on both sides of the Wall gathered and took it apart with their own hands.

## Los Angeles Festival, 1990 – Adelaide Festival, 2002

Two festivals, both directed by Peter Sellars, throw light on our attempts to play with LIFT as an 'experimental zone of sociability': Los Angeles, 1990, and Adelaide, 2002. Both festivals were radical experiments, undertaking wholesale re-examinations of the role of the arts in public and private lives. By telling the stories of migration and dispossession that shape our cities in the twenty-first century they drew new maps for international festivals.

The LA Festival was, in Peter's words, 'to re-fract the future of LA', and looked at the influence of Pacific Cultures on the city of Los Angeles. Embracing the city's eighty-five different cultural communities as a starting point, the Festival programmed 'outwards' towards Native Americans, Mexico, El Salvador, Hawaii, Australia, New Zealand, Japan, Korea, Burma, the Philippines and Thailand, and asked: 'Before we can talk to another human being, or touch them, or have dinner with them, or make a business deal, or support them politically, we have first to look at them. So how are we looking?

*The Bastille Dances*, Station House Opera, UK, LIFT'89, outside the National Theatre. Photo: Michael J. O'Brien Photography.

*The Seven Stages of Grieving*, Kooemba Jdarra Indigenous Performing Arts, Australia, LIFT'97. Photo: Tracey Schramm. Directed by Wesley Enoch with a virtuoso performance by Deborah Mailman, this story of resilience, strength and the will to survive was considered a landmark in the history of Aboriginal theatre.

What are we seeing?' It was a call to action, inviting participants to engage actively in thinking how global living could change lives for the better. 'Interculturalism', said Peter, 'is the basis for survival of the species.'

The LA Festival threw up unlikely juxtapositions: LA Gospel singers and Korean Shamans performed alongside Los Angeles Poverty Department actors drawn from the homeless on Skid Row and traditional Maori and Aboriginal dancers. Connections between people and definitions of art spilled in every direction. In the same day I (*LN*) saw Transvestite Likay Thai Street Theatre from Bangkok and an LA Philippino/Mexican Drag performance by Iranian-born Reza Abdoh, the former in a Thai Temple and the latter in the basement of a decaying hotel in a gang-warfare district of LA. To the visitor the Festival was unnerving: since everything was 'new' to you, even when, like the ancient Cambodian Royal Ballet, it was old, you had to take risks. The only way of gauging whether your time was best spent at an LA Chicano art exhibition or in preparing for an all-night Wayang Kulit shadow puppet theatre from Indonesia, was to accept that everything was interesting, disregard the city's 'no-go areas' and throw yourself into the action, hurtling down eight-lane freeways as you went. Nothing fitted the classic pattern of the 'best top ten' shows of the international festival circuit.

In Adelaide the experiment was even more radical. As an outsider arriving in a country that as recently as 1967 had classified its Indigenous Aboriginal population, sometimes hunted as animals, as flora and fauna, Peter declared that the Festival would be about Truth and Reconciliation with Australia's colonial past, Environmental Sustainability (particularly focussing on Aboriginal customs of living with nature) and Cultural Diversity. He wanted to deliver a Festival that could create 'a stronger community, more aware of itself'.

The ceremonial opening was entrusted to Waiata Telfer and Karl Telfer, Kaurna community artists, whose people had inhabited the land for 60,000 years. The Kaurna Palti Meyunna summoned spirit ancestors to stage a welcome to the city that embraced a crowd of 50,000 residents and visitors alike – a simple gesture denied to Australia's Indigenous population from the moment Captain Cook's ships landed in the late eighteenth century. The opening took place in Victoria Square, a sacred site for the Kaurna. Once called Tarndanyungga, in recent years it had become a major traffic intersection presided over by a statue of Queen Victoria. The ceremony gathered Indigenous people from Australia, South Africa, Tibet, New Zealand and New Mexico with festival-goers to join in 'healing' the square of its history. The lighting of a fire, with its traditional 'smoking', and the ritual (and literal) cleansing of Queen Victoria with water would rid her and the city of a toxic past, create civic space for the Aboriginal residents of Adelaide and return a sense of ownership, something that had been taken from them – along with land and children.

*Sadness*, William Yang, Australia, LIFT'95. Photo: Peter Elfes. In a lecture-cum-slide show, Yang traces his Chinese Australian ancestry whilst coming to terms with grief for friends who died from AIDS. A subsequent show, *Shadows*, looked at the 2002 Adelaide Festival's themes of Truth and Reconciliation.

In both LA and Adelaide I saw the transformations that occur when people are given public space to tell new stories of the past – to break free from the old stories that suffocate descendants of oppressors and oppressed alike. Both festivals gave glimpses of how our cities can be crucibles for the reconciliation of histories of cultural imperialism and conquest. But though they were grasped by some as inspiring opportunities for public celebration and realignment of social relationships, for others they proved threatening and even frightening. Both attracted their fair share of hostility, mockery and disparagement, and in Adelaide the Festival Board sacked Peter, shortly after proudly announcing that he was a contemporary visionary worthy of inheriting the mantle of Australia's finest festival tradition. Both festivals stirred controversies that resulted in discomfort and pride in equal measure, both created major shifts in the thinking of how future international festivals could be shaped – LIFT included. Both left legacies of rupture and change that are still being felt.


# LIFT'83

Urban Sax, France


On the evening of Sunday 7 August 1983, thirty French saxophonists dressed in white boiler suits, silver masks and insectoid antennae invaded the Piazza at Covent Garden (page 116). Accompanied by a chorus, dancers and a pair of huge Tibetan gongs, they arrived like futuristic aliens in a haze of coloured smoke and flashing lights, abseiling down the surrounding buildings or carried aloft on forklift trucks. The minimalist composer and creator of large-scale urban happenings Gilbert Artman and his troupe Urban Sax were in town to launch the second LIFT Festival. On arrival in London they had immediately thrown us into confusion by demanding they perform on the west side of the Piazza rather than the east side, as had originally been agreed. On the Saturday night before the show the licence would have to be renegotiated, and whilst officers at Westminster Town Hall were miraculously able to sanction the move, getting permission from English Heritage for performers to use the listed buildings as staging posts was proving an impossible task. With technicians all around us impatiently waiting to install the equipment, we rang Lord Birkett, the Greater London Council's Director of Arts and Leisure, at his home. He gave us the telephone number of the Chair of English Heritage, Lord Montagu of Beaulieu, where eventually we got through to an unsympathetic butler. No, he could not contact his lordship who was unreachable in the west wing. And, anyway, was this the sort of thing we should be troubling him with at 10.00 o'clock on a Saturday night? Repeated attempts to reach Lord Montagu the next morning failed. Completely impervious to our predicament and unable to understand why (in his view) some aristocrat-riddled preservationist institution should thwart his grand design, Gilbert Artman was now threatening not to perform. So with an estimated crowd of 5,000 people expected that evening we decided to go ahead. Health and Safety checks were legitimately in place, we reasoned, and as most of the buildings were being renovated they were protected by scaffolding.

We had not anticipated, however, that by 7.00 pm, with the Piazza filled to bursting point, much of that scaffolding would be squatted by eager spectators searching for the best vantage points. The police immediately moved in, clambering all over the Royal Opera House masonry to dislodge its illegal occupants. Across the Piazza, meanwhile, a gong clamoured. This was followed by a single guitar note, then a chord and suddenly there they were – a group of saxophonists playing from the roof of Jubilee Hall. From the opposite building came a response, a series of foghorn mating calls, which were echoed in turn by the increasingly excited congregation. A wailing, flashing ambulance screeched up and disgorged five saxophonists on stretchers, heralded by an exploding smoke canister that rolled through the crowds, coming to rest at the feet of a very angry police sergeant who had expressly forbidden the use of such devices. At the Society of West End Theatre Chambers above the Piazza, the LIFT opening night party was underway, with many of our guests perched on the scaffolding outside. We watched the evening unfold, not sure where reality ended and performance began and – more worryingly – where the true drama of the evening would ultimately lie.

Amazingly we got away with it. There were no recriminations and even the Metropolitan Police sergeant was grinning by the end. Miles Kington, writing in *The Times,* enthused that it had been 'the most stunning theatrical experience in my life . . . it is ludicrous and impossible, and it works perfectly.'

1. The Daily Dialogues were a series of open forums for public debate on topics arising from LIFT shows. Launched in LIFT'93 by Alan Read, who also curated them in LIFT'97, they quickly became a successful LIFT tradition, establishing the importance of not just talking about the current state of theatre but also of asking what it could be.
2. Walid Sadek, 'Laisser-passer', in *Tamáss 1: Contemporary Arab Representations. Beirut/Lebanon, Contemporary Arab Representations* series (Rotterdam, Witte de With; Barcelona, Fundació Antoni Tàpies, 2002).
3. Quoted by Stephen Wright, 'Like a Spy in a Nascent Era: On the Situation of the Artist in Beirut Today', in *Parachute*, 108, October 2002 (www.parachute.ca).
4. Delphine Minoui, 'Festival: l'occasion de la vingtième édition du festival de Téhéran, petit tour d'horizon de la création théâtrale en Iran. Entre audace et censure', in *L'Humanité*, January 2002.

Festival

# LIFT OUTGROWS ITS FESTIVAL CLOTHES

**Dragan Klaić**

## The proliferation of festivals

Since the end of the Cold War there has been a tremendous proliferation of festivals. How many exist in Europe today – 2,000? 3,000? Probably more, but the distinctive features of many of them have become blurred. What a festival programme must present in order to earn artistic approval, the prestige it must acquire, the number of visitors it should attract, the proportion of the budget that can be levied from sponsorship, the number of jobs, reviews, newspaper write-ups and minutes of media coverage it must generate have all become a matter of unrealistic expectation, controversy and quantity-obsessed debate. Nowadays *festival proliferation* provokes many cynical responses and, indeed, festivals are easy to criticise, even easier to gossip about. Pitted against each other and compared disparagingly with theme parks and the conference and events industry, or unfairly measured against the yardstick of visual arts biennials and film festivals, they face an increasing struggle as their artistic purpose becomes confused with market-driven entertainment.

At the beginning of the twentieth century, festivals such as Bayreuth (1876) and Salzburg (1918) addressed élite audiences and reflected the prestige that they brought with them. In post-Second World War Europe, new festivals of classical music promoted a spirit of reconciliation and reaffirmed traditional humanist values implicit in great art. With the founding of the Avignon and

*No Arrival, No Parking, Navigation Part III, Sound City Ensemble, Germany/UK, LIFT'01. Photo: Michael J. O'Brien Photography. An experiment led by composer and theatre director Heiner Goebbels who worked with young London musicians from the worlds of Electronica, Instrument Design, DJ Culture and Avant-Classical.*

Edinburgh Festivals in 1947, however, a new democratic spirit began to emerge. For theatre director Jean Vilar the Avignon Festival was in essence a try-out of his emancipatory programme to bring high culture to the masses, and, after he had founded the Théâtre National Populaire in Paris, Avignon became a summer extension of his regular season. That was of course long before the tourist industry boom, motorways and high-speed trains. In the not-yet egalitarian Netherlands of the 1950s, the Holland Festival (1948) attracted significant prestige and played to large devoted audiences, but it also brought more innovative foreign work into a rather provincial cultural climate. Early editions of the World Theatre Season in London or of the Automne à Paris similarly provided their own brand of cultural élitism but at the same time sought to establish their democratic credentials in order to justify public subsidy.

In the mid-1960s several international student festivals emerged – Nancy, Erlangen, Wroclaw, Zagreb. Venturing across the Iron Curtain, these were precursors of a new spirit of spontaneous international communication through the performing arts, but it was not until 1968 that there came an explosion of dynamic, irreverent theatrical expression, born out of a newly emerging and politically charged youth culture. During the student demon-strations in Paris and in many other cities across Europe, spontaneous festivals seemed to reshape everyday life. 'Festivalisation' was pervasive, inspiring the creation of new companies, festivals, studio theatres and summer schools. After the turmoil of those revolutionary years, the rebellious energy somewhat levelled out, but the élitist pretensions could no longer remain unchallenged and throughout the 70s and 80s a range of new independent festivals, conceived as provocatively 'alternative' to the established ones, appeared with clearly contesting agendas. LIFT was born in this new context, alongside, or after, the Festival de Théâtre des Amériques in Montreal, the Åarhus Festuge in Denmark, the Tampere Theatre Festival in Finland, the Zuercher Theater Spektakel in Zurich and Amsterdam's Festival of Fools.

How did such festivals fit into the wider landscape? In the big European cities a festival was perhaps little more than an extension of the normal cultural programme. In smaller places, however, a festival could provide an extraordinary impulse for creativity, community self-confidence and civic development. In the Cold War period some festivals successfully challenged the ideological divide between the West and the countries beyond the Iron Curtain and sought to display their artistic confluences and contrasts. Since

*End of Europe*, Teatr Nowy, Poland, LIFT'85. Courtesy of LIFT archive. Janusz Wiśniewski's nightmare of a Europe declining into black farce with white-faced refugees fleeing from strutting dictators and their puppet soldiers.

1989, festivals in former Communist countries, such as the International Theatre Festival in Sibiu, Romania, or the Malta Festival in Poznan, Poland, have become important in overcoming mutual ignorance between East and West, at the same time providing much needed new opportunities for artistic collaboration. During the 1980s specialised contemporary dance festivals made this art form popular all over Western Europe and after 1989 introduced it into Central and Eastern Europe, where it was previously almost unknown.

## Something special

Nowadays international performing arts festivals are sometimes criticised for presenting the same fashionable work as each other, although, in fact, some take advantage of co-production in order to share the cost and the risks. Another flippant remark is that festival directors travel to far lands simply so that they can import exotic fare and parade it as a solo scoop. But this, too, is unfair, because while they may appear to hopscotch to lesser known artistic realms in a search of novelty to surprise their constituencies, serious festival organisers seek a sense of distinctiveness and continuity in their overall programming, presenting a range of interdisciplinary works and often crossing boundaries of genre or discipline. In larger cities, where international performing arts works are regularly featured, festivals have to prove that they bring added value and must create events that go well beyond business as usual. The *raison d'être* of the more ambitious organiser is a flair for producing work that in the course of a normal season would not appear at all. A festival can initiate or facilitate original artistic collaborations that might never emerge from conventional theatre programming or within the mainstream institutions. British theatre director Deborah Warner could develop her unique experimental way of working outside theatre institutions primarily thanks to the support received from LIFT.

The best festivals make connections between different cultures not just as a celebration of 'diversity' or 'multiculturalism' but as an opportunity for truly daring intercultural engagement. In the 60s and 70s, US experimental groups survived chiefly because of the support of a few European festivals and therefore were able to influence many European theatre-makers. In the mid-60s a few curious festival programmers 'discovered' Jerzy Grotowski in the small provincial Polish town of Opole and from there he went on to make a world-wide impact, chiefly through the festival circuit. More recently, festivals have brought prominent Asian artists, such as Singapore's Ong Ken Sen, to work in Europe, while festival backing and commitment supported German theatre director Peter Stein and British director Declan Donnellan's adventurous productions in Moscow.

In areas torn by political strife and protracted conflict, festivals can have a consolidating, healing function, as we can see from the account in this book of the Beirut theatre festivals. Companies that went to the Sarajevo MESS Festival during and after the recent war in former Yugoslavia were clearly demonstrating solidarity with the martyred city and its artistic community. Elsewhere festivals can reinforce the self-confidence of an underprivileged community and celebrate its resourcefulness and new-found sense of purpose – the High Fest International Theatre Festival in Yerevan, for instance, seeks to reduce the cultural isolation of Armenia. Peter Sellars's agenda for the Adelaide Festival was to return a sense of ownership to the Aboriginal population and to reassert the regional context of Australian arts against the traditional Eurocentrism. International festivals have provided opportunities too for local artists and performance groups to show their work in the different context of the wider international arena, with much more media attention than they would normally receive at home in an ongoing season.

The worst mistake festivals can make is to neglect the artists in their immediate vicinity while reaching out to those in far-flung places. The best festivals succeed in creating new synergies from the dialectic between the local and the global and from the fusion and mutual inspiration of artistic energies from both realms. The success of festival directors is commensurate to their ability to gain the confidence of the more demanding artists, demonstrating a vision which radiates integrity, generosity, artistic discrimination and a readiness to take considerable risks (such attributes may even be set down as a job specification!). In essence, then, festival directors must be cultural superheroes and magicians. But might they not also be Devil's disciples?

## The art of partnership

The root of the word 'festival' suggest notions of festivity, feast and celebration. Who celebrates and what is being celebrated remain the key questions. LIFT has always had a firm artistic core and has successfully fused the celebratory aspects inherent in the tradition of festival with artistic experimentation and a vigorous re-mapping of the city topography. This has been achieved in collaboration with a wide range of UK and foreign artists but significantly also through the mobilisation of local people and social agencies, encouraging them to be protagonists and partners rather than just target audiences. Instead of falling from the skies as a parachute detachment, LIFT has involved many constituencies, sometimes widely divergent in socio-economic status, cultural background and artistic affinity, and systematically promoted them to the role of stakeholders. As we can see from the stories in this book, such partners have been cajoled and charmed, but, more importantly, offered a challenge, so that locally grounded projects have in turn served to enrich the overall artistic identity and social significance of the Festival.

Many festivals tend to regard the world of education as just one more niche or marginal target group. LIFT, on the other hand, has established long-term links with school teachers and pupils through its enlightened Education Programme, creating in effect a festive *intercultural learning zone.* This sort of association could be one of the best arguments for eliciting public support of

*The Factory of Dreams*, participants from Stockwell Park School, Out of LIFT'96 (pages 40–5). Photo: Michael J. O'Brien Photography.

festivals. Despite conditioning by an overwhelming cultural industry, secondary school pupils become protagonists when offered a chance to shape their own festival project and work alongside professional artists. In return, the Festival's artistic programme provides the school curriculum with unsurpassed material, a first-hand experience of arts in education, the chance to experiment and the opportunity to address the dialectics of tradition and innovation and the complexities of intercultural fusion. I cannot imagine a better way of recruiting *the audiences of tomorrow* to replace the rapidly shrinking traditional arts public.

At the other end of the spectrum LIFT has also engaged the corporate sector. All festivals are under pressure to chase sponsors and make them foot the bill for various aspects of the programme. Through its Business Arts Forum LIFT has managed to turn this relationship upside down, recruiting captains of industry to pay the Festival for the privilege of having top-notch artists teach *them* about intercultural leadership, stress reduction, crisis control, collaborative team building and other features of the managerial core curriculum in a fashion no management course can compete with and no executive MBA programme deliver. Once brought into the artistic kitchen, many 'corporate clients' have become admirers and advocates, recruiting other sponsors. But – and this *but* cannot be stressed enough – such a daring venture requires the involvement of artists who can talk about their work persuasively to constituencies outside the art world. Which drama school, which professional training programme offers such skills? How many artistic leaders can address the leaders of the business community with the vision and persuasiveness of Peter Sellars?

Until a few years ago most festival directors would claim that the prime aim of their festival was *artistic expression or experiment*. Nowadays, many would put the audience first. Both aims reinforce each other, though there may be tensions between them because if festivals are to pioneer experimental work outside the familiar cannon, they need to nurture appropriate core audiences for such adventurous and fragile activities. When productions from other cultures are presented, they often lose their original artistic and social contexts and need reinterpretation and relocation to gain the understanding of new and different audiences. LIFT's commissions for specific education and community group work have responded to this prerequisite.

## Artistic space/public space

Most performing arts events still take place in structures that originally emerged in the seventeenth to eighteenth centuries: the playhouse, the concert hall. For the last hundred years, however, festivals have been a driving force in the re-conceptualisation, expansion and inauguration of new artistic spaces. Whilst Richard Wagner believed he needed to adapt the Bayreuth playhouse to suit his own aesthetic notions, Max Reinhardt launched a more ambitious programme to reclaim central public spaces for artistic events, inspired by illustrious medieval and baroque predecessors – hence the staging of *Jedermann* in front of Salzburg Cathedral since 1920. Later festivals re-appropriated churches, castles, fortresses and other places of cultural heritage as settings for traditional and contemporary arts events, recreating them as places of collective memory (*lieux du memoire*).

The next generation of festival leaders challenged the prevailing notions of cultural 'centre' and shifted public attention to found sites on the peripheries and margins, to the forgotten, dilapidated combat zones of poverty and post-industrial debris – initiating in this way a major cultural recycling. Revitalisation of written-off urban zones through the arts usually leads to an inevitable gentrification, which pleases urban planners and real-estate developers but ultimately squeezes out the artists; they become victims of their own success when they cannot any longer pay the rents whose sky-rocketing they caused by the success of their artistic endeavour. If today international theatre can be experienced in Hackney or Brixton, in Docklands or King's Cross, as well as at the Barbican and the South Bank, this is certainly a credit to LIFT and its urban explorations.

## Politics of influence

Festivals have the capacity temporarily to alter social conventions and to usher in a tentative *utopian programme* requiring mutual trust and co-operation. This is a striking counterbalance to the business ethos of competition and marketing which prevails, especially in a city like London, which has a strategic role in contemporary capitalism. In the context of the theatre establishment LIFT has redefined the performing arts as a celebratory activity and this must have had an influence on statutory companies such as the Royal Shakespeare Company and the National Theatre, and even in the West End, although artistic institutions can be tremendously resistant to the alternative stimuli provided by a festival.

So where can LIFT's impact be discerned? I would argue that the primary beneficiaries are individual professional artists and theatre-makers, whose vision of performance has been transformed by many of LIFT's productions, whether experienced as spectators or participants. An artist's memory is his working capital as much as his talent.

My former colleague, Belgrade theatre critic Vladimir Stamenković argued as long as twenty years ago that international theatre festivals such as BITEF (Beogradski Internacionalni Teatarski Festival) can have a refreshing impact on theatre critics, expanding their ideas of what theatre can be and inspiring them to produce their most vigorous writing. When I myself was a regular critic in Belgrade, I felt that BITEF productions brought out my sharpest analyses and most nuanced responses. But some critics  are more narrow-minded when confronted with unfamiliar theatre practices in an international festival programme, their dismissive reviews revealing a low degree of intercultural competence and an arrogant over-confidence that what they know must be the norm, with everything else a futile aberration.

*Noiject*, Karas, Japan, LIFT'95. Photo: Chris Harrison FSP. Choreographer and sculptor Saburo Teshigawara's fast and frenetic contemporary dance production performed with breathtaking technical virtuosity. During the visit Teshigawara worked with London artists and young performers to create *Still Standing*, which explored ideas of time and space.

Rose Fenton and Lucy Neal's narratives in this book record how LIFT has affected the development of many community organisations, offering them artistic challenges and the often unexpected means of pursuing new goals and interests. Bureaucratic officials involved in checking regulations seem to have mellowed in response to LIFT's enthusiasm, to become seduced or at least sufficiently confused not to cause trouble. School groups have become hooked on experimental theatre and business people, especially those involved in LIFT's Arts Business Forum, have been beguiled, as is evident in their subsequent advocacy, sponsorship and donor recruitment. Urban planners, real-estate developers and local entrepreneurs have seen their localities transformed and this must have made an impact on the future shape of the city. Indeed, I'd like to see a *synoptic map* of changes in London over the years, with all the LIFT locations marked and explained 'before' and 'after'. And in terms of cultural policy-making, LIFT has altered the attitudes of the funding agencies, such as the Arts Council, whose officials have been converted from sceptics to supporters – and regular funders – not just of LIFT but of other experimental initiatives inspired by it.

## Dizzy from travel

Among festival directors there is no shortage of *Reislust* – the joy of travel – but routine, fatigue and disappointment with some of the mediocre work seen on the road inevitably take their toll. In the pages of this book I read hardly anything about those frustrations. Rose Fenton and Lucy Neal have been frequent flyers and curious explorers rather than self-indulgent shoppers. And in their reminiscences they skip the unsettling experiences and zoom in, perhaps rather selectively, to the trips that have brought them joy, excitement and revelation. To their credit, they have ventured courageously to many of the most troubled zones of the planet to measure what theatre means for communities in danger and distress, in order to assess the restorative and redemptive powers of performance. But it has taken real imagination and political astuteness to anticipate what those performances might mean when they are shipped  to London, how they can be anchored there and how they can make sense.

Festivals presume delicate *de-contextualisation* and *re-contextualisation*, a risky and complicated operation. A production is carved out from its natural surroundings, its inherent tradition and its audiences' expectations, and is made to travel to be hastily imposed on another theatrical, artistic, cultural, linguistic, and socio-political set-up, without time for much in the way of adjustment and try-out. Rehearsals concern technical matters; subtle issues of transition and linkage are taken for granted. If it works it works: if it doesn't, too bad. Rose Fenton and Lucy Neal have tended to focus on the positive side, on the dream match accomplished. And indeed, they seem to have been often successful in engineering the re-contextualisation of a de-contextualised production – perhaps because of the way they have prepared a nurturing ground for the transplant. Here the multicultural nature of London has provided a major advantage over many other festivals. I am sure, however, that an oral history of the experiences of major European festival directors (a project I would really like to undertake one day) would reveal stories of surprising failures, of unexpected and painful intercultural clashes, misunder-standings and rejections. Such risks are inherent to festival endeavours.

The LIFT spirit stands apart, especially from those festivals that succumb to the drudgery and mechanics of a template hospitality, of conveyor-belt arrangements that enforce on visiting companies a crushing routine of airport-hotel-venue. Theatre-makers who have been doing it for years, a dozen times a year, grow desperate from the numbing fatigue and disorientating sameness of festival circuits, prompting them to reject the platitudes of international cultural exchange, the facile *mantras of interculturalism*, and yearn for the peace and comfort of their own shabby studio and worn-out sofa.

## Beyond a festival formula

There is a clear sense of mission accomplished evident in the writing in this book and it is visible too in the way that long-term observers have witnessed the transformation of LIFT, developed from a traditional festival formula and reinvented as a research, reflection and development facility, now engaged in a systematic, prolonged LIFT Enquiry. LIFT's radical re-engineering prompts every festival operator to ponder on its longevity and purpose. There are ominous signs of *festival fatigue* in Europe and yet an urgent need for theatre to re-examine its social foundations and reconsider its capacity to shape the collective imagination and memory, to serve as a vehicle of debate, enhance intercultural relationships and affirm the public space as an essential feature of democracy. By ceasing to be a festival in the traditional sense LIFT has gained in stature in my view, and Rose Fenton and Lucy Neal have completed their festival adventure in a most open and tentative manner that leaves much freedom to their successor to determine LIFT's future course.

What I draw from this book on a very personal level is a painful sense of how much I have missed from the LIFT programmes. In all those years I was doing my own theatre-related work, travelling a lot, going to theatre frequently, often over a hundred times a year, regularly being disappointed, bored and even angry, but I was not often enough at LIFT and consequently clearly missed some exceptional adventures whose description here makes me curious and jealous. The feelings that LIFT productions have evoked among those fortunate enough to share them – appreciation, awe, envy – have created a sort of *emotional capital* that belongs to LIFT as much as to London. It remains to be seen how the new LIFT will go on from strength to strength. But its radical reformulation will act as a signpost in the continuing evolution of festivals in the twenty-first century, where they urgently need to assert themselves as *zones of creativity and sociability* against the proprietary claims of the tourist industry and the representational needs of public authorities and commercial sponsors.

# Theatre

I n ancient Greek, *theatron* means a 'place for seeing'. From the great Hindi epics to the medieval mystery plays, from Shakespeare through to the innovations of Chekhov, Pirandello and Beckett, each culture has searched for a theatre that can speak clearly and truthfully of its time. For us theatre has been the place where the world can be seen with different eyes, where truths can be tested, a disturbing yet exhilarating space, fuelling dreams and provoking fundamental questions about our lives. In this chapter we look at new experiments with theatre form, audience engagement and artists' risk-taking.

From the outset LIFT has questioned the nature of theatre, perhaps particularly in relation to its location – not just traditional theatre buildings – and its participants – not just traditional theatre practitioners and theatre audiences. Experimentation, collaboration and encounters with other cultures have characterised the LIFT quest: Anatoli Vasiliev 'jumbling up and destroying' everything he has known so far in the theatre; De La Guarda deliberately avoiding the 'treachery of words'; the artists of *Things Fall Apart* engaged in a three-fold encounter between Africa, Britain and the Caribbean; Raffaello Sanzio pushing the essential elements of theatre – performance, image, sound – to their uttermost limits.

Place has often been a key protagonist – the deserted corridors of the St Pancras Hotel or the corn-filled glades of *Oráculos* – not an 'empty space' waiting to be filled, but one charged with a history, eliciting active personal engagement from its audiences. Forced Entertainment artist Tim Etchells[1] talks about the distinction between being an audience member, a spectator and a witness: 'To witness an event', he says, 'is to be present at it in some fundamentally ethical way, as an onlooker. The art-work that turns us into

**Anatoli Vasiliev and Company, USSR, on the set of *Cerceau*, LIFT'87. Photo: Valery Plotnikov.**

witnesses leaves us, above all, unable to stop thinking, talking, reporting what we've seen . . . borne on by our responsibility to events.' Many of the artists with whom we have worked allow a lot of creative space for the audience's own imagination, who are drawn in as participating creators in the work, complicit in the process of making, not just receiving, theatre.

## Six Characters in Search of an Author
Anatoli Vasiliev and Company, USSR, LIFT'89

The Russian director Anatoli Vasiliev, before whom all trembled, brought to LIFT'97 his controversial production of Pirandello's enigmatic meditation on artistic illusion and reality, *Six Characters in Search of an Author*. The 1921 play is a classic piece of theatre modernism, in which six characters wander into a rehearsal demanding that the author complete their story.

'I've long been wanting to jumble up, destroy and forget everything I have known so far,' Vasiliev declared before embarking on the production, in many ways echoing Pirandello's original desire in writing the play. Over a period of three years Vasiliev had worked in his Moscow studio, The School of Dramatic Art, with students from all over the Soviet Union, using Pirandello's text as a basis for a broader re-evaluation of theatre relevant to life in the 1980s, exploring new forms and principles of expression – and in doing so, almost driving his group of students to the point of collapse.

We chose to stage *Six Characters* in the Brixton Academy, an extravagantly baroque 1920s fun palace, more accustomed to rock concerts than theatre. Vasiliev's white-box theatre unit was placed in an illuminated corner of the vast, dark interior, underneath the soaring proscenium arch, which is modelled on the Venice Rialto. It was effectively a theatre within a theatre, reflecting perfectly the structure of Pirandello's play within a play, an entrance into a dizzying hall of mirrors. Throughout the evening a guitarist wandered in and out of the action, a dog cavorted round the stage, the sound of jazz floated across the room from unseen corners, so the whole event took on a dream-like quality.

For us LIFT organisers, though, it had its nightmarish aspects. One evening we almost did not have a performance. The show had been going up fifteen minutes late, causing problems with our child licence, which stipulated that the child actor had to be off stage by 11.00 pm. Hearing that the Inner London Education Authority inspectors would be in that night, we asked Vasiliev to ensure that the show went up on time. Outraged at the request he deliberately started the show five minutes early, leaving some forty members of the public clamouring outside in the foyer, indignantly pointing at their watches. Defying Vasiliev's orders, we let them in. In a black-eyed fury Vasiliev stormed across the stage and stopped the show. We held our breath behind the main entrance doors, hoping he would relent and start the performance again. The audience waited in bemused silence, not quite sure what was part of the performance and where reality took over. Vasiliev did relent and after ten minutes the play resumed, but it was then all the more confusing when a very attractive late-comer arrived, waved at her friends in the audience and crossed the stage where she began to dance in wild abandon. She turned out, of course, to be the stepdaughter in the play.

Each of the characters in Vasiliev's production was played by a number of different performers, developing Pirandello's idea that personality is not unitary but multiple. Passages of the action were repeated several times in succession, giving often radically divergent interpretations of the same piece of text. Everything became fluid and open to re-interpretation, depending on who was taking part and from which vantage-point a scene was viewed. The audience, which was moved three times during the evening, was seated on white bentwood chairs in the midst of the action and, as in the play, the boundaries between theatre and life became blurred. When the lecherous, pot-bellied father seduced his stepdaughter, pulling her on to his knee, he literally brushed up against us, and we were all implicated. Afterwards we shared the stepdaughter's violent anguish as, stripped to her underwear, she beat her head against the wall. We were further implicated when she became a giggling coquette, wandering amongst us wiggling her hips, perching on laps and caressing the men in the audience. Yet when the seduction scene was reconstructed by a mincing actor in a green pork-pie hat singing *'Beso me Mucho'* to an inappropriately grandiose leading lady, the action became preposterously funny.

Critics were divided about the piece. Charles Spencer in *The Daily Telegraph* dismissed it as a 'monstrously egocentric exercise in cultural vandalism', but *The Guardian*'s Michael Billington hailed it as a production that 'transcends the language barrier and welcomes us into the realm of pure theatrical poetry.' The director Katie Mitchell, who later went to study with Vasiliev in Moscow, remembers the impact of seeing his work in LIFT. 'Even now I am still digesting the implications . . . the sheer dexterity of the ensemble acting and the unobtrusive delicacy of the directing that left me speechless. I had never seen anything like it in my life. How did they do it?'

## The St Pancras Project

Deborah Warner, UK, LIFT'95

A meandering journey all over London in 1995 with Deborah Warner led us to George Gilbert Scott's magnificent St Pancras Chambers, the former Midland Grand Hotel, on the Euston Road; Deborah was curious about the idea of architecture as hidden text for a LIFT site-specific commission.

Lying derelict since the last guests left in 1935, the inside of St Pancras had rarely been seen in sixty years, except by architecture and railway enthusiasts. The building's Neo-Gothic splendour, we discovered on entering, was matched by its interior, with a curved dining room, floors with Minton tiles and mosaics, a ladies' smoking room and a spectacularly spacious wrought-iron staircase sweeping up towards a frescoed ceiling painted with stars. The back staircase,

by contrast, was known as the 'suicide staircase', because unhappy chamber-maids, exhausted from running between the 250 bedrooms with coal scuttles and bowls of hot water, threw themselves off it.

'Suspended between two lives,' said Deborah, 'its effect on the imagination is extraordinary, disturbing, powerful. I thought about putting a piece of theatre in it – a corridor play – but the building itself is far bigger an event than any play I would do.' Along with her designer, Hildegarde Bechtler, she created a 'fantastical walk' through the empty building for audiences of one, who departed on it at fifteen-minute intervals. With no words and no narrative to the piece, their imaginations were given full rein to create their own show, as though they were ghosts haunting the building from another age.

After signing an insurance indemnity form advising them of floors in a dangerous condition and of rats, the public entered the building alone through creaking front doors and followed a white line through a labyrinth of deserted corridors, up narrowing staircases to maids' attic bedrooms and down into a dank basement piled high with pristine white sheets. Details of the past were delicately evoked along the way: rows of discarded breakfast trays with bone china and silver coffee pots outside bedroom doors; shoes put out to be polished; and a door left ajar revealing signs of habitation – a dress coat on a door hook, a pair of stays, a petticoat.

A sudden movement alerted the viewer to a glimpse of a bell-boy in green uniform, or of a maid, startled like a pigeon, scurrying up the staircase above. Perhaps you saw them, perhaps you didn't. Here and there were more surreal touches: a room planted with grass, a pianola that burst into jaunty life. A canary sang in a cage suspended over a stairwell. An abandoned lift-shaft whirred as a girl far off was heard sobbing. Through an open window, meanwhile, came the sound of traffic on the Euston Road. Audience members remarked on how alone they felt. The 'text' of their solo journeys, the building, its ghosts and reminders of mortality became inextricably linked.

The success of *The St Pancras Project* led Deborah Warner on to further site-specific explorations: *The Wasteland,* with Fiona Shaw, in 1998, and *The Tower Project* in LIFT'99 (which was developed into *The Angel Project* in Perth and New York).

*The Tower Project*, Deborah Warner, UK, LIFT'99. Photo: Michael J. O'Brien Photography. Angels occupy the thirty-fourth floor of Euston Tower in London.

## Genesi – From the Museum of Sleep

Sòcietas Raffaello Sanzio, Italy, LIFT'01

*'To encounter Castellucci's theatrical forms . . . is to feel yourself face to face with some sort of alien life form, which is, at the same time, profoundly and frighteningly familiar.'*
Joe Kelleher, Senior Lecturer in Drama, Theatre and Performance Studies at Roehampton University

*Forsennare* is a verb invented by the French philosopher Gilles Deleuze to describe the work of Antonin Artaud. It combines *forzare*, to force, with the adjective *forsennato*, which means out of reason, or *fuori di senno*, and conveys a lunatic sense of exertion, forcing the materials you work with beyond their ordinary possibilities. It is a brilliant word to describe the work of the Italian company Sòcietas Raffaello Sanzio, which takes the essential elements of theatre – sound, image, light, the human voice, body and text – and pushes them to their utmost limits.

The work disturbs and delights in equal measure, transcending the ordinary vocabulary of theatre. Beauty goes hand in hand with violence. The company's Director, Romeo Castellucci, rarely employs trained actors and often uses animals, children (usually his own), automated machines that jerk to life and performers chosen for their physical attributes: an actor with an open laryngotomy playing Mark Antony; one with a withered arm, Cain; a contortionist, Adam; an actress who has had a mastectomy, Eve; while others are exceptionally tall, thin, large or fat. His inspirational sound composer, Scott Gibbons, works at the edge of what the human ear is able to hear. Recalling a performance is akin to describing a dream. Although almost unapproachable with words, the depth of its visceral communication demands your entire attention, moment by moment. It is in the following days and weeks that one succeeds in distilling the show, through the filter of one's own experiences, and in gaining revelation from it.

A few nights after the opening of *Genesi – From the Museum of Sleep*, presented at Sadler's Wells in June 2001, the company's second appearance at LIFT,  a sequence of events allow me to enter into a dialogue with their work, to observe how the 'alien' and 'familiar' go cheek by jowl and, in particular, to see how their theatre is informed by a responsible and unsentimental vision of children and childhood. 'Our work is closely related to childhood,' says Romeo. 'Childhood is a radical thinking process, childhood does not trust words, it chooses other forms of expression to reach its aims. It trusts what one can feel with one's body. Childhood seizes the world through its eyes, its mouth, the whole surface of its body like an animal, like a cat; it wants to know the world by brushing against it and rubbing itself against it.' Many of the most controversial scenes in the work of Societas Raffaello Sanzio involve children, either on stage or imagined. Many scenes are deeply disturbing and employ images that are brutal or sexual: a masturbating woman, a child being prepared for sacrifice, a shrouded sphinx-like head. What is the creative logic that shapes such theatre work?

Sadler's Wells June 2001. It is after 10.00 pm and I (*LN*) am backstage. Theatre-maker Chiara Guidi, wife of Romeo Castellucci and mother of their six children, stoops to pick up socks and children's clothes strewn across two dressing-room floors. I have read about the experimental theatre school for children she ran for two years in their home town of Cesena from 1996–7, where their work involved a live bull, a dead fish and masks. Chiara had spoken at a LIFT gathering in London the day before on the subject of the child's imagination and what it can contribute to theatre-making.

We fold clothes and talk about how well this last performance of the *Genesi* run is going. Over a sound link we can hear the dying falls of Henryk Górecki's music from Act 3. In the theatre, one man lies on top of another on a stage bathed in soft ochre light. Cain is attempting to embrace his brother Abel, whom he has just killed in a wrestling match. The audience is hushed, for what seems an eternity, absorbed in the scene.

Upstairs in the dressing rooms, though, it is noisy. I have traded my duties as a Festival Director for those of looking after my two youngest children, Madeleine (7) and Xanthe (4), to allow my husband, Simon, to watch the show. My excursion backstage began three hours earlier when we decided to pay a visit to Chiara and her six children: Teodora (13), Demetrio (12), Agata (10), Cosma (9), Sebastiano (7) and Eva (5), all of whom appear in the show. We arrived to find them prancing around their dressing rooms preparing to be on stage for Act 2.

In *Genesi – From the Museum of Sleep*, Romeo Castellucci sets out a narrative of the Holocaust, framed by stories of creation and destruction. 'Genesis', he said, 'is more frightening than the apocalypse because it presents the sheer terror of possibility.' Divided into three acts, the production moves from the opening book of the Bible and Madame Curie's discovery of radioactivity in Act 1, to the Nazi death camps in Act 2, back to humankind's first 'murder', that of Abel by his brother Cain, in Act 3.

Bearing witness to the horrors of Auschwitz on stage had proved a challenge for Romeo: 'The word Auschwitz itself is radioactive,' he said. 'We found it was impossible to approach.' His eldest daughter, Teodora, however, was reading Primo Levi at the time and joined in the discussions about the show. That a child could read and talk about such things prompted Romeo to a creative solution. A depiction of Auschwitz could, he decided, be approached by working with children.

Although I had seen *Genesi* a few times during the run, I found I was still wrestling with images from the play that had disturbed and disorientated me: the bars of radium glowing in Madame Curie's dark laboratory; Lucifer, tall and anorexically thin, singing an unearthly Hebrew lament, his elongated fingers dancing over the brilliant material that killed its discoverer. The ghostly scene fills one with a truly terrible sense of foreboding. Lucifer steps suddenly into the light, stripping off his clothes, layer after layer, in an attempt to squeeze through the thin space between two vertical poles which stretch up to the ceiling. Naked, he finally forces himself through with excruciating difficulty and is hurled screaming into an exile of chaos and darkness. The soundtrack blasts agonisingly into a rip of feedback. It is the noise of hell, and as Lucifer screeches and flails around, it is viscerally terrifying. A tank of water overhead, in which more radium rods are glowing, bubbles away. The floor swells as though alive.

This evening, back in the dressing rooms, the Castellucci children are introducing Madeleine to the contents of a giant wicker prop basket filled with Raffaello Sanzio trademark objects: a mechanism for pumping blood through a hand, a rubbery dark foetus (*'Questo é Artaud, conosci Artaud, Madeleine?'*). Cosma holds up bowls of brown sludge: '*É caca*'. Everyone laughs. 'No, not really, it's brown paint.' Agata's friendly curiosity in Madeleine is energetic and only occasionally in need of interpretation: 'How do you say Dad? How do you say dead?' Xanthe sticks with me, but Madeleine is absorbed in the children's play and the thrill of theatre-making and is pulled towards another room where the children are preparing for their entrance. They are changing into soft white robes with strange long necks and floppy rabbit ears. Agata explains: 'We are the ghosts of children whose parents have been killed.' '*Guarda, guarda.*' They show Madeleine how the skirts and collars work, asking all the time if she wants to try it all on, and the make-up too. I turn around and there she is with a white face, gleefully all made up. Although the show is strong on the stomach and strictly for adults, I decide on the spur of the moment to let my children watch the second act in isolation to see this family of artists 'in action', and ask Agata to explain 'the  story'.

'There were these men', Agata explains, 'who were very bad and they killed all these children who didn't even have parents, and they killed them in a

*Genesi – From the Museum of Sleep*, Societas Raffaello Sanzio, Italy, LIFT'01. Photo: Luca Del Pia.

shower, putting a piece of soap into their hands so that they think that it's a real shower, but it's not, it's a gas chamber and they all died. Some of them weren't killed though, they were made to work in the gas chambers.' 'Do you mean like Anne Frank? She was a Jew,' Madeleine pipes up. 'Yes,' says

Agata, and she goes on to the story of the Mad Hatter in *Alice in Wonderland,* a rabbit and a man who kills someone, 'but he comes back to life.' I make a mental note never to underestimate the capacity of children to engage with ideas and discourse.

The six costumed children make for the wings and I and my two go into the auditorium, leaning over the circle rails to get a good look at the stage. The audience seems edgy and disturbed. For the second act, 'Auschwitz', the stage is draped in soft white musliny fabric and has the look of a children's nursery. The Castellucci children, now joined by two dogs, drift across the stage, the elder ones in choreographed precise movements, the younger ones in simple play. There is a both a serenity and a fearfulness to the scene. A Mad Hatter chinks a teaspoon playfully against his teacup, and a toy train 'hoots' as it is driven to and fro. As a child dismounts from the train, we see a large yellow star of David on his back. Utterly compelling, like both a dream and a nightmare, this soft, harrowing scene exemplifies the 'double emotion' that Castellucci wishes to be at work in his theatre, 'so you should not know what to think'.

Madeleine and Xanthe are absorbed, watching the children they have just met inhabiting the stage with such ease. Initially they ask, 'Is that Eva? Is that Cosma?' but are then frightened by loud deranging music. A chandelier swings to and fro and a child claws with a large chicken's foot at a barely perceptible white gauze, which covers the whole aperture of the proscenium. One child kills another by slitting his neck with a knife; blood comes spurting out. Madeleine and Xanthe are appalled and look at me. I, in turn, am wondering fearfully if I am 'doing the right thing' and receive glances from members of the public around me who are clearly as horrified by what they are seeing as they are by seeing my children watching it. I breathe deeply, reminding myself of something Romeo had said about his decision to use his own children in the show: that children can process information intellectually at their own level. Reminding myself that they have already *seen* this blood, and even played with it, I say, 'Remember it's pretend,' and Madeleine replies, 'Oh yeah, that's right.' On stage, a child with a stethoscope round her neck matter-of-factly attempts, and fails, to revive a dead foetus. This is beyond sadness. A child killing a child and a child reviving a dead child. Castellucci speaks of *From the Museum of Sleep* as the death of death and the loss of death's intimacy – there was no possibility of marking death in Auschwitz, or of burying or honouring the dead.

Afterwards in the dressing rooms there is great excitement. The Castellucci children have a shower and look for clean pants and shoes. Chiara's tidying is in overdrive as she sorts clothes into bags for each child, one for dirty, one for clean. (I remember Flaubert's advice to the artist, to 'maximise the benefits of your environment, be regular and orderly in your life, then you can be violent and original in your work.')

Madeleine, meanwhile, behaves as though she has also been on stage. At the end of the show there is a rush to the wings for the '*applauso*' (Chiara: 'It's the best first experience of theatre for children'). Agata *insists* that Madeleine joins the cast for the curtain call and without any hesitation she does just this. They run on to the stage of Sadler's Wells together, with nearly 1,000 people applauding. I watch from the wings, stunned at my daughter grinning at the standing ovation, simply doing what all the other children are doing – gambolling, having a lot of fun. Her mouth drops open when, beside her, Adam, played by the contortionist Vadim, takes his bow by standing on his hands and placing his legs around his neck. A crown rolls off someone's head and Madeleine steps right to the front of the stage, very cool, picks it up, puts it on her own head and continues to smile and bow. Through Madeleine's eyes I see the stage transformed as a big playroom. It's a revelation for me at that moment to understand that the theatre, without contradiction, can be a place of play at the same time as a place of disturbing realities. 'Alienation is a perfect word', says Castellucci, 'for the only thing that matters in the theatre: *surprise*, or to find oneself outside yourself.'

Madeleine brings armfuls of flowers into the foyer rejoicing in her debut as a surprise-applause heroine of the night. The children go home with their even more surprised father, leaving me to resume duty as a Festival Director and take the company out to eat a meal. For months, the words of one of the children in *Genesi* go round and round in my head. She shouts waving a big stick, saying, 'Pay Attention! Pay Attention!'

## Brace Up!

The Wooster Group, USA, LIFT'93

For the last thirty years the Wooster Group have been deconstructing – and disrupting – the dramatic classics that animate theatre history, filtering them through a late-twentieth-century sensibility. When working on his translation for the Wooster Group's production of Chekhov's *Three Sisters,* Russian scholar Paul Schmidt asked: 'How are we in 1990 to stage the plays of a writer who announced as he worked on *The Seagull* that he was "flagrantly disregarding the

basic conventions of the stage"? A writer who invented young Konstantin Treplev, a playwright, who proclaims that, "we need new forms, and if we can't have them, let's have no theatre at all." Is it possible to find "new forms" for Chekhov, whose own theatre has found no new forms in almost a hundred years?'

The result was *Brace Up!,* a multimedia deconstruction of *Three Sisters,* featuring TV screens, Noh Theatre, vaudeville routines and samurai movies. The host and narrator of the show, Kate Valk, fast-forwards and freeze-frames the action, describing the surroundings and quizzing different characters as to how they are feeling. The technicians, sitting upstage, complain that no one knows their lines, while those actors who are 'on vacation' or 'not here yet' appear on video. Conversations are exchanged between characters on stage and those on screen, and speeches, delivered in fast, inexpressive tones, are intercut with Bob Dylan's *Blowing in the Wind* or TV muzak. Nothing is as it seems. The youngest sister, Irina, is played by an elderly woman and the boorish Solyony is represented, on video, by a roaring B-movie dinosaur. On stage, Willem Dafoe as Andrei acts out acting Chekhov, occasionally breaking into a 'Japanese' dance, while the actor Kenneth Branagh, as Henry V, rides forth to battle across the screens.

Coming out of the show, Richard Eyre, at that time Director of the National Theatre, commented that he did not see the point. 'Why', he asked, 'could they not write their own plays, rather than messing up other people's?' 'Appropriation', said Ron Vawter, founder member of the Wooster Group who played Vershinin in *Brace Up!,* 'is such a fundamental thing . . . That's how I'd describe what's gone on in twentieth-century art. It's a kind of recycling . . . What we tend to do in the Wooster Group is to appropriate from several different sources at the same time. That way we can juggle all these separate things until the weights are familiar and then a new kind of theatre text is created between these different places.'

Whilst the Wooster Group has had a major influence on generations of theatre-makers, critics are divided. 'Phoney, sub-Brechtian . . . a Chekhov of scraps and fragments, all coherence gone . . . the technology of meaningless,' raged Nicholas de Jong, reviewing *Brace Up!* in the *Evening Standard*. Lyn Gardner in *The Guardian* enthused, 'Deeply moving and totally absurd . . . genuinely a play for today . . . Anyone with an interest in the future of British theatre should see *Brace Up!* and wise up.' And for the director Peter Sellars the Wooster Group has quite simply created 'The most important theatre I have ever seen.'

*Brace Up!,*
The Wooster
Group, USA,
LIFT'93. Photo:
Simon Annand.

## Período Villa Villa

De La Guarda, Argentina, LIFT'97

Between 1976 and 1982, 30,000 people 'disappeared' in Argentina's dirty war; debate was stifled and the murderous hand of military repression ruled. Argentina's defeat by Britain in the 1982 Falklands War precipitated the fall of General Galtieri and the country began to rebuild a fragile democracy. In 1987 LIFT had presented *Potestad*, written by the actor and psychiatrist, Eduardo Pavlovsky, well known for his gruelling analysis of the mentality of the torturer and an advocate of psychodrama. In *Potestad* a broken man, a doctor, grieves for the loss of his daughter, and for most of the play we share his eloquent anguish. But towards the end of the play comes the chilling realisation that this charming and sensitive man collaborated with the military in abducting the children of the *fanáticos* who were systematically hounded down and slaughtered by the Junta's death squads. It emerges that he had discovered the girl alone with her murdered parents and claimed her for his own. But with the restoration of democracy, the now adolescent girl has been tracked down and reclaimed by her grandparents. That is the nature of his 'loss'.

A few days before the show opened at the Royal Court, we received a phone call from the Foreign Office. Did we realise that the Falkands issue was still unresolved, that Britain was still officially at war with Argentina and therefore no government subsidy could be used in presenting an Argentinian company? We pointed out that the visit was being supported by the Baring Foundation whose Director, Nicholas Baring, a passionate friend of Argentina, saw the visit as an opportunity of reconnecting the country with Britain at a human level beyond the corridors of political wrangling and territorial claims. The Foreign Office backed down.

Almost ten years later in March 1996, Buenos Aires was getting ready to mark the twentieth anniversary of the Junta. The tragic human consequences of this era were still very much alive and the ageing *Madres de Plaza de Mayo*, Mothers of the Disappeared, continued their candlelit vigil outside Government House in Buenos Aires, demanding the truth about their loved ones. To mark the anniversary the mothers' symbol, a tied headscarf, had been stencilled on all the pavements around the city centre. In the main square an open-air concert was in rehearsal, bringing together protesting voices from the 70s and 80s with those of a new generation of music-makers. Buenos Aires's elegant streets and squares, built by prosperous Italian, Spanish and French immigrants, had a down-at-heel feel. The economy was faltering, shops were boarded up and cafés were empty. But there was another Argentina, led by a younger, irreverent generation who were out to have fun. At five o'clock in the morning every day of the week cars filled with exuberant clubbers going home created traffic jams worse than any rush hour.

In the early 90s a young street theatre company, Organización Negra, had stormed Buenos Aires's landmark obelisk, the symbol of military might and conquest that dominates the city's grand boulevard, the Avenida Nueve de Julio. Their action attracted thousands to participate in an all-night happening, complete with fire, bands, rock climbers and abseilers. The event was deliberately wordless. They were, they declared, tired of the treachery of words and were going to express their dissent purely through acrobatics.

Organización Negra joined forces with the dance company El Descueve and formed De La Guarda to create what became the world-storming *Período Villa Villa*, an anarchic, gravity-defying show that owed as much to rave culture as to circus, theatre and modern dance.

Totally unsubsidised and all but ignored by the established theatre, the show had been a huge success and was preparing to open for a second run. I (*RF*) attended a rehearsal in their specially constructed scaffolded tent, situated right next to La Recoleta Cemetery, where Argentina's great and good are buried, Eva Peron included. We were ushered into a dark claustrophobic space under a low translucent ceiling. Something was happening above. To gentle music, human shadows flitted across our gaze and strange amplified crunching sounds, accompanying what appeared to be illuminated water droplets, further disorientated us. Then in a breathtaking moment the whole ceiling was transformed into a night sky, a constellation of incandescent stars. Cracks appeared in the heavens and we were showered with plastic toys. We kept looking up and suddenly, to wild drumming and chanting, demonic spirits burst through the ceiling and began to swing wildly round the space, chasing each other, frenziedly racing up and abseiling down the walls, spinning down to embrace and then swoop up audience members from below. A tropical storm swept through the makeshift auditorium. We were soaked and caught up in a drama of desperate callings out for loved ones who had disappeared, swept away by torrential rains.

After the rehearsal I watched a video of the full show which tantalised with yet more unimaginable theatricality. *Villa Villa* was wild, exciting, great entertainment. But more than that, there was something that seemed to capture the defiant spirit of a generation navigating their recent history, caught

*Período Villa Villa,*
De La Guarda,
Argentina,
LIFT'97. Photo:
Gavin Evans.

in a dialectic of remembrance and forgetting and determined to move beyond the empty posturings of the ineffective state and its corrupt politicians.

'There is a sense of the spirits coming down to earth,' co-director Pichón Baldinu explained to me. 'We want to be with people. We don't want to frighten them. We are not here to provoke. We lost so much in our military period in Argentina and forgot feelings. Now perhaps we need to look inside more, consider more personal politics. Argentineans have always looked outside their country for inspiration. This is another approach.'

Bringing *Villa Villa* to London presented LIFT with a huge challenge as this was a show that seemed to break every rule in the licensing book. The only possible space that could accommodate it was at Three Mills Island, but Newham's Chief Licensing Officer was concerned about the safety of densely packing a standing audience, including children, into a dark, enclosed space and sprinkling them with plastic toys, to say nothing of the torrential rain which was to shower down from great hoses while the performers whirled dangerously above their heads. We negotiated. We argued. We made some concessions. There was to be a reduction in audience capacity from 800 to 600 (not good news for the box office), the performers had to wear new custom-made double-strength harnesses, and the water canon had to be strategically placed so the audience were less than soaked. We agreed: they agreed – still reluctantly, we felt.

We proposed to the Chief Licensing Officer that he should attend the first performance, something he didn't usually do himself. 'It wasn't his kind of thing,' he said but he would come. As the show proceeded and the audience's mood altered from cautious curiosity to wide-eyed amazement and foot-stomping endorsement, we cast nervous glances his way. The music pulsated loudly, the paper ceiling ripped open and the performers burst through. The Chief Licensing Officer came over to us. Was he going to stop the show? 'I wonder', he asked, rather sheepishly, 'whether I might have a few tickets for this weekend so I can bring my granddaughter and her friends?'

This energetic, breathtakingly beautiful and very sexy show caught the imagination of Londoners overnight. The sheer acrobatic brilliance of the entertainment, the violent playfulness of the mischievous spirits, the rock-concert exuberance, the exhilaration of the tropical storm were greeted with enthusiasm. Some audience members found themselves – literally – in a passionate clinch with the performers, others were pulled into the heavens. All were caught up in the changing moods of the show's internal dramas – a comically tender love scene between a wildly swinging couple striving and failing to embrace, a brutal act of masochism as a woman repeatedly smashed herself against the canvas walls, a whooping headlong race between two competing wall-scaling teams, and all to a manic drumbeat which, more than anything else, spoke of the anger, pity and defiance of a severely bruised nation.

Soon after the LIFT season ended, De La Guarda went on to play for almost a year to packed audiences from across London's many constituencies at the

Roundhouse in a production which though still wild, felt safer, more familiarly rock-circus. Whilst a little of its rebellious spirit had certainly been lost in its transition from Buenos Aires to Three Mills Island, at the Roundhouse it was received simply as a piece of theatre, unconventional certainly, but ultimately perhaps just another piece of razzmatazz entertainment for London's sensation-seeking audiences.

## *Murx den Europäer! Ein Patriotischer Abend* (Kill the European! A Patriotic Evening)

The Volksbühne Theatre, Germany, LIFT'95

In an enormous empty waiting room (or is it an employment agency or a government office? – it is never made clear) eleven men and women sit at tables and ... wait. Staring vacantly into space, they are held in a Beckettian limbo. Slapstick routines and strange rituals break an uneasy silence. A middle-aged couple bicker over the poisoning of a dog. A man fools around at the piano. Neon lights flicker and tiles fall from the ceiling. It is a place of lassitude and stasis.

On the back wall is a clock that has stopped and a notice, '*damit die Zeit nicht stehen bleibt*' ('so that time doesn't stand still'). As the hours pass, the letters on the back wall fall to the ground one by one. Time passes slowly – on some nights, too slowly for some members of the audience, who show their protest and walk out.

A caretaker stokes an ominously large furnace down stage, while another distributes glasses of water, followed a while later by teabags – maybe after all it's a factory canteen? A buzzer goes and the rituals begin all over again. A violinist falls over. The pianist starts to sing a song of thanks for little joys, beginning each new verse on a higher and higher note. As the other ten join in, one by one, ripples of laughter run through the audience. It is disturbing, hilarious, compelling. Only when their voices swell in unison do the performers emerge from the isolation of their separate worlds, singing music closely woven into the German consciousness, although meaning different things to East and West: songs of the Fatherland and of the Hitler Youth movement; a Schubert string quartet; evangelical hymns; and the national anthem of the old GDR. A Yiddish song drifts out of the large oven.

With every second East German losing their job and forty years of the GDR reduced to rubble, Swiss director Christoph Marthaler's brilliantly evocative play

*Murx den Europäer! Ein Patriotischer Abend (Kill the European! A Patriotic Evening)*, The Volksbühne Theatre, Germany, LIFT'95. Photo: David Baltzer.

marked a particular moment in time and place. Exploring the complex process of German reunification, the show went on to become a cult hit, running for ten years and touring the world.

Commissioned in 1993, four years after the fall of the Berlin Wall, *Murx* was created at the Volksbühne theatre on Rosa-Luxemburg-Platz in former East Berlin. Built in 1914 as a *Volks* (people's) theatre, the venue's grassroots traditions were established under artists such as Erwin Piscator. Post-reunification, the theatre enjoyed a renaissance under the iconoclastic Frank

Castorf, whose policy of retaining the old GDR company whilst inviting guest directors in and staging political cabaret alongside rock concerts reconnected the Volksbühne to its populist past.

Too big to fit on any stage in London, LIFT created a theatre space for the show in an old gin distillery at Bromley-by-Bow near the River Lea, which became the Three Mills Island Studio.

## Things Fall Apart

West Yorkshire Playhouse and Collective Artistes, UK/Nigeria, LIFT'97

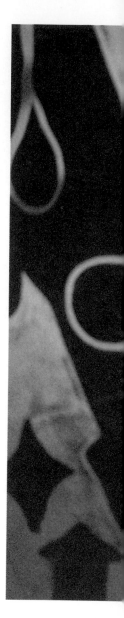

'The drums were still beating, persistent and unchanging. Their sound was no longer a separate thing from the living village. It was like the pulsation of its heart. It throbbed in the air, in the sunshine, and even in the trees, and filled the village with excitement.'
Chinua Achebe, *Things Fall Apart* (1958)

There are no passive sentences in Chinua Achebe's classic African novel about the impact of colonisation on an Ibo village community. Lines jump out at you, like the lizards the book describes leaping from the Oroko trees, with an energy that connects the characters' interior lives to their external environment. In this way, the novel draws everyone, including the reader, into the collusions of history to ask 'Who is responsible when things fall apart?'

Playwright Biyi Bandele first read the novel when he was 7 years old, making his way voraciously through all his father's books: Conrad, Soyinka, the King James Bible, Rider Haggard. At 9, inspired in part by Achebe's book, Biyi decided to become a writer himself. Obsessed by the story, he wanted to tell people about its proud, tragic hero, Okonkwo – known in the Nigerian village of Umuofia as the man who threw Amalinze the Cat in a wrestling match and who survived the worst yam harvest in living memory. Okonkwo was grand enough to impersonate the gods at tribal rituals and had three wives, many children and great wealth. 'When he walked, his heels hardly touched the ground.' How was it then that one of the greatest men in Umuofia fell foul of his own anger and was driven to kill himself and be buried like a dog?

Achebe wrote the novel in 1958, two years before Nigeria declared its independence. An unsentimental rendering of tribal village life at the end of the nineteenth century, it resists the temptation of depicting pre-colonial life as a kind of Eden. It exposes violence and war, balanced with a strong sense of

Okonkwo in
*Things Fall Apart*,
West Yorkshire
Playhouse and
Collective
Artistes,
UK/Nigeria,
LIFT'97. Photo:
Richard Moran.

traditional ritual and social coherence. Achebe said, 'I would be quite satisfied if my novels ... did no more than teach my [African] readers that their past – with all its imperfections – was not one long night of savagery from which the first Europeans acting on God's behalf delivered them.'[2] His desire was to hear Africa speak for itself after a lifetime of hearing Africa spoken about by others.

Biyi's own life was not without its own dramatic upheavals. Born into a large family in 1967 in the small town of Kafanchan in the Muslim north of Nigeria, his book-reading father turned to the bottle. Biyi saw John Osborne's *Look Back in Anger* on the first television set ever to arrive in Kafanchan and recognised the play's rage. He left home at 12 and by the age of 16 was living dangerously, managing thirty-two betting shops in a part of Nigeria where gambling was illegal. A surprisingly mild-mannered man with a characteristic long chuckle, Biyi tells stories about driving a car stashed with large quantities of Naira (Nigerian currency) in cash and getting knifed in the back. A wake-up call came later, when as a student at Obafemi Awolowo University, Ile-Ife, he saw a British Council advertisement for a playwriting competition. His play, *Rain,* won and he found himself in the rainy north of England, under the guidance of Alan Ayckbourn at the Theatre in the Round, Scarborough.

In 1994, Biyi called us to ask if LIFT would be interested in staging an adaptation of *Things Fall Apart.* With plays produced at both the Bush and Talawa Theatre and a TV commission from BBC 2 called *Bad Boys,* he was now a rising star in the UK. His circular stories of the unborn and the dead, of shamans and maverick villains, elided into one another, revealing a common thread only as the narrative moved on. We liked the spacey world he created, where fiction and magic blurred into the reality of the present.

We felt that a British adaptation wouldn't bring Okonkwo's quintessentially African story to life, so proposed to Biyi that we find a co-producer with whom we could create the play in both Nigeria and Britain, involving artists from each country. A LIFT'95 commission, *Zumbi,* about Brazil's legendary slave hero, had set a precedent for us. This cross-cultural collaboration between the UK's Black Theatre Co-operative and a team of Brazilian artists had been successfully led by Brazilian theatre director Marcio Meirelles.

Once we'd negotiated the rights of *Things Fall Apart* with Achebe in the US, Sue Higginson at the National Theatre Studio agreed to offer Biyi an eight-week residency to write the play, though Biyi had to be led into the writing room many times before he would produce the script ('and I'm not letting him out!'). Half-way through we held a workshop with British and Nigerian actors to help us decide if a full-stage version would work, and we needed a director. Biyi suggested Chuck Mike, an African-American who had lived in Nigeria since 1976 and had built a reputation leading ensemble projects at Collective Artistes and the Performance Studio Workshop in Lagos. In 1986, when I (*LN*) had met Chuck myself, he was working on 'guerilla' community theatre projects with Wole Soyinka, the great man of letters and human rights activist, at Obafemi Awolowo University.

Chuck had known Biyi at university and thought an adaptation of the book was timely, seeing in the story of one man's pride the decimation of an entire culture. He considered that in the complex character of Okonkwo, Achebe had identified a means of signalling 'a need for those on the continent of Africa to look inward for solutions towards progressive change'. 'Who *is* responsible when things fall apart? The book is a lament for an individual and for a society,' said Chuck, in a LIFT Daily Dialogue. Nigeria *was* falling apart. General Sani Abacha's violent and corrupt rule was condemned within Nigeria and internationally. The two million barrels of oil being exported daily were extracted at monstrous human and environmental cost. Led by the writer, Ken Saro-Wiwa, campaigns against the military government and the oil corporation Shell were gaining support internationally in favour of the Ogoni people of the Niger Delta, whose land was polluted after decades of drilling, its communities restless and dispossessed.

While Chuck prepared to travel to London from Nigeria with a musician, a choreographer and one performer, LIFT's Administrative Producer Angela McSherry drew up lists of black British actors she thought might be interested in the play. It was her belief that *Things Fall Apart* offered a rare chance for British actors to celebrate an African classic at a time when most black theatre in the UK focused on African-Caribbean culture. It was an emotional opportunity, particularly for performers whose cultural origins were West African, to travel to Nigeria and explore a contemporary African theatre idiom. 'For many UK-based actors,' said Chuck Mike, 'their cultural identity is three-fold, combining as it does a British identity with African ancestry and often Caribbean cultural roots.' The company finally consisted of six Nigerians (two of whom were second-generation British citizens), four Caribbeans, two Ghanaians (all second-generation British citizens) and one British Caucasian.

Each day during the subsequent week's workshop in London, Ken Saro-Wiwa's face appeared on the front pages of the newspapers. Bill Clinton and John Major joined the pleas for clemency and the world was up in arms. Abacha's government was proposing to hang Saro-Wiwa, along with eight others, for killing pro-government leaders at a rally they did not attend. There were uncanny parallels to be drawn between the lives of Saro-Wiwa and Okonkwo that made us feel queasy: here were visionary men underestimating the invading forces they were up against in defending their people.

At the National Theatre Studio, to a battery of drums, we joined the fledgling British-Nigerian ensemble to watch the results of the workshop. When Wole Soyinka strolled into the rehearsal room to join us we realised a theatre production of significance was in the making. Biyi opened the play with the book's closing scene: Okonkwo's suicide. A District Commissioner arrives in the village to arrest Okonkwo for killing a clansman at a recent funeral in the village and has arrived too late. He is directed to the tree where the body no one will touch is hanging. By committing suicide he has committed the greatest sin against the Ibo tradition he is fighting to defend. Solemn, brief, but also comic, the short scene carried a charge and we all agreed that Biyi should complete a full-length script. But on 10 November 1995, as Biyi returned to 'the room', the world was informed that Ken Saro-Wiwa had been hanged.

Chuck returned to the climate of oppression and danger in Lagos. Conditions there were deteriorating, with frequent power cuts and low water supplies. Despite this, he and his colleagues prepared for the reciprocal visit of the British cast, a versatile ensemble who would play the fifty characters of an entire Ibo village. However, when they could no longer access their rehearsal space with ease because the roads were up, we had to look for a UK co-producer and return the workshop to Britain.

Although Stephen Daldry had agreed to stage the play at one of the Royal Court's two West End bases as part of LIFT'97, it proved harder than we expected to find producers to engage with African theatre. But Jude Kelly, at the West Yorkshire Playhouse, had premièred Soyinka's *Beatification of Area Boy* the year before and her travels around Nigeria had opened her eyes to West African culture. She also had the trust of Soyinka, who had been Chuck's one-time mentor and wasn't shy of plays that articulated ideas 'politicians are happy to skirt around'. Somewhat at the eleventh hour we secured West Yorkshire's offer to share the financial risk and open the play in Leeds. With the Royal Court still prepared to stage it in London, we could get down to production details:

Jude: 'So Chuck, how many actors are you thinking of having?'

Chuck: 'Not that many. Thirty. Or forty?'

'How about twelve? Or thirteen?'

We settled on thirteen.

Everyone was determined to stick to the original plan to part-rehearse in Nigeria so the British cast went out there, the designer Niki Turner travelling to the Ibo east to buy the goatskins, machetes, cow horns, calabashes and kola-nut bowls required to stage nineteenth-century Ibo village life in Britain. Chuck found the British company whose training had been so text- and character-based initially wary of engaging with his exuberant performance style, which incorporated song, dance, drumming, music, movement and story-telling. On their return from Africa, however, we observed how the company could act with

*New Earth*, Kufena, Nigeria, LIFT'87. Photo: Tomas Steenborg.
A LIFT commission directed by Peter Badejo, *New Earth* explored Nigerian land conflicts using Bata and Bori traditional ritual dances in a contemporary dance drama form.

a lack of inhibition about characterisation, passing the story's telling between themselves. Chuck would later remark on the collective abilities of the company as a model for African diasporic work: 'The ensemble nature of the production gave it a lightness in attitude, an effortlessness comparable to the lyrical and eloquent nature of the text.'[3] Time spent in Nigeria, however brief, had been essential, allowing the British company to become immersed in Nigerian culture. British-born Nigerian actress Antonia Coker said: 'It was the first time I understood that we Africans have our own story. Visiting Nigeria for *Things Fall Apart* was a time when things came together for me.'

The play opened at West Yorkshire Playhouse on 23 May 1997 and at the Royal Court for LIFT on 12 June. Beginning and ending with the death of

Okonkwo (played by Yomi A. Michaels), it was staged in a circular, sand-covered pit. A formidable ensemble company brought Ibo tribal culture alive, switching genders and roles with remarkable fluidity. It was exhilarating to see evidence of the relationships between the British and Nigerian ensemble, indistinguishable from each other on stage.

A mixed audience of black and white theatre-goers, unusual at that time in a West End theatre, confirmed the shift in cultural references that the play had achieved. There was an air of respect in the auditorium as people listened to the play's stories of the gods, of harmattan winds and heavy rains that drown the yams. Some acknowledged that they weren't familiar with such stories, while others, particularly those from an African diasporic community for whom the play was a classic knew them so well they could finish off the actors' lines – and did. When the gods demand that Ikemefuna, Okonkwo's beloved adopted son, be killed, Okonkwo doesn't question the demand, he is too wrapped up in the fabric of Ibo laws and traditions. As the actor, Freddie Annobil-Dodoro, playing the child moved across the stage in a 'death-walk', the audience watched in silence, deeply moved.

Biyi was applauded for capturing the nuances of Achebe's tale of redemption and hope, Chuck for a production that was lithe and lean. When Achebe himself saw the production in America he sat in silence for a long while at the end. It was the first time, he declared afterwards, that he had actually 'seen what he had written'.

In 1999, Collective Artistes and the Performance Studio Workshop in Lagos initiated a tour of the production, working in association with Jan Ryan's Fifth Amendment. *Things Fall Apart* took in New York, Princeton and Washington in America, then Manchester, Bristol, Nottingham and Plymouth in the UK before arriving ceremoniously home on Nigerian soil in April 1999, twenty-five years on from Biyi's first reading of the novel and five from his initial call to LIFT.

## Oráculos

Taller de Investigación del Imagen Teatral, Colombia, LIFT'97

Fanny Micky is the exuberant, red-headed, larger-than-life diva who runs the Bogotá Festival. Every two years she brings together a roll-call of Latin American, North American and European companies to play on the street, in the decaying splendour of the opera house, in cavernous sports halls, scented courtyards and rickety studio theatres. The Wooster Group from New York performs alongside Britain's Cheek by Jowl, with shows from Lithuania, Chile and Peru as well as a clutch of newly commissioned productions from Colombian companies.

At the 1996 Festival we were bussed every day from our soulless hotel on the outskirts of a rapidly expanding Bogotá, a journey which sometimes took two hours to complete through the traffic. The city had changed immensely since my (*RF*) first visit in 1982. Then the centre was pot-holed and muddy and at every turn we were confronted by the desperate pleading of street children. One day we came across an emaciated donkey dying pitifully at the bottom of the cathedral steps. Fourteen years later the roads were immaculate, the street children had been shunted off to some less public part of town and all around were ostentatious high-rise office buildings and smart shops for the privileged few. The old Spanish colonial quarter, La Candelaria – in 1982 a crime-infested slum under threat of demolition – had become the principle tourist destination with renovated streets, chic bars and restaurants. All this development had been largely financed by the drug barons against whom the government was waging a war. Yet it was their money that was creating an economic and social infrastructure for the country, building schools, houses, hospitals and business centres. The misery produced by years of military dictatorship in the 60s and 70s had been replaced by the rule of the traffickers, with its attendant social unrest, violence and anarchy.

Many of the Colombian productions in the 1996 Festival revolved around the country's recent history. One performance re-enacted the moment in November 1985 when guerrilla forces had come down from the mountains and forced their way into the Supreme Court where they had taken everyone hostage, killing more than seventy people before they fled. Seated on the wooden balcony of a large communal house, we were drawn into the everyday reality of the siege, witnesses to the agonising days of the family living in our midst, waiting for news of their daughter who never returned from work. The performances of the CCT (Corporación Colombiana de Teatro), in contrast, had a strong social and political agenda, grappling with the issues of the day and fighting for better conditions for the dispossessed. Patricia Ariza, CCT's remarkable founder-director, works with women who have been violently evicted from their land, as well as with street children, offering them a haven from the city's dangers.

Toward the end of the Festival I had a totally unexpected theatrical experience, one that hit a completely different register. The rain had not stopped for days and the sprawling, sodden tent which housed the labyrinthine passages and chambers of Enrique Vargas's *Oráculos* was shored up with sandbags. Steaming in the tropical warmth, I entered a waiting room and took off my shoes, as instructed. A gnome-like lady gently pulled me into a huge dark wardrobe filled with clothes and smelling of mothballs. She dressed me in a dashing feathered hat and a red velvet cloak then led me into a long corridor of mirrors, closing the door behind and leaving me alone with my disorientating reflections. I waited for a long time before deciding to make my own way out. Increasingly panic-stricken, I desperately pushed at every opening, only to be mocked by the distant sound of hidden laughter. It was a relief when at last a figure appeared out of nowhere and beckoned me forward. Now I was fumbling through fabric pathways until I reached an open glade, filled with refreshing light, the smell of newly cut grass and the sounds of oceans and bird song, my bare feet trudging sensuously through sand. And here was a girl swinging on a rope who slipped off and began to chase me in a game of hide-and-seek through a maze of gauzy white curtains where I fell into piles of grain, whose sweet, slightly fusty smell and hard, slippery texture immediately evoked childhood memories of playing in the huge corn silos of our neighbour's farm. Instructed by a silent figure, I helped grind some corn. In the next chamber there was a pile of dough waiting to be kneaded. I shaped it into a small loaf and placed it alongside the other loaves about to go into an oven, from which came the comforting smell of freshly baked bread. At the end of the corridor, past a window overgrown with ivy, was a small dark room with a solitary desk, lit by a lamp. On the desk lay an open book and fountain pen. I recorded my impressions then continued the journey, following the sound of a bell coming from behind a broken door which opened to lure me into the lair of a gorgeous androgynous devilish creature. She invited me to arm-wrestle with her and then dance a tango. Uncertain as to how to respond to her increasingly sensual and provocative game, I was relieved when she stopped abruptly and pushed me into a claustrophobic barred space, slamming the door behind her. It became clear that my release could only be effected through climbing into a velvet-lined coffin on the other side of the grille in the next room. But once in the coffin I lay curiously relaxed and closed my eyes as I felt myself turned upside down by a creaky contraption. The movement ceased, there was no one there and after a silent pause I stepped out. Feeling my way forward, I found a bridge and at last arrived in a dim, carpet-covered room where previously unseen fellow travellers were resting on cushions drinking mint tea and eating the bread they had helped to prepare during the journey.

I had never experienced anything quite like this before. Puzzled, almost irritated and impatient to begin with, I now felt calm, uplifted, as if I had taken a break from everyday life and been on a long holiday. *Oráculos,* as Enrique Vargas explains, is about a surrender to the world of the senses. It challenges the binary mind-body split in Western culture and draws the traveller into a non-intellectual experience where one loses oneself. The idea is based on the Eleusian mysteries – some say the origin of theatre – where pre-Homeric Greeks disappeared on a drug-induced voyage of self-discovery. 'Oracles enable you to listen to yourself, labyrinths to set off in search of yourself,' says Enrique.

Enrique works with a host of performers, including trained actors, aroma specialists, psychotherapists and anthropologists, all of whom inhabit the labyrinth. He tours the world with a core group of twelve, augmented by people drawn from the host city. It was an enticing and exciting proposition to stage *Oráculos* in London. But had I been seduced by the experience because I was far away from home, feeling both more open and vulnerable in a very different culture? How would it survive in cool, sceptical London? A chance encounter with *Oráculos* two months later convinced me that we had to do it. I was on my way across Europe from the Exit Festival in Ljubljana to Toruň in Poland and had missed the early morning train by five minutes. Across the road from the station *Oráculos* was about to open in a vast abandoned power station. I went over and booked into the 11.00 am performance, which I found even more powerful than before. I invited Enrique to LIFT the following year.

To find a venue large and flexible enough to accommodate the labyrinth in London was a huge challenge. We booked it in at Wapping Pumping Station, but then discovered that an adjacent housing development planned for completion had overrun its schedule and the experience would be drowned out by the noise of heavy machinery and drilling. When we tried to relocate to the vaulted chambers of the Undercroft beneath the Roundhouse we were refused a licence, owing to the lack of safety exits. Our increasingly frantic search for a space took us to a derelict power station deep in Deptford which proved too dangerous. With days to go before the team of Colombian performers were due to arrive to construct the labyrinth, we finally tracked down an abandoned coach station at the heart of the drug-dealing and prostitution pick-up area near King's Cross station.

The London response to *Oráculos* was startling. Cynical, hardened critics talked about a 'deeply affecting . . . moving and beautiful event' from which they emerged 'spiritually refreshed'. The show was a 'playground of the imagination' and succeeded in transcending the sterile debates often provoked on such occasions as to whether this was or was not theatre.

## The Theft of Sita

Nigel Jamieson *et al.* and Performing Lines, Indonesia/Australia/UK, LIFT
Enquiry 2001

Along with the Internet, the ancient story-telling tradition of Wayan Kulit shadow
puppetry became the main source of independent news and commentary in
Indonesia during the turbulent period prior to the overthrow of the Suharto
regime in 1998.

British-born, Australian-based director Nigel Jamieson took this example of
tradition meeting modernity as inspiration for *The Theft of Sita,* a stunningly
inventive cross-cultural production created in Bali by young Indonesian artists,
puppeteer I Made Sidia and musician I Wayan Gde Yudane, with a team of
theatre-makers, musicians, puppeteers, designers and film-makers from
Europe and Australia.

*The Theft of Sita* told the story of the *Ramayana* from the perspective of two
comic Wayan Kulit characters, *punkawan* servant clowns Twalen and Merdah,
while progressively moving the action to contemporary Indonesia. The demons
of the great Sanskrit epic of good and evil, representing greed, the destruction
of the natural environment and political corruption, were transposed to the
modern world. Using hundreds of puppets, traditional and newly created, *Sita*
combined the magical beauty of a popular Indonesian shadow play with
contemporary politics, fart jokes and slapstick humour. The spiritually sublime
was to meet, in Jamieson's own words, 'The Simpsons on Speed'. Throughout
the piece, the exquisite timeless sound of the Balinese gamelan blended
seamlessly with song and improvised rhythms led by Australian jazz musician
Paul Grabowsky. (It took the musicians weeks to tune the Western and
Indonesian instruments so that they could be played together.)

At the outset, a traditional Wayan Kulit shadow play is set up: a crocodile
stalks a duck, a buck mounts a doe, humans live like gods. King Rama and his
wife Sita are seen loading an idyllic existence in the pristine forest until an evil
spirit, the demon Rawanna, kidnaps the beautiful Sita – embodiment of the
natural environment.

The tranquil old world of the *Ramayana* then shifts to the modern industrial
world. Giant animated logging-machine beasts rampage through the forest,
wood-chip factories (for toilet paper) spoil the beauty of the landscape, while
rice terraces are drained dry of water for tourists' white-water rafting. In search
of Sita, the clowns Twalen and Merdah approach the city of Lanka and meet
the horror of the urban jungle. The production reaches its climax in an epic

*The Theft of Sita*,
Nigel Jamieson *et
al.* and Performing
Lines, Indonesia/
Australia/UK, LIFT
Enquiry 2001.
Photo and design
by Julian Crouch,
based on the
graphic work of
Reg Mombassa.

battle, in which King Rama destroys the corrupt Rawanna (who has sold off
the precious Sita to save his toppling empire). With chilling footage from the
Indonesian riots of 1998, and the head-on collision of shadow play and TV
screens, the two clowns find themselves thrown on to the violent streets. Sita
is finally returned to Rama, a fragile promise of democracy is born and the
show's clown heroes can approach the ballot box.

The Theft of Sita created something fresh and forceful from the meeting of
the two different theatre traditions. Presented in both New York and London in
the weeks after September 11, the show's example of cross-cultural
collaboration was uplifting. Audiences commented that the performance
allowed them to see how a more hopeful future for the world could be
imagined.

1. Tim Etchells, *Certain Fragments: Contemporary Performance and Forced Entertainment*
   (London, Routledge, 1999).
2. Chinua Achebe, 'The Novelist as Teacher', in *Hopes and Impediments: Selected Essays*
   (London, Heinemann, 1988; New York, Doubleday, 1989).
3. Chuck Mike, 'Since and Sensibility: Case Study on *Things Fall Apart*', Intersection
   Conference, New World Theater, Massachusetts, October 1997.

# Theatre

# THE JESTER IN THE PACK

## Lyn Gardner

In Chekhov's *The Seagull*, the young playwright Konstantin declares: 'We need new forms, and if we can't have them, let's have no theatre at all.' For twenty-four years LIFT has given London's theatre-goers new forms and challenged our safe and tidy definitions of theatre. By bringing the world to us, it has expanded the boundaries of our London theatre consciousness – geographically, culturally, stylistically and aesthetically – and opened our eyes to the many possibilities of theatre. In the process it has made us question what theatre can, could and should be, where it takes place, and even who it is for. Over the years I have seen that theatre can happen anywhere, in any space, and that it speaks an international language that crosses national and cultural boundaries, so that a community in one part of the world can speak directly to a community of theatre-goers here. LIFT has provided me with geography, history and cookery lessons all rolled into one great theatrical experience. My contact with so many LIFT performances through the years has helped teach me how to live and dream, how to embrace the new and the unfamiliar. In short, it has opened me up.

*Kitchen Show*, Bobby Baker, the first of five commissions in the *Daily Life* series, LIFT'91–LIFT'01 (page 191). Photo: Andrew Whittuck.

It is worth remembering that the theatre landscape of 1981 was very different from what it is today. The worst of the public spending cuts that were to decimate funding of the arts during that grim decade were yet to be fully felt. Nonetheless the antipathy that Prime Minister Margaret Thatcher and her Conservative government felt towards the arts – and in particular theatre, with its ability to question the world around us – was already clear. Even so, London theatre was largely insular and smug, confident that it was the theatre capital of the world and yet almost entirely ignorant of developments beyond these shores. It was eight years since the last of Peter Daubeny's World Theatre Seasons at the Aldwych, and while the need to export British theatre was understood by funders, the idea of importing theatre from abroad was considered laughable, as Rose Fenton and Lucy Neal discovered when they approached the Arts Council with the idea of a London-based international theatre festival. After all, we did theatre better than the rest of the world – why would we want to pay to bring foreign theatre here?

The truth is that we did a certain kind of theatre better than the rest of the world, a kind of theatre that was heavily text-based, literary, witty and grounded in social realism; a theatre that still owed much to the traditions of George Bernard Shaw, who had introduced Henrik Ibsen to the London stage, and Harley Granville-Barker. What we did was the well-made play. Twenty-five years after it was first put on, *Look Back in Anger* was still the point of reference for most critics and many theatre-goers, and while the state-of-the-nation plays of younger playwrights such as David Hare and Howard Brenton were considered radical because of their espousal of socialist ideals, nobody found it curious that in terms of form they were extraordinarily old-fashioned. That is just how plays were meant to be.

It was a play by Hare, the much trumpeted *Fanshen*, a documentary-style drama about the Chinese Revolution, that helped open Rose Fenton and Lucy Neal's eyes to other kinds of theatre. For when they took a production of it to the student theatre festival in Portugal in 1978 they were astonished to discover that their contribution seemed dull alongside the visually fizzing and physically dynamic productions by students from other countries. In that moment the seeds of LIFT were sown, a festival that has always very clearly known that there is a distinction between drama and theatre.

Prior to the arrival of LIFT, 'going to the theatre' usually meant going to one of the Victorian chocolate-box theatres on Shaftesbury Avenue, to the faded grandeur of the Royal Court in Sloane Square or perhaps to the purpose-built concrete slab on the South Bank that is the National Theatre. True, younger audiences had discovered the excitement of seeing an intimate production in a small room above a pub, or at Riverside Studios or the Roundhouse, and many were stimulated and excited by the work of innovative home-grown companies such as Pip Simmons, Hull Truck and the People Show. But for most of us 'going to the theatre' still involved sitting in neat rows in the dark, as often as not on plush velvet seats, and hardly acknowledging the presence of the strangers with whom we sat shoulder to shoulder, certainly never expecting the actors to invade our space or dreaming that we could stake a claim to theirs. LIFT changed all that.

First of all it introduced the idea that theatre didn't have to take place actually in theatres. LIFT performances were as likely to happen in a disused cellar, a shop window, a cage at the zoo, a derelict hotel or a church as in a traditional theatre building. LIFT shows spilled out into the streets and invaded our shared spaces – the parks, the squares and the river. When Els Comediants' carnivalesque orgy of fireworks, drumming and dragon-slaying tumbled across Battersea Park at the opening of the 1985 Festival, it was much more than a mere performance. It represented an artistic occupation of the city in which the lines between performance and life and art and everyday activity, between the play and playing, were increasingly blurred. On an entirely different scale, LIFT's radicalism was also typified by the work of the art school-trained Bobby Baker, whose canvas is women's domestic lives and whose work owes as much to the visual arts as it does to theatre. In her *Daily Life* series, supported by LIFT during the 1990s, Baker placed the ordinary and the extraordinary, the absurd and the sacred, the inconsequential and the searing, cheek by jowl in performances such as *Kitchen Show* (1991), in which she threw open her own North London kitchen, playing the perfect hostess, albeit one festooned with spinach and kitchen utensils (page 188).

In Fiona Templeton's 1989 *YOU – The City,* London itself became the stage, with each member of the audience transported about the city via foot and taxi to a series of secret locations. In twenty-one years LIFT has expanded my geographical knowledge of London no end, taking me to its hidden corners and forgotten nooks and crannies. Over the years these places became part of my landscape, my memory, my personal geographical and emotional map of the London where I live. The journeys to the productions became part of the performance itself, teaching me that theatre is not a passive experience. We do not just go to watch, but take ourselves to every show. And I am not alone. It was LIFT's determination always to match performance and site – whether it was Anatoli Vasiliev's version of Luigi Pirandello's *Six Characters in Search of an Author* (1989) in the rackety splendour of the Brixton Academy, or Bobby Baker's *Grown-Up School* (1999) set in a real primary school – that encouraged subsequent experiments such as the Almeida's residencies in the Gainsborough Studios and the Hackney Empire. As the Almeida discovered, *Hamlet* in run-down Hackney

means something different to *Hamlet* in chic Islington. LIFT established the precedent, demonstrating that the performance does not exist in isolation but always within a social, political, geographical and architectural context.

So when the Lottery-funded refurbishments of theatre buildings in the mid to late 1990s led to enforced exile for a number of theatres, many followed LIFT's example in looking for found spaces. For several seasons the Almeida took up residence in the old coach station at King's Cross that LIFT had discovered for the 1997 presentation of *Oráculos,* the large-scale labyrinth show created by Enrique Vargas. Even when the Royal Court, in exile from Sloane Square, took over the traditional New Ambassadors Theatre in St Martin's Lane it reconfigured the auditorium and played with the space. More recent experiments, such as Out of Joint's promenade *Macbeth*, Shunt's occupation of thousands of square feet under London Bridge for *Tropicana* (in collaboration with the National Theatre), and the work of site-specific artists Wilson + Wilson, owe much to LIFT's pioneering activity. Without Deborah Warner's raising of ghosts in a derelict hotel in *The St Pancras Project* (1995) or her conjuring of angels in *The Tower Project* (1999), without Theatre-rites' extraordinary transformation of an ordinary Brixton house into something mysterious and magical in *Houseworks* (1996), British theatre might still be locked in purpose-built theatre buildings. LIFT, along with Artsadmin and later Artangel, were among the few British producing organisations that helped set it free.

Even when LIFT used traditional theatre buildings it often did so with a certain cheekiness or gave us productions that broke theatre conventions. Rose English's show *The Double Wedding* (1991) not only took performance art to the heart of Britain's new-writing culture, it also imported an ice rink into the theatre. LIFT showed us that rules are there to be broken and that the fourth wall can be battered down, even in the case of classic texts – in Matthias Langhoff's 1989 production of Strindberg's *Miss Julie*, Julie headed towards her suicide by clambering over the audience in the stalls, with the audience offering her a helping hand towards her death. British theatre has taken note and in recent years it has been not uncommon to find ourselves seated on the stage with the actors occupying the auditorium. The work of companies such as Kneehigh that directly engage with the audience across the footlights belongs to a folk-theatre tradition that has been strongly represented in LIFT shows over the years. With its mixture of clowning, female impersonators, singing, dancing, and elemental use of water, fire and ashes, writer Surit Patar's 1993 version of Lorca's *Yerma* transposed a

*Miss Julie*,
Comédie de
Genève,
Switzerland,
LIFT'89.
Photo: Michael J.
O'Brien
Photography.

European classic to an Indian village (page 10) to create an experience in which the spectacular and the poetic collided head-on and which reached out to British audiences with extraordinary generosity. It didn't matter whether we spoke a word of Punjabi or not, this was a universal story told in a universal style that audiences everywhere could understand emotionally.

Taking theatre out of theatre buildings immediately changed the relationship of audience and performers, often making us participators not just passive spectators. But it also changed the relationship of the audience with each other. In shows such as De La Guarda's *Período Villa Villa*, pyrotechnician Christophe Berthonneau's *Un Peu Plus de Lumière* or Alicia Rios's *La Feria de Los Cinco Sentidos*, all 1997, the giddily social nature of the performance encouraged the audience to become a community. In some cases, such as *Los Cinco Sentidos* or Opera Transatlantica's *Variations on a Concierto Barroco* (1999), the communal nature of theatre was demonstrated through the ritualised sharing of food. During these performances traditional English reserve was swept away as audiences rediscovered the joy of play. Young and old, rich and poor, white and black, we became as one, all with an equal stake in a shared experience, no longer divided in the way the Victorian playhouse isolated audience from action through its segregation of playing and passive space, segregating the audience from each other with separate entrances to the theatre, so the rich need never brush shoulders with the poor. In turning every performance into an 'event' LIFT democratised theatre and in the process freed us from notions of good art and bad art, high art and low art. The LIFT policy of making theatre for all was reflected in programmes where high and low art stood side by side, with circus and Shakespeare rubbing shoulders. This was to the astonishment of some theatre critics who found it difficult to accept that watching circus performer Johann Le Guillerm painfully battling his way across the floor of a tent on the narrow necks of eight wine bottles (*Cirque Ici*, 1997) could be as moving and meaningful, and tell us as much about the human condition, as watching King Lear rail against the heavens on the blasted heath. Or indeed that Shakespeare in a foreign language might be worth seeing at all. What was Shakespeare without the poetry? asked many, only to discover that Shakespeare was not only our contemporary but also the contemporary of the Romanians, Italians and Lithuanians. Instead of finding it confusing or baffling to see familiar texts performed in a foreign language, it proved unexpectedly liberating. Robbed of our usual reference point – the text – we suddenly had to read what was going on on stage in an entirely different way. It forced us to plunge deeper into the emotional and visual subtext of productions.

In our literary and often literal theatre culture, LIFT performances were distinctly different because they opened the door on other ways of conveying meaning. They encouraged ambiguity and allowed space for the audience to put its own meanings into the event, making us pay closer attention and turn detective, using our deductive skills. LIFT recognised something that British theatre had previously ignored: that the audience brings as much to the performance as the actors do, that without our contribution there can be no theatre. On occasion the idea was taken to the extreme: *YOU – The City, The Tower Project* and *Oráculos* were performances for an audience of one – you were in effect the star of your very own show. The intensity of such experiences was beyond doubt, but there was perhaps a danger that these introspective performances owed more to therapy than to theatre – as in the case of *Oráculos's* sensuous aromatherapy – and when so much of LIFT's work has been about the transforming possibilities of bringing people together there was something curious about a strand of work that isolated them. Is theatre really theatre when it has no public dimension? Surely a performance exclusively for one is also in danger of making what is already perceived as an élitist art form seem even more restrictive and beyond access for the majority?

Of course most LIFT performances were the very opposite of élitist in their experiments, which extended not just the boundaries of theatre, but of theatre-going itself. Those in parks, in open spaces and on the river were free events, making theatre available to anyone who wanted to see it. In 1989 the anniversary of the French Revolution was marked by Station House Opera's *The Bastille Dances,* a continual week-long performance involving the daily dismantling and reassembly of 8,000 breeze blocks outside the National Theatre. It not only reminded us of the relationship of street theatre to revolution but during its run many more people would have seen it as they passed by over Waterloo Bridge than had watched all the performances in the National Theatre's three auditoria in the whole of the previous ten years. The more recent arrival of an outdoor summer programme of street arts outside the National Theatre is a belated recognition of the fact that if you can't expect people to come to the theatre you can take theatre to the people. In some cases this has meant taking it to the communities to whom it belongs. Jamaica's Groundwork Theatre Company found a ready-made audience for *Fallen Angel and the Devil Concubine* (1989) in Brixton, just as

*Houseworks*,
Theatre-rites, UK,
Out of LIFT'96.
Photo: Andy
Goss.

the Indian production *The Mad Woman of Our City* (1995), a musical version
of Jean Giraudoux's *The Madwoman of Chaillot*, was perfectly sited at
Watermans Arts Centre in Brentford, where there is a large Punjabi
community. It is doubtful if either of these productions would have been
embraced by the Caribbean or Punjabi communities if they had played the
Old Vic. They would simply have been a piece of theatrical exotica.

If free performances removed the barrier of buying a ticket that may well deter people from going to the theatre, then LIFT also ensured that age wasn't a barrier to theatre either. Theatre for children and young people has often been perceived as the Cinderella of British theatre, but with its espousal of the work of Theatre-rites and, for example, Societas Raffaello Sanzio's *Buchettino* (2001) and Les Deux Mondes' *The Tale of Teeka* (1995) for older children, LIFT helped kick-start a revolution that has made theatre for the under-fives one of the most radical and least text- and hide-bound areas of British theatre. When LIFT commissioned Theatre-rites to transform an ordinary Victorian house in South London in 1996 into an unreal imagined space, custom-made for the small child, it was paying homage to the pioneering work of under-acknowledged British children's theatre artists, inviting them to realise their ideas on a much larger scale in site-specific venues and with exceptional budgets – and then giving them the promotion they deserved. Theatre-rites' Penny Bernand had been co-founder of the pioneering company for under-fives Pop-Up Theatre, and with *Houseworks* she developed earlier ideas, creating the first show in a body of work that has explored the imaginative and transforming possibilities of theatre and which has embraced Einstein's suggestion that 'the most beautiful thing that we can experience is the mysterious'.

Many LIFT performances have welcomed children, unlike traditional theatre which is inclined to erect invisible Keep Out signs around its work. The 1996 Out of LIFT Festival went further still by showing how theatre could be relevant to young people and their lives by encouraging participatory performances. Young teenagers were even allowed to 'play with matches' when 120 of them from Stockwell Park School created a ritualistic spectacular with Christophe Berthonneau in *The Factory of Dreams*, where fireworks became symbols for the hopes, dreams and aspirations of a generation of inner-city kids.

This was work that embraced the future not just in content but also in form. One of my most memorable LIFT moments came in 1999 with *Be Yourself*, in which groups of British and South African teenagers made connections in a piece where the personal and political were intimately entwined, the relationship between theatre and ritual explored through the washing of the audience's hands in bowls of water handed around by the cast.

There is a danger that any kind of theatre festival simply becomes a market-place with each performance representing another stall showing off its exotic wares. The careful siting of LIFT shows in the right environment

*The Dragons' Trilogy*, Théâtre Repère, Canada, LIFT'87. Photo: Claudel Huot. The epic story of two French Canadian girls, spanning seventy-five years from turn-of-the-century Quebec to contemporary Vancouver. Robert Lepage's visually inventive production created a sensual theatrical experience and established Lepage as an international artist.

ensured that this was seldom the case. But the sheer width and breadth of LIFT's vision have meant that commentators have often been at a loss to describe exactly what LIFT is, such has been the Directors' determination not to have the organisation's work pigeon-holed. In a British theatre culture where performance art and new writing view each other with suspicion, and the worlds of straight and musical theatre hardly ever meet on equal terms, LIFT has thrown everything into the melting pot and demonstrated that every kind of theatre deserves an equal place in our culture. Without LIFT there would be no Barbican International Theatre Events (BITE) – the Barbican's programme of international work – nor might there have been an invitation for Robert Lepage to play at the National.

The success of LIFT has been in turning theatre into a series of events that divert and entertain but which also open windows on the world to help us see beyond our self-imposed geographical, mental and psychological boundaries. Long before the current vogue for documentary-style theatre, LIFT was bringing us the news, whether it was in shows such as *Alive from Palestine*, the Ramallah's al-Kasaba Theatre 2001 series of monologues subtitled 'stories under occupation', or in Alexandru Darie's post-Ceausescu staging of *A Midsummer Night's Dream* (1991), which helped us understand what it was like to live under a dictatorship. It was possible to glean as much about the bankruptcy of Communism from Gabor Zsambeki's version of Gogol's *The Government Inspector* (1989) as it was from any newspaper report. In the age of 24-hour news reporting, LIFT has shown that theatre still has a role to play as a reflection of what is going on in the society in which it is made.

Perhaps most of all LIFT has proved that through performance we can share our dreams. By taking theatre out of the stuffy playhouses and back to its origins as a shared celebration and a safe way of letting our devils out to play, it can bring us together and help us tell the stories we want to recount in new and exhilarating ways. LIFT has shown us that theatre can be many things – a well-made play, an outdoor firework spectacular, a shared feast of dancing and singing, a 14-year-old telling us of his reactions to the murder of Stephen Lawrence – it can be anything we want it to be. The jester in the pack of British theatre, LIFT has always led us on a merry dance to somewhere unexpected and often disconcerting. I wouldn't have missed a single one of those strange, unsettling and often thrilling evenings. They have helped to shape the theatre-goer in me and they have given me a map of the world, a map of the city and a map of myself.

# Epilogue

The South African theatre director Barney Simon believed that theatre could 'nurture' a changing society. In 1980 Nelson Mandela was in prison, Pinochet in power in Chile and the Berlin Wall stood firm. The stories in *The Turning World* demonstrate how the artists of the day challenged the status quo, making possible with poetry what politics had yet to achieve. They show that theatre offers us courage to engage collectively in an imagined future, and that people gathering together can be a radical act in itself.

Gurpreet Kaur Bhatti, a young British Sikh writer whose play, *Behzti*, was cancelled after attacks on its performance at Birmingham Rep in December 2004, wrote a month after the incident:

> *'The dramatists whom I admire are brave. They tell us life is ferocious and terrifying, that we are imperfect, and only when we face our imperfections truthfully can we have hope. Theatre is not necessarily a cosy space, designed to make us feel good about ourselves. It is a place where the most basic human expression – that of the imagination – must be allowed to flourish'* (The Guardian*, January 2005).*

When we started LIFT, the Cold War dominated our European view of the world. Youthful as we were, there were perhaps more certainties for us then. Twenty-five years later, the contexts we operate in are politically and culturally both more complicated and more polarised. The artists LIFT is working with, whether from the Middle East, South Africa, the former Eastern-bloc countries, Western Europe or the Pacific Rim, grapple with these new uncertainties, playing with their ambiguities and contradictions.

In the beginning LIFT simply set out to give Londoners a window on the world through theatre. As we worked with artists, staging performances in unconventional spaces, the richer complexities of our work revealed themselves. The very fabric of the city, its hidden corners, communities and links across the world, became an integral part of the Festival. By 2001, LIFT projects had evolved into a series of interconnecting chambers, spilling out of the biennial Festival format. How, we reflected, could we continue to experiment with performance, how develop learning led by artists, sustain relationships across the city and world and bring London audiences into the process? Was the biennial Festival format still the best? There was a great deal more international work regularly on offer in the capital. To stay true to our feel for experiment, we took stock of our role in this evolving landscape.

We decided to break with our own traditions. LIFT'01 would look back at a twenty-year history of one kind of Festival and look forward to the creation of another. We would 'unframe' the biennial Festival format to embark on a five-year venture: the LIFT Enquiry (2001–6), a year-round staging of 'an exuberant and public exploration of theatre in these times worldwide'. The Enquiry would be playful and practical, open to exploring new possibilities.

Soon after LIFT'01, the September 11 attacks on New York and Washington brought latent tensions across the world to centre stage. President Bush's response, 'You're with us or against us', divided people still further. Our plans for the Enquiry gained urgency and purpose. We would have to be even bolder with the questions that interested us. With its multiplicity of voices and stories, how does theatre exist within a polarised global order? Where does a renewal of engagement in the theatre lie?

Away from the demands of a biennial LIFT, the LIFT Enquiry was able to initiate research and evidence-gathering around performance and learning, in addition to commissioning new theatre work. We could investigate, year round, the creative processes of both artists *and* audiences, triggering growing circles of conversations between them and including teachers, children, business people, community activists, scientists, anthropologists, journalists, international barristers and economists. What meaning does theatre have? For whom? And why? When the play ends, we asked, what begins? Over the course of five years we wanted answers to our questions to accumulate, providing a rich understanding of theatre as a place for public dialogue and civic engagement.

At a series of events held at Bargehouse on the South Bank during the summer of 2004 a hundred LIFT Enquirers were invited to give testimonies in answer to the questions 'What is theatre to you? And if it weren't there, what would be missing from your life?' These opportunities allowed a hundred

Londoners of different ages and from different cultural and professional backgrounds to talk of theatre as a place of survival, an intimate space of exchange across cultural barriers, of renewal, of play, of resistance, reconciliation, joy, and confrontation with painful pasts. Together they re-imagined international theatre today: a place of listening as much as a place of giving forth.

The LIFT Enquiry was a gamble – for artists, for LIFT audiences and for us. As we publicly questioned LIFT's role as a producer of international theatre, we investigated whether festivals could be less 'masterminded'. Could they find a more ecological basis? LIFT would turn its attention towards the public in order to regard them not merely as consumers but also as *producers* of culture.

The experience of the LIFT Enquiry, which has run parallel with the writing of this book, has felt like a collective act of faith. Its process of engaging with the unknown has proved reminiscent in many ways of the spirit of those first days of LIFT. Creating space for a multiplicity of voices, the Enquiry has proved a logical evolution of LIFT's earlier ideals, and is ongoing. With a new Director picking up the reins in 2005, the end of this book marks a new beginning for ourselves and for LIFT. So it is that after twenty-five years we pass the baton on to another generation of LIFT-makers, recognising that the ownership of LIFT belongs to many and trusting that seeds have been sown for it to flourish for a good twenty-five years more.

*Road to Heaven*, Young@Heart Chorus, USA, 2000. Photo: Ellen Augarten. The 28-strong company from Massachusetts, ranging in age from 73 to 92, investigate how to stay forever young by taking the songs and music of their children and grandchildren's generations, from Talking Heads to Led Zeppelin, the Doors, Bob Dylan and the Clash, and singing them, outrageously, themselves.

# Postscript

The twenty-first century is exploding in front of us – can we replace fear with festival? Festival means stunning reversals and re-imaginings of reality, not just an idea, but an experience we touch, we taste and we feel. Festivals are zones where people can come together to work through difficult things in an atmosphere of multiple truths, simultaneous translation, blazing, tender contradiction.

In this charged, contested and energised environment, which can be located in a school hall, in the human heart, or on the back of a swift horse, the confrontation is real, but not terrifying. We are offering our lives as metaphors. In this space no one needs to die to speak the truth. And perhaps the person who is the problem is also the solution.

Theatre keeps holding out hope for shared space in a segregated world, public life in the age of privatisation and participation in the midst of an enveloping corporate culture of spectatorship. It invites us to enter 'the space between', the unspoken, the unspeakable. For twenty-five years LIFT has opened this space and helped us as we approach and step inside, to lift our eyes, our minds, our standards, our expectations, our voices and our hearts.

Peter Sellars

# LIFT Business Arts Forum

In the early 1990s we felt a growing dissatis-faction with business sponsorship models in the arts, which were designed primarily to satisfy the commercial demands of marketing and brand promotion. In association with the *Financial Times* and strategic thinkers from a range of fields, LIFT set out to explore how businesses might be interested in a different relationship with the arts, one which would help them reflect on their own long-term development through the medium of international contemporary performance.

The 1995 LIFT Business Arts Forum was the result. Around forty participants from the private and arts sectors were invited to attend LIFT performances and to reflect on how they might do their work differently as a result of this shared experience. The first Forum was designed as a professional development programme for emerging leaders; as described by Forum advocate Charles Handy, 'The goal is to help business people learn from the arts, in a way that enriches their work, their businesses and in the end their lives.'

Over the ten years since it began, Forum participation has widened to include people working in government, health and other public-sector institutions, and to involve a group of young performing-arts students. This wider membership has enabled the Forum to explore imaginative responses to concerns that transcend boundaries of culture, generation and sector. In the words of Forum adviser Barbara Heinzen: 'Most of our institutions focus on the politics of delivery, which provide us with the services we want. LIFT is experimenting with the politics of invention and the skills of agreement needed to survive an unpredictable future.'

Forum participants expressed a wish to engage others in similar debate. A lecture series, *Imagining a Cultural Commons,* was initiated in 2003 to focus on the contemporary impact of commerce on culture and civil society worldwide. Speakers have included Indian biodiversity and water-rights activist Dr Vandana Shiva; US attorney Lawrence Lessig, inventor of a new form of copyright, Creative Commons; and US economist Jeremy Rifkin, advocate of the hydrogen economy.

Julia Rowntree
Director of Development 1986–95, Director of Business Arts Forum 1995–2005
Author of, *Performing Change: The Business of Theatre in a Global Age* (working title) (London, Routledge 2006).

# LIFT Teacher Forum

Throughout the 1990s, as LIFT investigated its relationship with the city through LIFT Learning participatory projects, LIFT staff and their teacher partners struggled to balance such arts-based activities in schools with the demands of an increasingly prescriptive national curriculum. By 1997 the situation was reaching a crisis point. Teachers were becoming wary of exploring ideas with artists within the mainstream curriculum and there was a real danger that the latter would be reduced to the status of occasional visiting specialists.

In this context LIFT set up the LIFT Teacher Forum, an experimental professional-development programme for teachers from a mix of primary, special and secondary schools, in partnership with artists associated with the LIFT programme. The Forum was organised from 1999 as a cycle of practice-based learning sessions over a period of a year. Each cycle involved reflection on the

*Buchettino*, Socìetas Raffaello Sanzio, Italy, LIFT'01. Courtesy of Socìetas Raffaello Sanzio. The scary tale of Thumbkin for children and grown-ups together, in which every member of the audience was tucked up in a bunk bed. *Buchettino* provided the inspiration for *Stones in My Boots*, a week-long residency at BAC by choreographer Madalena Victorino and photographer Agnès Desfosses with twenty-three 8-year-old children from Shaftesbury Park Primary School, and *Into the Woods*, a day conference for education professionals who considered issues of childhood, creativity and censorship.

shared experience of theatre, as well as jointly planned arts-based investigations in school. By 2001 a total of twenty-eight teachers involved with the Forum had received accreditation towards the Advanced Diploma of Professional Studies from the University of London Institute of Education.

After two cycles of the Forum, in the spirit of the LIFT Enquiry, LIFT began to play a wider role, in partnership with others, in investigating the nature of the collaboration between artists and schools. In 2002, with the Guildhall School of Music and Drama and Animarts, LIFT took part in the Animarts Action Research Programme, which examined the roles and responsibilities of artists working in education. The 2003–4 Teacher Forum graduation and review coincided with the publication of the Animarts Report.[1] In a climate of increased resourcing for the arts in schools, both of these served to accentuate the urgent need to increase the pool of artist and teacher practitioners equipped to work in effective partnerships in arts education. A transferable professional-development model was needed that could demonstrate that jointly training artists and teachers would provide an effective template for preparing a future generation of arts educators. To this end LIFT combined forces with seven other organisations to form the TAP (Teacher Artist Partnership) Professional Development research initiative,[2] in order to devise the curriculum for a continuing professional-development initiative, to run, initially, for two years, from April 2005.

Anna Ledgard
Director of Teacher Forum 1999–2004

---

1. *The Art of the Animateur: An investigation into the skills and insights required of artists to work effectively in schools and communities* (London, Animarts, 2003).
2. The TAP Consortium comprises: Animarts, CAPEUK (Creative Partnerships in Education), Guildhall School of Music and Drama (GSMD), LEAParts (formerly London Education Arts Partnership), LIFT, NewVIc (Newham Sixth Form College), LONSAS (London Schools Arts Service) and PLEY (Proactive Learning from Early Years).

# Project Phakama

Project Phakama is an international arts exchange programme that involves young people, arts practitioners, teachers and educationalists. Since its inception in 1996, a programme of intense cultural training has established a process of equitable exchange that builds creative skills amongst young artists internationally. Combined with a series of adventurous public performances, Phakama has developed new paradigms for an artistic process grounded in personal encounters and stories.

Over the years Phakama's network has grown to include Botswana, Namibia, Lesotha, Mozambique, Mauritius and India, as well as cities in the UK, where Phakama now works with young refugees and unaccompanied asylum seekers. The productions resulting from Phakama's work have been seen in LIFT seasons and in locations such as Robben Island in South Africa or Pune in India. Theatre critic Lyn Gardner called Phakama production *Be Yourself* 'one of the most moving, exuberant and visually stunning shows to see in London' (*The Guardian*, June 1999). Crucially, in every location the projects are a direct result of an interaction between the local realities and international cultural exchange; they respond to the specifics of each place and reflect them across the world.

Phakama is committed to promoting a participant-centred, non-hierarchical educational philosophy through the medium of the arts. Through a process of 'Give and Gain', the learning is two-way, acknowledging that everybody has something they can give to the project and everybody has something they can gain. This approach, which transcends age, experience and culture, is driven by the desire to make inspirational theatre, fuelled by the different viewpoints of each individual. Sixteen-year-old Cynthia Skhosana, from South Africa, commented: 'The experience was empowering . . . I have learnt to work with people from different cultures with patience and dignity, because we are not all the same and yet we can share everything.'

Many 'graduates' of Phakama go on to become trainers themselves, thereby seeding possibilities for Phakama projects in new areas.

Fabio Santos
Creative Co-Ordinator Phakama UK

# Companies performing in LIFT 1981–2004

## as part of the biennial Festival 1981–2001 and subsequent LIFT Enquiry

| | COMPANY | PROJECT | COUNTRY OF ORIGIN | VENUE/SITE |
|---|---|---|---|---|
| **LIFT'81** | | | | |
| | Cuatrotablas | Caminatas e Insomnios (Wandering and Sleeplessness) | Peru | ICA |
| | Die Vaganten | Urfaust – after Goethe | West Germany | Tricycle Theatre |
| | Greta Chute Libre | Glâces (Mirrors) | France | Old Half Moon |
| | Grupo de Teatro Macunaíma | Macunaíma | Brazil | Lyric Theatre, Hammersmith |
| | Het Werkteater | Zus of Zo (One of Them) | The Netherlands | ICA |
| | Suasana | Jentayu | Malaysia | Shaw Theatre |
| | Tamagawa | Bekkanko – an Ogre | Japan | Tricycle Theatre |
| | Teatr Ósmego Dnia (Theatre of the 8th Day) | More Than Just One Life Oh, How Nobly We Lived | Poland | New Half Moon |
| | Teatr Provisorium | It is Not for Us to Fly to the Islands of Happiness | Poland | ICA |
| Street Theatre | Medieval Players, Natural Theatre, Ompholos, The Beach Buoys, and others | | UK | Covent Garden Piazza, Paternoster Square, St Martin-in-the-Fields, the South Bank |
| Festival Club | Forkbeard Fantasy, Lol Coxhill, Mike Westbrook, and others | | UK | The Piccadilly Suite, Piccadilly Hotel |
| Forums and Talks | | | ICA | |
| | | | | |
| **LIFT'83** | | | | |
| | Cardiff Laboratory Theatre | The Heart of the Mirror The Wedding | UK | ICA |
| | Georges Coates Performance Works | The Way of How | USA | Bloomsbury Theatre |
| | IVT: International Visual Theatre | La Boule (The Seashell) | France | Lyric Studio |
| | Jozef Van Den Berg | Message from One-eye Mother and the Fool | The Netherlands | Almeida Theatre |
| | La Compagnia del Collettivo | Hamlet Henry IV Macbeth | Italy | Riverside Studios |
| | Le Théâtre de la Marmaille | L'Umiak Taller Than Tears | Canada | Battersea Arts Centre |
| | Natsu Nakajima | Niwa (The Garden) | Japan | Lyric Studio |

| | COMPANY | PROJECT | COUNTRY OF ORIGIN | VENUE/SITE |
|---|---|---|---|---|
| | Naya Theatre | Bahadur Kalarin | India | Lyric Theatre, Hammersmith |
| | Sistren Theatre Collective | QPH | Jamaica | Drill Hall |
| | Tabule Theatre | Bohboh Lef (Boy be Careful) | Sierra Leone | Battersea Arts Centre |
| | Urban Sax | Urban Sax | France | Covent Garden Piazza |
| | * Welfare State International | The Raising of the Titanic | UK | Regent's Canal Dock, Limehouse Basin |
| Street Theatre | Cardiff Laboratory Theatre, Jozef Van Den Berg, Pookiesnackenburger, Tabule Theatre, Teatro Títeres La Tartana, Théâtre de Complicité, The Kosh, The Natural Theatre Company, The 2 Reel Company, Zippo and Co | | | Covent Garden Piazza, Lakeside Terrace Barbican Theatre, outside National Theatre, Paternoster Square, Trafalgar Square |
| Festival Club | Desperate Men, Harvey and The Wallbangers, Théâtre de Complicité, The Bouncing Czechs, The Joeys, The Kosh, and others | | | Drill Hall |
| Workshops | | | | Drill Hall |

## 1984

| | COMPANY | PROJECT | COUNTRY OF ORIGIN | VENUE/SITE |
|---|---|---|---|---|
| | * Greta Chute Libre | Ceremonies: A Melodrama | France, UK | The Place Theatre |

## LIFT'85

| COMPANY | PROJECT | COUNTRY OF ORIGIN | VENUE/SITE |
|---|---|---|---|
| Alberto Vidal | El Hombre Urbano (Urban Man) | Spain | London Zoo |
| Bahamutsi Theatre Company | Dirty Work Gangsters | South Africa | Lyric Studio, Albany Empire |
| Dr Hot & Neon | Dr Hot & Neon | The Netherlands | Albany Empire |
| Els Comediants | Alè (Breath) The Devils (A Night In Hell) | Spain | Sadler's Wells Battersea Park |
| Ko Oku Jin | Ko Oku Jin | South Korea | Riverside Studios |
| La Gaia Scienza | Il Ladro Di Anime (Thief of Souls) | Italy | Shaw Theatre |
| Mladinsko Theatre | Mass in A Minor | Yugoslavia | Riverside Studios |
| Pelican Players | Dear Cherry, Remember the Ginger Wine Martha and Elvira | Canada | Battersea Arts Centre |
| Teatr Nowy | End of Europe | Poland | Lyric Theatre, Hammersmith |
| The 4th Beijing Opera Troupe | The Three Beatings of Tao San Chun | China | Royal Court Theatre |
| Traci Williams | Journey | USA | Battersea Arts Centre |
| Winston Tong | Sings Duke Ellington | USA | ICA |

*Il Ladro Di Anime* (*Thief of Souls*), La Gaia Scienza, Italy, LIFT'85. Georgio Barberio Corsetti's intensely physical dance theatre production conjured an imaginary Mediterranean city, ingeniously combining the geometrical illusions of Escher and the surrealism of Magritte. Courtesy of LIFT archive.

| Festival Club | De Spiegeltent (The Mirror Tent) Harvey and the Wallbangers, Pookiesnackenburger, Ra-Ra-Zoo, Rose English, Spitting Image, and others | The Netherlands | Camden Lock |

Discussions and Workshops

## LIFT'87

| Anatoli Vasiliev and Company | Cerceau | USSR | Riverside Studios |
|---|---|---|---|
| Circus Oz | Circus Oz | Australia | Big Top, Coin Street South Bank |
| Compañia Divas | Donna Giovanni | Mexico | Shaw Theatre |
| Eduardo Pavlovsky | Potestad | Argentina | Royal Court Theatre Upstairs |
| Ethyl Eichelberger | Great Women From History Leer | USA | ICA |
| Free Street Theater | Project! The Cabrini Green Musical | USA | Theatre Royal Stratford East |
| Jim Neu | Duet for Spies (The Whole Story) | USA | ICA |
| * Kufena | New Earth | Nigeria | Riverside Studios, Albany Empire |

| COMPANY | PROJECT | COUNTRY OF ORIGIN | VENUE/SITE |
|---|---|---|---|
| La Cubana | La Tempestad | Spain | Sadler's Wells Theatre |
| Needcompany | Need to Know | Belgium | The Place |
| New York Shakespeare Festival, Joseph Papp | The Colored Museum | USA | Royal Court Theatre |
| NSK (Neue Slowenische Kunst), Kosmokinetical Theatre Red Pilot | Fiat | Yugoslavia | Riverside Studios |
| People Show | The Unofficial Heavyweight and Entertainment Championship of the World | UK | Watermans Arts Centre |
| Pep Bou | Bufaplanetes | Spain | Battersea Arts Centre |
| * South East Asia Arts Project and Pip Simmons | Gor Hoi (Crossing the Water) (produced by Artsadmin) | UK | Shadwell Basin |
| Théâtre Repère | The Dragons' Trilogy | Canada | ICA |
| * The Bow Gamelan Ensemble | Offshore Rig (produced by Artsadmin) | UK | Watermans Arts Centre |
| Vusisizwe Players | You Strike the Woman, You Strike the Rock | South Africa | Riverside Studios, Watermans Arts Centre, Albany Empire |
| **LIFT'87 Children's Programme included:** All Day Suckers | Don Quixote | UK | Almeida Theatre, Festival Club |
| Pop-Up Children's Theatre | Spilt Milk | UK | Almeida Theatre, Festival Club |
| Teatro Dell'Angolo | Robinson & Crusoe | Italy | Battersea Arts Centre |
| The Oily Cart Company | Box of Tricks | UK | Battersea Arts Centre |
| Umoja | Tiger Fly | UK | Battersea Arts Centre |
| **Street Theatre** La Cubana | | Spain | South Molton Street and various locations |
| **Festival Club** Beverly Bell, Circus Oz, Ethyl Eichelberger, Hattie Hayridge, Jenny Éclair, People Show, Raw Sex, Shikisha, The Merry McFun Show, The Strange and Frightening James Macabre, and others | | Spain | Almeida Theatre |
| **Discussions and Workshops** | | | Africa Centre, ICA, Riverside Studios |
| **Exhibitions, Films, Music** Including NSK (Irwin and Laibach) | | | ICA, Riverside Studios |
| **LIFT'89** | | | |
| Abbey Theatre | A Whistle in the Dark | Ireland | Royal Court Theatre |
| Anatoli Vasiliev and Company | Six Characters in Search of an Author | USSR | Brixton Academy |
| Celavek Studio | Cinzano | USSR | Almeida Theatre |
| Comédie de Genève | Miss Julie | Switzerland | Lyric Theatre, Hammersmith |
| Derevo | Derevo | USSR | ICA |
| El Gran Circo Teatro | La Negra Ester | Chile | Riverside Studios |

*The Colored Museum*, New York Shakespeare Festival and Joseph Papp, USA, LIFT'87. Directed by George C. Wolfe, *The Colored Museum* was a runaway success in New York before coming to London. Black America laughed at itself and at white stereotypes of it in a masterpiece of sardonic wit. Photo: Martha Swope.

| COMPANY | PROJECT | COUNTRY OF ORIGIN | VENUE/SITE |
|---|---|---|---|
| * Fiona Templeton | YOU – The City (produced by Artsadmin) | USA, UK | Bishopsgate, Spitalfields and Brick Lane |
| Groundwork Theatre Company | Fallen Angel and the Devil Concubine | Jamaica | Almeida Theatre, Brixton Village |
| Jawaharlal Nehru Manipur Dance Academy | Keibul Lamjao | India | The Place |
| Katona József Theatre | The Government Inspector Three Sisters | Hungary | The Old Vic |
| Reduta Deux | Song of Lawino | USA | ICA, Riverside Studios |
| Roadside Theater | Pine Mountain Trilogy | USA | Albany Empire |
| Royal de Luxe | Roman – Photo Tournage | France | Broadgate Arena, Liverpool Street, Westminster Cathedral Piazza |
| * Station House Opera | The Bastille Dances (co-commisisoned by the City of Cherbourg and produced by Artsadmin) | UK | Outside the National Theatre |
| * The Bow Gamelan Ensemble | The Navigators (produced by Artsadmin) | UK | River Thames between Richmond and Twickenham Bridges, Watermans Arts Centre, Bow Creek at Three Mill Lane, South Bank Centre |
| Street Theatre   Derevo, El Gran Circo Teatro | | USSR, Chile | Covent Garden Piazza, Hyde Park |
| Conferences, Discussions, Talks and Workshops | | | ICA |

## LIFT'91

| COMPANY | PROJECT | COUNTRY OF ORIGIN | VENUE/SITE |
|---|---|---|---|
| Battimamzel Productions | The Man Who Lit Up the World | Trinidad, UK | Hackney Empire |
| * Bobby Baker | Kitchen Show (commissioned in association with and produced by Artsadmin) | UK | Bobby Baker's North London Kitchen |
| Comedy Theatre, Bucharest | A Midsummer Night's Dream | Romania | Lyric Theatre, Hammersmith |
| Footsbarn Travelling Theatre | A Midsummer Night's Dream | European (based in France) | Highbury Fields |
| Jerzy Kalina | Cathedral Welcome to Poland (part of Heatwave at the Serpentine Gallery) | Poland | Serpentine Gallery Lawn |
| * Keith Khan | Flying Costumes, Floating Tombs (co-commissioned and produced by Arnolfini, Bristol) | UK | Paddington Basin |
| Konic Theatre | Natura Morta (part of Heatwave at the Serpentine Gallery) | Spain | Serpentine Gallery |

| COMPANY | PROJECT | COUNTRY OF ORIGIN | VENUE/SITE |
|---|---|---|---|
| * Los Angeles Poverty Department | LAPD Inspects London (in association with North Lambeth Day Centre and Mickery Theatre, Amsterdam) | USA, UK | Abbey Community Centre |
| Maly Drama Theatre, Leningrad | Brothers and Sisters Gaudeamus (19 Improvisations) | USSR | Lyric Theatre, Hammersmith Riverside Studios |
| * Mayhew and Edmunds & Co | The Divine Ecstasy of Destruction (co-commissioned and produced by the Green Room, Manchester) | UK | ICA |
| * Nancy Reilly | Assume the Position (UK version commissioned in association with Artsadmin) | USA, UK | ICA |
| New York Shakespeare Festival, Joseph Papp | Spunk | USA | Royal Court Theatre |
| * Pants Performance | Democracy (co-commissioned and produced by Third Eye Glasgow) | UK | ICA |
| Rajatabla | No-one writes to the Colonel | Venezuela | Riverside Studios |
| Rose English | The Double Wedding (part of Barclays New Stages at the Royal Court Theatre) | UK | Royal Court Theatre |
| * Royal Court Theatre, National Theatre Studio | Cross References series (plays co-commissioned in association with the Royal Court Theatre and National Theatre) | | Royal Court Theatre Upstairs |
| Ariel Dorfman | Death and the Maiden | Chile, Argentina, UK | |
| Gcina Mhlophe | Love Child | South Africa | |
| Griselda Gambaro | Putting Two and Two Together | Argentina | |
| Harold Pinter | The New World Order | UK | |
| Stefan Tsanev | Paranoia | Bulgaria | |
| * The Damned Lovely | Neglected English Monuments (co-commissioned by Cambridge Darkroom and the Arts Theatre, Cambridge) | UK | ICA |
| * The Market Theatre Company | Starbrites (co-commissioned with Tricycle Theatre and the International Theatre Festival of Chicago, UK tour produced by Artsadmin) | South Africa | Tricycle Theatre |
| The Puppet Centre, Handspring Puppet Company, Faulty Optic and Queen's Park Community School | The Life of Themba | UK, South Africa | Kilburn High Road, Tricycle Theatre |
| Welfare State International | Lord Dynamite | UK | Three Mills Centre, Bow Creek |

| COMPANY | PROJECT | COUNTRY OF ORIGIN | VENUE/SITE |
|---|---|---|---|
| Angell Town Festival | Community Festival featuring LIFT artists | | Angell Town Estate, Brixton |
| Festival Club | Music, Talks | | ICA |
| Lifting the Lid A programme of conferences, talks and workshops | | | Abbey Community Centre, Commonwealth Institute, ICA, Serpentine Gallery |

LIFT Education and Access Programme curated by Michael McMillan and Pol Brown

## 1992

| | | | |
|---|---|---|---|
| Lifting London Conference | Trevor Phillips (Chair); Angell Town; Islington – New Approaches to Post-16 Education; Korda and Company; Theatre Royal Stratford East | A cross-sector celebration of local innovation | Cabot Hall, Canary Wharf |

## LIFT'93

| COMPANY | PROJECT | COUNTRY OF ORIGIN | VENUE/SITE |
|---|---|---|---|
| Anne Bean and Paul Burwell | Bankside Launch Event | UK | Bankside Power Station |
| Beijing Jing Ju Opera Troupe | The Little Phoenix | China | Queen Elizabeth Hall |
| * Bobby Baker | How to Shop: The Lecture (an Artsadmin project) | UK | Tuke Hall, Regent's College |
| Chengdu Theatre Company | Ripples Across Stagnant Water | China | Riverside Studios |
| Druid Theatre Company | At the Black Pig's Dyke | Ireland | Tricycle Theatre |
| * En Garde Arts | Bad Penny | USA | Regent's Park Boating Lake |
| * Gabriel Villela and Company | A Guerra Santa (The Holy War) (co-commissioned with Banco Brasil) | Brazil | Riverside Studios |
| Geremie Barmé and He Yong | Red Noise: Bringing the Streets of Beijing to London | China, Australia | ICA |
| Ghana Dance Ensemble | The King's Dilemma | Ghana | Old Spitalfields Market |
| Graeme Miller | The Desire Paths (an Artsadmin project, part of Barclays New Stages at the Royal Court Theatre) | UK | Royal Court Theatre |
| Hanoi Water Puppets | Hanoi Water Puppets | Vietnam | Highbury Fields, National Maritime Museum, Greenwich Park |
| * Keith Khan | Moti Roti Puttli Chunni (an Artsadmin project, produced by Theatre Royal Stratford East) | UK | Theatre Royal Stratford East |
| Mac Wellman | Terminal Hip | USA | ICA |

| COMPANY | PROJECT | COUNTRY OF ORIGIN | VENUE/SITE |
|---|---|---|---|
| * Platform | Homeland, Minha Terra, Szulofold, Fy Ngwlad I (an Artsadmin project) | UK | Various, including Jermyn Street (near the HQ of Rio Tinto Zinc); Shortlands (UK HQ of General Electric); St Dunstan's Road (Hungarian Reformed Church); and Wren Street (opposite the London Welsh Centre) |
| Ron Vawter | Roy Cohn/Jack Smith | USA | ICA |
| The Company | Yerma | India | Tricycle Theatre |
| * The Costume Designers Club | Journeys from Jourouvert (produced by Artsadmin) | UK, Europe, Caribbean | Old Spitalfields Market |
| Intercult, Sarajevo Company | Sarajevo – Tales of a City (by Goran Stefanovski and company from an original idea by Haris Pašović) | Europe | Riverside Studios |
| The Wooster Group | Brace Up! | USA | Riverside Studios |
| Caetano Veloso, Mario Bauza, NG La Banda and Sierra Maestra, and others | Gran Gran Fiesta! | Latin America | Clapham Common, Le Palais, South Bank Centre |

Debates and Talks (based on a concept proposed by Antonia Payne and Joanna Scanlan)

| | | | |
|---|---|---|---|
| Daily Dialogues curated by Alan Read | | | South Bank Centre |
| Lectures and Conversations | * Gayatri Spivak | Lecture | USA, Bangladesh | The National Theatre |

| | | | | |
|---|---|---|---|---|
| | * Guillermo Gómez-Peña | Lecture: The New World Border | USA, Mexico | |
| | * Peter Adegboyega Badejo | Lecture | UK, Nigeria | |
| | * Rustom Bharucha | Lecture: Somebody's Other | India | |
| | The Wooster Group | Conversation | USA | |
| BT LIFT Education Programme | * Emergency Exit Arts and Greenwich Primary Schools | Sang Song – River Crossing | UK | National Maritime Museum, Greenwich Park |
| | * The Puppet Centre | Fantastic and True | UK | Roundwood Park |

## LIFT'95

| COMPANY | PROJECT | COUNTRY OF ORIGIN | VENUE/SITE |
|---|---|---|---|
| Bak-truppen | Super – per | Norway | ICA |
| * Black Theatre Co-Operative, Bando de Teatro Olodum | Zumbi | UK, Brazil | Theatre Royal Stratford East |
| * Bobby Baker | Take A Peek! (co-commissioned by the South Bank Centre, an Artsadmin project) | UK | South Bank Centre |
| Cirque Plume | Toiles | France | Highbury Fields |
| Coco Fusco and Guillermo Gómez-Peña | Mexarcane International – Ethnic Talent for Export | USA, Mexico | Whiteley's Shopping Centre |
| * Deborah Warner | The St Pancras Project | UK | St Pancras Chambers |
| Familia Productions | Familia | Tunisia | Riverside Studios |

| COMPANY | PROJECT | COUNTRY OF ORIGIN | VENUE/SITE |
|---|---|---|---|
| * Gary Stevens | Sampler (an Artsadmin project, in association with Barclays New Stages in Nottingham) | UK | ICA |
| Groupe F | Birds of Fire | France | River Thames |
| Karas | Noiject | Japan | QEH, South Bank Centre |
| Les Deux Mondes | The Tale of Teeka | Canada | Riverside Studios |
| Lyric Theatre, Hammersmith in association with LIFT | Splendid's | UK, USA | Lyric Theatre, Hammersmith |
| National Theatre of Craiova | Phaedra | Romania | Riverside Studios |
| The Company | The Mad Woman of Our City | India | Watermans Arts Centre |
| The Market Theatre Company, Theatre Connections | Jozi Jozi | South Africa | Theatre Royal Stratford East |
| The Market Theatre Company | The Suit | South Africa | Tricycle Theatre |
| The Seka Barong of Singapadu | The Seka Barong | Bali | QEH, South Bank Centre |
| The Volksbühne Theatre | Murx den Europäer! Ein Patriotischer Abend (Kill The European! A Patriotic Evening) | Germany | Three Mills Island Studios |
| William Yang | Sadness | Australia | ICA |
| Xi Ju Che Jian Theatre | File O | China | ICA |

*Phaedra*, National Theatre of Craiova, Romania, LIFT'95. A chorus of forty cloaked actors told this epic story of forbidden love. Silviu Purcarete's dreamlike and sinister production was adapted from texts by Euripides and Seneca. Photo: Sean Hudson.

| | COMPANY | PROJECT | COUNTRY OF ORIGIN | VENUE/SITE |
|---|---|---|---|---|
| Lecture and Playreading | Charles Handy | Lecture: The Search For Meaning | UK | ICA |
| | Fatima Gallaire | Playreading: Princesses | Algeria, France | Royal Court Theatre |
| Lifting the Lid Conferences, Daily Dialogues and Films | | | | ICA, Riverside Studios |
| LIFT'95 Education Programme | Baggard Teatret | Take One | Denmark | Queens Park Community School |
| | In association with Circus Space | Sirk Uzay – Celestial Circus | UK, Turkish, Kurdish | The Circus Space, The Big Top Highbury Fields |
| | In association with SBC | Still Standing | UK | South Bank Centre |
| | In association with TRSE | Streets of London – North/South/East/West | UK | Theatre Royal Stratford East |
| | In association with WAC | Rush! (in collaboration with Black Theatre Forum and Black Theatre Co-op) | UK | Weekend Arts College |
| Business in the Arts Forum | | | | |

**Out of LIFT'96  A season of theatre for, with and by young people**

| | COMPANY | PROJECT | COUNTRY OF ORIGIN | VENUE/SITE |
|---|---|---|---|---|
| | Bando de Teatro Olodum | Erê | Brazil | Young Vic |
| | Bando de Teatro Olodum and Brazilian and UK artists | Carnival | Brazil, UK | Gabriel's Wharf, South Bank |
| | * Groupe F with UK artists and pupils from Stockwell Park School | The Factory of Dreams | France, UK | Brockwell Park |
| | * Reich and Syzber | Visions of Earthly Paradise (in association with BAC Young People's Theatre) | Sweden, UK | St Peter's Church, Vauxhall |
| | Theater La Balance | Cordelia | Denmark | Young Vic |
| | * Theatre-rites | Houseworks | UK | A House in Brixton |
| Conference | Shared Values | Shared Values conference on theatre for, with and by young people | UK | The Oval House |
| Daily Dialogues | | | | Young Vic |
| Business Arts Forum | | | | |
| | Phakama | Bulang Dikgoro (Open the Gates) | South Africa, UK | Benoni, South Africa |
| | Phakama'96/'97 | The Gates are Open Wide | South Africa, UK | Seshego, Benoni, Cape Town, South Africa |

**LIFT'97**

| | COMPANY | PROJECT | COUNTRY OF ORIGIN | VENUE/SITE |
|---|---|---|---|---|
| | * Alicia Rios | La Feria de Los Cinco Sentidos | Spain | Grand Hall, BAC |
| | al-Kasaba Theatre | Ramzy Abul Majd | Palestine | Royal Court Theatre at Ambassadors |
| | Cirque Ici | Cirque Ici | France | Clapham Common |
| | De La Guarda | Período Villa Villa | Argentina | Three Mills Island Studios |

| COMPANY | PROJECT | COUNTRY OF ORIGIN | VENUE/SITE |
|---|---|---|---|
| Deutsches Schauspielhaus, Hamburg | Stunde Null | Germany | QEH, South Bank Centre |
| el-Warsha | Tides of Night | Egypt | Royal Court Theatre at Ambassadors |
| * Ewan Forster and Christopher Heighes | Preliminary Hearing – An inquiry into the loss of the Mary Ward House Story | UK | The Mary Ward House |
| Gesher | K'Far (The Village) | Israel | Lyric Theatre, Hammersmith |
| * Groupe Γ | Un Peu Plus de Lumière | France | Battersea Park |
| Juliana Francis | Go Go Go | USA | ICA |
| Karas | I Was Real Documents | Japan | QEH, South Bank Centre |
| Kooemba Jdarra Indigenous Performing Arts | The Seven Stages of Grieving | Australia | BAC |
| Maya Krishna Rao | Khol Do (The Return) | India | BAC |
| * Phakama | Izimbadada – If I were in your Shoes (in association with Lewisham Youth Theatre and Sibikwa Community Theatre Project) | South Africa, UK | The Albany Theatre |
| * STEP | Invisible Room (in association with The Place and Karas) | Japan, UK | ICA |
| Taller de Investigación del Imagen Teatral | Oráculos | Colombia | The Former Coach Station, King's Cross |
| * TEA (Those Environmental Artists) | Now and Again | UK | Meard Street, Soho |
| The Geography of Haunted Places Company | The Geography of Haunted Places | Australia | Royal Court Theatre at Ambassadors |
| * Utshob Company | Utshob (in association with Watermans Arts Centre) | India, Bangladesh, UK | Trinity Buoy Wharf |
| * West Yorkshire Playhouse, Collective Artistes | Things Fall Apart (co-commissioned with West Yorkshire Playhouse in association with National Theatre Studio, produced by West Yorkshire Playhouse) | UK, Nigeria | Royal Court Theatre at Ambassadors |
| William Yang | The North | Australia | BAC |
| Zuni Icosahedron (curator), various artists | Journey to the East '97 | Beijing, Hong Kong, Taipei | ICA |

| Lifting The Lid | | | |
|---|---|---|---|
| Daily Dialogues curated by Alan Read | | | Royal Court Theatre at Ambassadors |
| Publication | * RealTime: Four Special Issues in Response to LIFT'97 | Australia, UK | Distribution all LIFT venues |
| Seminars | | | |
| Business Arts Forum | | | |

| COMPANY | PROJECT | COUNTRY OF ORIGIN | VENUE/SITE |
|---|---|---|---|
| Phakama | Ka Mor Walo Ka Seatleng (With a Suitcase in My Hand) | South Africa, UK | Seshego, South Africa |

**1998**

| | | | |
|---|---|---|---|
| Phakama | Met'n Sak Onner die Blad | South Africa, UK | Cape Town, South Africa |

**LIFT'99**

| COMPANY | PROJECT | COUNTRY OF ORIGIN | VENUE/SITE |
|---|---|---|---|
| al-Rasif Theatre | Ismaël Hamlet Memory of Ashes | Syria | ICA |
| * Bobby Baker | Grown-Up School (an Artsadmin project) | UK | A Camden Primary School |
| * Deborah Warner | The Tower Project (co-commissioned with the Perth Festival, Australia) | UK | Euston Tower |
| Ensemble Modern | Schwarz auf Weiss (Black on White) | Germany | Barbican Centre |
| * Forced Entertainment | Who Can Sing A Song To Unfrighten Me? (co-commissioned by the Royal Festival Hall and SpielArt Festival Munich) | UK | QEH, South Bank Centre |
| Itim Theatre Ensemble | Va Yomer. Va Yelech (And He Spoke. And He Walked) | Israel | Three Mills Island Studios |
| * Maya Krishna Rao, Gavin O'Shea, Abhilash Pillai, Bea Haut | Departures | India, UK | Union Chapel |
| Mehlo Players with the Khulumani Support Group | The Story I'm About To Tell | South Africa | Tricycle Theatre |
| Neil Thomas, Andrew Morrish, David Wells, Nick Papas and Richard Jeziorny | Urban Dream Capsule | Australia | Arding & Hobbs, Clapham Junction |
| Opera Transatlantica | Variations on a Concierto Barroco | Venezuela | Three Mills Island Studios |
| * Phakama | Be Yourself | South Africa, UK | Tricycle Theatre |
| Societas Raffaello Sanzio | Giulio Cesare | Italy | QEH, South Bank Centre |
| Theatre Nanterre-Amandiers | Le Jeu de l'Amour et du Hasard | France | Barbican Centre |
| * Theatre-rites | Cellarworks | UK | Belfast Rd, N16 |
| William Kentridge and Handspring Puppet Company | Ubu and the Truth Commission | South Africa | Tricycle Theatre |

| | COMPANY | PROJECT | COUNTRY OF ORIGIN | VENUE/SITE |
|---|---|---|---|---|
| Festival Club | Allegra McEvedy | The Good Cook Café Chef | UK | HMS President |
| | * Maurice O'Connell | The Stowaway | Ireland | |
| | Laia Gasch (curator), Amel Tafsout, Amy Lamé, DJ Ritu and The Asian Equation, Duckie, Frank Chickens, Marisa Carnesky, Max Reinhart, People Show, Rita Ray, Stayfree, Ursula Martinez, Wendy Houston, Zenzile, and others | Club programme | | |
| Daily Dialogues | Professor Lisa Jardine, Wesley Enoch (Chairs) | | UK, Australia | HMS President |
| Teacher Forum 1999 | | | | |
| Business Arts Forum | | | | |

### 2000

| | COMPANY | PROJECT | COUNTRY OF ORIGIN | VENUE/SITE |
|---|---|---|---|---|
| | * William Patten Primary and Stoke Newington Secondary Schools | Style of Our Lives | UK | Stoke Newington and its environs |
| | Young@Heart Chorus | Road to Heaven | USA | Lyric Hammersmith |
| Lecture | Roy Faudree | What Has Age Got To Do With It? | USA | Lyric Hammersmith |

### 2001

| | COMPANY | PROJECT | COUNTRY OF ORIGIN | VENUE/SITE |
|---|---|---|---|---|
| | Théâtre des Bouffes du Nord | Le Costume (The Suit) | France | Young Vic |

### LIFT'01

| | COMPANY | PROJECT | COUNTRY OF ORIGIN | VENUE/SITE |
|---|---|---|---|---|
| | al-Kasaba Theatre | Alive from Palestine | Palestine | Royal Court Theatre |
| | * Bobby Baker | Box Story (an Artsadmin project in association with Warwick Arts Centre) | UK | St Luke's Church, Holloway |
| | * Colin Prescod (programme curator), Mannafest, para active, JazzXchange | Critically Black | UK, USA | Riverside Studios |
| | Declan Donnellan, Nick Ormerod, Russian ensemble | Boris Godunov | Russia, UK | Riverside Studios |
| | * Groupe F | Garden of Light | France | Victoria Park |
| | * Hannah Hurtzig | Information Retrieval | Germany, UK, USA | King's Library, British Museum |
| | * Heiner Goebbels, Sound City Ensemble | No Arrival, No Parking, Navigation Part III (in association with Almeida Opera) | Germany, UK | Almeida at King's Cross |
| | * Hittite Empire, Chakra Zulu | Skeletons of Fish | UK, USA | Riverside Studios |
| | László Hudi, Mózgo Ház Társulás | Tragedy of Man | Hungary | Riverside Studios |

| COMPANY | PROJECT | COUNTRY OF ORIGIN | VENUE/SITE |
|---|---|---|---|
| Reich and Szyber | The Night Manager | Sweden | Sightseeing Boat on the Thames |
| Royal Court Theatre | New Plays From Uganda Scenes from work by Charles Mulekwa, Isaac Muwawu, Phillip Luswata | Uganda, UK | Royal Court Jerwood Theatre Upstairs |
| Socìetas Raffaello Sanzio | Buchettino Genesi – From the Museum of Sleep | Italy | BAC Sadler's Wells Theatre |
| Zuidelijk Toneel Hollandia | Voices | The Netherlands | Riverside Studios |

| **Festival Club** | | | | |
|---|---|---|---|---|
| | Maurice O'Connell | House of Miracles | Ireland | HMS President |
| | Laia Gasch (curator), Duckie, Halloween Society, OMSK, People Show, Shunt, and others | Club programme | | |

| **Conference** | | | | |
|---|---|---|---|---|
| | Including Deborah Warner, Phelim McDermot, Rachel Clare, Romeo and Chiara Castellucci, Sita Brahmachari, and others | Into the Woods: A conference on the experience of theatre for children | | BAC |

| **Residency** | | | | |
|---|---|---|---|---|
| | Madalena Victorino, Agnès Desfosses and Shaftesbury Park Primary School | Stones in My Boots | Portugal, France | BAC |

| **LIFT Conversations** | | | | |
|---|---|---|---|---|
| | Declan Donnellan, George Ibrahim, Peggy Phelan and Adrian Heathfield, Romeo and Chiara Castellucci, and others | | | |

| **LIFT Lectures** | | | | |
|---|---|---|---|---|
| | * Alan Read | 20/20 Vision, Seeing Through Theatre | UK | Sadler's Wells Theatre |
| | * John Fox | Steps in Rehearsing Utopia | UK | Bargehouse, South Bank |
| | * Rustom Bharucha | Between Past and Future, Re-Imagining 'Our Times' in Theatre Today | India | Riverside Studios |

**LIFT Learning**
Teachers' Forum 2001/02, Business Arts Forum 2001/02 and Network, US/UK Learning Partnership

| **LIFT ENQUIRY 2001** | | | | |
|---|---|---|---|---|
| | Nigel Jamieson, Paul Grabowsky, I Made Sidia, I Wayan Gde Yudane, Peter Wilson, Julian Crouch | The Theft of Sita (produced by Performing Lines) | Indonesia, Australia, UK | Riverside Studios |
| **LIFT in Conversation** | | The Theft of Sita: Tradition Into Modernity | Indonesia, Australia, UK | Riverside Studios |

| **LIFT ENQUIRY 2002** | | | | |
|---|---|---|---|---|
| | al-Kasaba Theatre | Alive from Palestine | Palestine | Young Vic |
| | Anne Bean and others | Many Hands – Midsummer Eve Event | UK | Battersea Park |
| | The Wooster Group | To You, The Birdie! (Phèdre) | USA | Riverside Studios |

| | COMPANY | PROJECT | COUNTRY OF ORIGIN | VENUE/SITE |
|---|---|---|---|---|
| Symposium | Adrian Heathfield and Andrew Quick (curators), The Wooster Group | The Wooster Group Symposium | USA | Cochrane Theatre |

### Landscape of Childhood 2002

| | COMPANY | PROJECT | COUNTRY OF ORIGIN | VENUE/SITE |
|---|---|---|---|---|
| | Acrobat | Acrobat | Australia | The Roundhouse |
| | * Clare Patey, Cathy Wren, Mark Storer, and invited artists | Old Dog New Trick (in association with the Roundhouse) | | The Roundhouse |
| | Teatr Rozmaitości | Festen | Poland | Sadler's Wells Theatre |
| | Victoria , Josse de Pauw | Übung | Belgium | The Place Theatre |
| Conference | Seth Honor (curator), Alan Read, Andrew Quick, Biyi Bandele, Marina Barham, Tim Etchells, and others | Why Do We Play? | UK | The Roundhouse |
| Research Programme | Animarts with the Guildhall School of Music and Drama | | | |

Business Arts Forum 2002/03

### LIFT ENQUIRY 2003  A Family Friendly Season

| | COMPANY | PROJECT | COUNTRY OF ORIGIN | VENUE/SITE |
|---|---|---|---|---|
| | * Anne Bean, Guildhall School of Music and Drama, Sovanna Phum, Rev. Nagase | Midsummer Eve Event | UK, Japan, Cambodia | Battersea Park |
| | Back to Back | Cow | Australia | BAC |
| | * Clare Patey, Cathy Wren and Rosendale School | Feast – Winter Solstice (P) | UK | Rosendale Allotments |
| | * Fevered Sleep | The (once in a blue moon) Ball | UK | BAC |
| | Gruppe 38 | Hansel and Gretel | Denmark | Lilian Baylis Theatre |
| | * Heather Ackroyd, Dan Harvey, Graeme Miller | Dilston Grove (P) (in association with Café Gallery Projects and Artsadmin) | UK | Dilston Grove |
| | Inad | Miladeh and Ramadan Until When? | Palestine | Schools in Southwark Oval House |
| | * MoMo | MoMo (in association with Natural History Museum) | Australia | Natural History Museum |
| | Oškaras Korsunovas Theatre Company | A Midsummer Night's Dream | Lithuania | Riverside Studios |
| | Phakama | Strange Familiars | UK | Stephenson Hall, National Children's Home |
| | Sovanna Phum | Rousey Dek | Cambodia | BAC |
| | TAG | Dr Korczak's Example King Matt | Scotland | BAC |
| | * Theatre-rites | Shopworks (co-commisioned with Vienna Festwochen, Austria) | UK | 220 Upper Tooting Road |
| Broadcast | LIFT/ BBC Radio 3 | Packet of Seeds (P) | | Radio 3 |

| COMPANY | | PROJECT | COUNTRY OF ORIGIN | VENUE/SITE |
|---|---|---|---|---|
| International BAC Debate | | The Rights and Roles of Young People and Arts Makers | | Grand Hall, |
| Lectures | * Dr Vandana Shiva | Imagining a Cultural Commons Lecture Series | India | Natural History Museum |
| Research Paper | Mafra Gagliardi | A paper on the experience of theatre for children | Italy | BAC |
| Teacher Forum 2003/04 | | | | |
| Business Arts Forum 2003/04 | | | | |

## LIFT 04: ENQUIRY

| COMPANY | PROJECT | COUNTRY OF ORIGIN | VENUE/SITE |
|---|---|---|---|
| Christine Tohme, Ashkal Alwan (curator) | Laughter: A progamme of performances, installations and videos | Lebanon | Bargehouse, ICA |
| Akram Zaatari | Excavation | Lebanon | |
| Atlas Group | My Neck is Thinner than a Hair: A History of the Car Bomb in the 1975–1991 Lebanese Wars Volume 1: January 21, 1986 | Lebanon, USA | |
| Joana Hadjithomas, Khalil Joreige | Lasting Images | Lebanon | |
| Lamia Joreige | Replay | Lebanon | |
| Marwan Rechmaoui | Beirut Caoutchouc | Lebanon | |
| Nadine Touma | Sayyidi Milady | Lebanon | |
| Rabih Mroué | Looking for a Missing Employee | Lebanon | |
| Rabih Mroué and Lina Saneh | Biokhraphia | Lebanon | |
| * Clare Patey, Cathy Wren and Rosendale School | Feast – Spring Equinox (P) | UK | Rosendale Allotments |
| * Clare Patey, Cathy Wren and Rosendale School | Solstice (P)Feast – Midsummer Rosendale Allotments | | UK |
| * Clare Patey, Cathy Wren and Rosendale School | Feast – Autumn Equinox | UK | Rosendale Allotments |
| * Groupe F | Joueurs de Lumières (Players of Lights) | France | Victoria Park |
| * Roma Patel, Trudi Entwistle, Graham Nicholls | Living Image (P) | UK | The Dana Centre at the Science Museum |
| * Societas Raffaello Sanzio | L. #09 London, Tragedia Endogonidia IX Episode (co-commissioned by Societas Raffaello Sanzio; Festival d'Avignon; Hebbel Theater, Berlin; Kunsten Festival des Arts, Brussels; Bergen International Festival; Odéon – Théâtre de l'Europe with Festival d'Automne à Paris; Romaeuropa Festival; Le Maillon – Théâtre de Strasbourg; Théâtre des Bernadines with Théâtre du Gymnase, Marseilles) | Italy | Laban |
| Lectures    * Jeremy Rifkin | The Hydrogen Economy – A Question of Culture Imagining a Cultural Commons Lecture Series | USA | London School of Economics |

| | COMPANY | PROJECT | COUNTRY OF ORIGIN | VENUE/SITE |
|---|---|---|---|---|
| | * Lawrence Lessig | Creative Commons in a Connected World Imagining a Cultural Commons Lecture Series | USA | Royal Geographical Society |
| LIFT Evidence | * Angad Chowdhry | On the Theatre that Watches Us | UK, India | Bargehouse |
| | * Cris Bevir | Connecting Circles | UK | Bargehouse |
| | * Jenny Sealey | And Seven | UK | Rargehouse |
| | * Mark Lythgoe | Perception and Realities: The Science of Theatre | UK | Purcell Room, South Bank Centre |
| | * Pamela Carter | Theatron | UK | Bargehouse |
| LIFT Enquirers | | * 100 Enquirers give a public testimony in response to the question 'What is theatre to you? And if it was not there what would be missing from your life?' | UK | Bargehouse |
| LIFT Learning Symposium | | Growing by Design | | Bargehouse |

## Indoor Fireworks

| | COMPANY | PROJECT | COUNTRY OF ORIGIN | VENUE/SITE |
|---|---|---|---|---|
| | Tim Etchells, Forced Entertainment (curator) | | | Riverside Studios |
| | Atlas Group | The Loudest Muttering is Over | Lebanon, USA | |
| | Davis Freeman, Random Scream | Reflection | Belgium, USA | |
| | Edit Kaldor with Cecilia Vallejos | Or Press Escape | Hungary | |
| | Eva Meyer-Keller | Death is Certain | Germany | |
| | Forced Entertainment | Bloody Mess Instructions for Forgetting Marathon Lexicon The Voices | UK | |
| | Gob Squad | Super Night Shot | Germany, UK | |
| | Tim Etchells | Video Works | UK | |
| | Tim Etchells and Hugo Glendinning | Years 0–20 | UK | |
| Dialogues | Adrian Heathfield (curator), Emma Kay, Jonathan Burrows, Steven Connor, in conversation with Tim Etchells | On Contemporary Performance and Visual Culture | | |
| Talk | Peggy Phelan | | | |

* LIFT commission
(P) Part of a series of LIFT commissions exploring the Poetics and Politics of London

# LIFT Staff, Board of Directors, Patrons, Advisers, Student Placements and Volunteers 1981–2004

Ruanne Abou-Rahme
Richard Adams
Mukul Ahmed
Tom Albu
Fiona Alexander
Lesley Allan
Christopher Allen
George Allen
Kirk Allen
Lulu Allott
Camilla Ander
Andy Anderson
Helen Anderson
Neil Anderson
Tereza Araujo
Timo Arnall
Kate Ashcroft
Dame Peggy Ashcroft
Jane Ashdown
Paul Askew
Harriet Atkinson
Ute Axmann
Bolaji Badejo
Peter Badejo
Mutinta Bailey
Brian Baker
Raef Baldwin
Tiffany Ball
Polonca Baloh-Brown
Biyi Bandele
Rob Barling
Kaye Barnham
Gabrielle Barraclough
Rachael Barraclough
Jonathan Bartlett
Randip Basra
Acushla Bastible
Nora Batchelor
Sasha Bates
David Baxter
Edwin Belchamber
Cathy Bell

David Bell
Jane Bellai
Patricia Benecke
Joseph Benjamin
Annie Bennett
Emma Bennett
Lesley Bennett
Camille Bensoussan
Theresa Bergne
Kate Berney
Emma Berry
Petrus Bertschinger
Jane Bevan
Suman Bhuchar
Sally Bibb
Ellen Birley
Lady Marcia Blakenham
Maria Blanco
Rachel Blech
Angie Board
Guillame Bodin
Rachel Borchard
Mark Borkowski
Fiorella Boscia
Chantal Bougnas
Stephanie Bouton
Sara Bowen
Lawrence Brandes
Simon Breden
Rebecca Brewin
Charles Brian
Emma Brooke
Karen Brooks
Patricia Brown
Tim Brunsden
Sophie Bruun
Maz Bryden
Jimmy Buchanan
Marianne Buckland
Joanna Buggy
Traci-Lin Burgess
Ruth Burnett

Josephine Burns
Lynne Burton
George Butler
Kim Byung What
Fiona Callaghan
Erica Campayne
Maureen Carroll
Robert Carsons
Jo Carter
Vicky Carter
Jamie Cason
Maylene Catchpole
Anne Caulfield
Rosalind Cavaliero
Tina Cawt
Deborah Chadbourn
Ben Chamberlain
Mark Chamberlaine
Debbie Chambers
Michael Chance
Chris Chandler
Terri Chandler
Nicola Cherry
Nicky Childs
Elly Ching
Mukid Choudhury
Lara Clark
Robert Clover-Brown
Rachel Cohen
Nigel Coke
Amanda Colbenson
Elizabeth Cole
Lo Cole
Danni Colgan
Sam Collins
Emma Comfort
Grainne Cook
Theo Cook
Andree Cooke
Jamie Coomarasamy
Muriel Cordoba
Joshua Cornbleet

Stephen Cornford
Glenn Cottenden
Jean-Charles Coulibeuf
Neil Craig
Rebecca Craig
Belinda Creswell
Simon Crompton
Lord Dahrendorf
Rachel Dale
Sarah Daniel
Lady Molly Daubeny
Jason Davidge
Sally Davies
Sam Davies
Tiffany Davies
Joanna Davis
Chief Dawethi
Thrith Dawnschild
Alan Dawson
Rebecca Dawson
Suzana Day
Rachel d'Cruze
Samantha de Bendern
Arie de Geus
Ana de Skalon
Rufus Dealish
Lizzie Dekkers
Cathy Delacy
Neil Dempsey
Dame Judi Dench
Martine Dennewald
Alison Denning
Jerry Dennis
Tia Destiya
Anne Dewey
Emma Diamond
Mick Dickinson
Sam Dickinson
Siobhan Docherty
Katrin Dominik
Beth Dorey
Claudette Douglas

Lucy Doyle
Jeni Draper
Patrick Driver
David Duchin
Alan Dufton
Anne Duncan
Wiss Duncombe
Ian Dunlop
Cathy Dunn
Ali Dwyer
Sony Dyakova
James Dyer
Andy Edwards
Lynette Edwards
Barbara Egervary
Pat Elliot
Richard Elsner
Orpheas Emirzas
Rudy Engelander
Brian Eno
Tim Etchells
Adrian Evans
Gavin Evans
Simon Evans
Ronald Eyre
Gerard Fairtlough
Lisa Fairtlough
Donatus Fai Tangem
Tanja Farman
John Farquhar-Smith
Amelia Fawcett
Andrew Fay
Tony Fegan
Alison Fellows
Leona Felton
Rose Fenton
Katrina Ffiske
Ralph Fiennes
Jeff Fisher
Jenny Fisher
Mark Fisher
Kimberly Fisk
Tashi Fletcher
Anthony Fletcher
Sharon Flindell
Tony Flynn
Rebecca Fortey
Clare Fox
John Fox
Kate France
Tish Francis
Karen Freed

Jackie Friend
Norman Frish
Emma Frost
Vince Frost
Daisy Froud
Caroline Galmot
Cristina García Tenerio
Laia Gasch
Gabriel Gbadamosi
Nina Gebauer
France Gelinas
Stephanie Gerra
Maria Gibbons
Ben Gibson
Philicia Gilbert
Sammy Jane Gildroy
Alan Gilmour
Emma Glackin
Adam Glasser
Rachel Glittenberg
Amanda Glyn
Charles Godfrey
    Faussett
Fi Godfrey Faussett
Jeremy Goldstein
John Good Holbrook
Heather Goodman
Pamela Gordon
Mickey Gould
Jane Gower
Lord Gowric
Clare Grainger
Lisa Grech
Amy Greenbank
Laura Gribble
Matt Grierson
Becky Griffith
Hilary Groves
Tim Groves
Ana Guadalupe
Ragga Gudmundsdottir
Krishna Guha
Sir Alec Guinness
Dave Gunstone
Sarah Gurcel
Christabel Gurney
Rachel Gurney
Kenny Guthrie
Matthew Gwyther
Karin Hackensoellner
Michelle Haffner
Rick Hall

Stella Hall
Gamal Hammad
Charles Hampden-
    Turner
Libby Hampson
Sylvia Han
Charles Handy
Elizabeth Handy
Li-Mei Haong
Cinzia Hardy
Daniel Hardy
Martha Hardy
Serena Harragin
Jenny Harris
Kieko Hattori
Debra Hauer
Bea Haut
Justin Hay
Jo Hayes
Vivien Hayman
Adrian Heathfield
Carin Heidelbach
Silja Heikkila
Barbara Heinzen
Sarah Hemming
Michelle Hendry
Franziska Henner Regier
Kate Henriques
Andrew Hepburne-Scott
Sheyla Hernandez
    Elosua
Georgie Hewitson
Vikki Heywood
Jenn Higginson
Paul Highfield
Natalie Highwood
Dean Hill
Lam Ho
Sasha Hoare
Ruth Hogarth
Ruth Holdsworth
Nigel Hollidge
Tamsyn Holloway
Christopher Holt
Sally Homer
Seth Honnor
Moti Hooper
Alpha Hopkins
Julie Hornsby
Aziza Horsham
Jean Horstman
Tanja Hosch

Gaie Houston
Joost Houtman
Geoffrey Howard-Spink
Jon Howes
Delphine Hsin Yi Ku
Chloe Hughes
Sue Hughes
Jill Hutton
Will Hutton
Nicholas Hytner
Joanna Igham
Kalu Ikeagwu
Mirijana Ilic
Kerstin Illing
Ailsa Ilott
Dada Imaroqbe
Anna Ingleby
Laura Inskip
Risa Ip
Liza Irvine
Noriko Ishihara
Oana Jackson
Bianca Jakubowski
Ian James
Tracy Jaques
Paul Jenkins
Alex Jennings
Mary Jeremiah
Xian Jiang
Joanna Jones
Phillip Jones
Sally Jones
Sian Jones
Echoe Ju Ying Chang
Anna Julian
Alex Julyan
Gemma Jupp
Greg Kahn
Edith Kaldor
Alexandra Kamenetski
Portia Kamons
Tomoko Kanaka
Jeremy Kane
Jessie Kaner
Maurice Kanereck
Yun Hee Kang
Tosh Kara
Kumi Kato
Tadashi Kato
Tony Kavanagh
Huw Kennair-Jones

Baroness Helena Kennedy
Sophie Kennedy-Martin
George Kessler
Sarah Kessler
Louise Keyworth
Sami Khan
Tilney Kirkbride
Chia-Che Klsieh
Judith Knight
Oliver Kranz
Mary-Agnes Krell
Michael Kruger
Hsinyi Ku
Laure Kwiatkowski
Adelina La Scaleia
Alex Laird
Agnes Lajot
Elke Laleman
Maria Lamb
Karen Lancaster
Yvonne Lang
Helen Lannaghan
Steven Larkin
Alice Lascelles
Karen Lath
Vanessa Lecointe
Anna Ledgard
Claire Lee
Sharon Lee
Dorothy Legrand
Sanna Lehtonen
Gerard Lemos
Adrian Lesurf
Michael Levine
Tessa Liebschner
Irene Lifske
Jessie Lim
Martin Lloyd-Evans
Jennie Long
Victoria Long
Laura Longrigg
Richard Lydon
Juliet Lygon
Monica Ma
Claire MacDonald
Brian MacStay
Simon Maggs
Ghiniva Mamari
Antonio Mandralis
Nathalie Marie Currie
Dilson Marino

Sylvia Maroino
Helen Marriage
Karon Maskill
Rebecca Mason-Jones
Kim Masterman
Richard Masterman
Margaret Matheson
Dave Matthews
Rebecca Matthews
Susan Maxwell
Kate Mayne
Bill McAlister
Alison McAlpine
Caoimhe McAvinchey
Ruth McKenzie
Jamie McLaren
Maria McLaughlin
Adele McLoughlin
Brian McMaster
Michael McMillan
Angela McSherry
Colette Meacher
Carien Meijor
George Melly
Sarah Menzies
Carien Meyer
Michael Meyer
Corinne Micalleff
Daniella Michaels
Anne Middleton
Anne Millman
Katie Mitchell
Rob Moffett
Helen Molchanoff
Alison Molloy
Collette Molloy
Nick Moore
Christopher Moorsom
Lynnette Moran
Holly Morris
John Morris
Michael Morris
Joumana Mourad
Virginia Moutlia
Debbie Mullins
Jodee Mundy
Irene Musemeci
Stella Myeong Kim
Steve Nagy
Malcom Nash
Anthea Neagle
Gub Neal

Lucy Neal
Michael Neal
Tabitha Neal
Karen Newby
Elise Newman
Evie Newman
Simon Notton
Clare O'Brien
Michael O'Brien
Jenny O'Connell
Maurice O'Connell
Charlene O'Ferrall
Jonquille Okhiria
Peter Oldham
Toby Oliver
Vanessa O'Neil
Sally Orihuela
Karen Otazo
Caroline Owen
Kate Owen
Katie Owen
Anna Paige
Abi Palmer
Robert Palmer
Nick Pamphlett
Evy Papadimitriou
Penelope Paraskeva
Victoria Parker
Rosemary Parkinson
Steve Parsons
Julia Pascal
Clare Patey
Katie Paton
Helena Paul
Thomas Pausz
Antonia Payne
Elaine Peake
Christopher Pearce
Anna Peitch
Stephen Penty
Daniela Perazzo
Sean Perry
Manuela Perteghella
Claudia Pestana
Veronique Petit
Nicky Petto
William Plowden
Cindy Polemis
Denis Poll
Costas Polydorou
Zsuzsanna Posta
Alison Pottinger

Sally Power
Colin Prescod
Paul Prescott
Christopher Price
Margred Pryce
Charlotte Purton
Andrew Quick
Yasemin Rachet
Isabella Radcliffe
Beverley Randall
Elizabeth Rathman
Alan Read
Nicky Read
Alex Reedijk
Alexa Reid
Nell Reid
Peter Renshaw
Dawn Richards
Jacqueline Richardson
Karen Richardson
Sir Ralph Richardson
Marina Rigato
Kim Ringsell
Agostino Riola
Sally Robarts
Sorrel Roberts
Matthew Robinson
Frank Rodgers
Jane Rogoyska
Simona Rossett
Bruno Roubicek
Julia Rowntree
Patricia Roy
Ruth Rutstein
Emma Sadler
Anjalika Sagar
Ruth Sallis
Dani Salvadori
Honey Salvadori
Marrianne San Miguel
Mila Sanders
Fabio Santos
Rosey Sawkins
Joanna Scanlan
Nona Schulte-Roemer
Ceri Seel
Lorraine Selby
Kerry Sellens
Euan Semple
Katy Sender
Sonia Serafin
David Serame

Debbie Serrant
Carlie Sharman
Fiona Shaw
Rachel Shaw
Jim Shen
Clare Sheridan
Andrew Siddall
Elke Sigg
Ruth Silver
Pete Skelley
Rob Skinner
Dijana Skondric
Lizzie Slater
Colin Small
Amanda Smith
Ellie Smith
Rupert Smith
Deborah Smookler
Naomi Soetendorp
Cathy Sollars
Tamás Soocz
Ahdaf Soueif
Martin South
Pen Spally
Angela Sparks
Leslie Spencer
Toby Spencer
Peter Spong
Judith Squires
Christophe St Lambert
Lord St Oswald
Vanessa Stanley
Julie Starling
Geraldine Steen
Gina Stein
Miranda Stevens
Debbie Stevenson
Juliet Stevenson

Gary Stewart
Seonaid Stewart
Angela Stewart Park
Polly Stokes
Chris Stooke
David Strickland
Simon Sturgess
Suvida Sudthisote
Camilla Summers
Daniel T. Summers
Andrew Sutton
Janet Suzman
Franklyn Sweeney
Lisa Swerling
Alysha Sykes
Leo Sykes
Teresa Szczotka
Anne Tagg
Carlo Tailleux
Faizou Tairou
Sylvia Tan
Yuki Tawada
Danielle Taylor
Edward Taylor
Imogen Taylor
Annette Telesford
Alda Terracciano
John Terry
Elly Thomas
Sharon Thomas
Ana Thomaz
Bridget Thornborrow
Shira Thorne Hess
Emelia Thorold
Sam Thorpe
Dominic Tickell
Achilleas Tilegrafos
Barbara Tincher

Tina Toeberg
Anna Tolputt
Margreth Tolson
Marc Tomlinson
Anne Torreggiani
Mark Trezona
Sarah Tuck
Jennifer Tuckett
Jenny Turtill
Dorothy Tutin
Kerstin Twachtmann
Christine Tweddle
Kate Tyndall
Prue Upton
Sir Peter Ustinov
Isabelle Van Lennep
Bridgette Van Leuven
Georgina Van Welie
Rebecca Vargas
Joana Velasco
Hazel Vidler
Jenny Vila Carpe
Beate Voigt
Alex Von Koettlitz
Beata Von Oelreich
Theresa Von Wuthenau
Anna Votsi
Gede Wahyu
Andrew Walby
Jenny Waldman
Charlotte Wales
Jessica Wall
Mike Wall
Moke Wall
Richard Walton
Brian Wang
Hilary Waters
Tim Waterstone

Heidi Watson
Fiona Watt
Louise Watts
Sally Watts
Janet Waugh
Nicky Webb
Elke Weiler
Jenny Weston
Ian Whitaker
Jo White
Michael White
Em Whitfield
Teresa Whitfield
Fields Wicker-Miurin
Sophie Wietzman
Robin Wight
Helen Wilding
Peter Wilkinson
Machteld Willemsc
Russell Willis Taylor
Alice Wilson
Paul Wilson
Peter Wilson
Jane Winder
Carole Woddis
Bettina Wohlfahrt
Richard Wong
Hilary Wood
Matt Wood
Alice Woodhouse
Gini Woodward
Claudia Woolgar
Everton Wright
Jemma Yarwood
Okyung Yoon
Jonathan Young
Nigel Young
Jaffer Zahir

# Index

# Picture Credits

Annand, Simon  10, 48, 168

Augarten, Ellen  202

Baltzer, David  175

Bartlett, Neil  25

Beloff, Zoe  37

Beu, Thilo  135

Corio, David  82

Coudyzer, Ruphin, FPPSA, www.ruphin.com  53, 54

Crouch, Julian/Mombassa, Reg  187

Crummay, Patricia  28

de Lahaye, Guy  47

Del Pia, Luca  165

Douet, Mark  101

Elfes, Peter  141

Ellis, Richard  60

Els Comediants  41

Evans, Gavin, www.gavinevans.com  172

Glendinning, Hugo  122

Goss, Andy  196

Groupe F/Nava, Thierry  Frontispiece

Hadjithomas, Joana/Joreige, Khalil  130

Han Lei  Cover

Harrison, Chris, FSP  153

Hudson, Sean  217

Huot, Claudel 198

Laure de Decker, Marie, courtesy of Katona József Theatre, Hungary  102

LIFT archive  72, 74, 93, 99, 109, 118, 147, 210

Michael J. O'Brien Photography  42, 44, 49, 58, 63, 88, 121, 127, 138, 145, 150, 160, 192

Moti Roti  65

Pearce, Christopher, PanicPictures.co.uk  19

Pedrotti, Federico, Munich  57

Phakama archive  114

Plotnikov, Valery  156

Pozorski, Irmgard  116

Richard Moran Photography,  177

Salvadori, Honey  12

Schramm, Tracey  140

Shakespeare Lane, Catherine  24

Shank, Theodore  33

Shen Yantai  77

Sistren Theatre Collective  69

Sociètas Raffaello Sanzio  205

Steenborg, Tomas  181

Swope, Martha  212

Topolski, Feliks, courtesy of Daniel and Teresa Topolski  26

Vassiliev, Victor  105

Whittuck, Andrew  188

# Biographies

**Rose de Wend Fenton** is an independent arts producer. She co-founded LIFT with Lucy Neal in 1981 and was its co-director for twenty-five years, receiving an OBE in 2005 for her services to drama. Rose Fenton contributes to arts advisory panels in the UK and abroad, in addition to occasional writing and broadcasting. She is on the board of the performance company Moti Roti, a member of the Roundhouse Trust Advisory Board and President of Theorem, a pan-European organisation that supports the work of emerging arts from Eastern and Central Europe.

**Lucy Neal** is an independent arts producer. She co-founded LIFT with Rose Fenton in 1981 and was its co-director for twenty-five years, receiving an OBE in 2005 for her services to drama. Lucy Neal contributes to arts advisory panels in the UK and abroad, in addition to occasional writing and broadcasting. She is a Trustee of the Roundhouse Trust and a Board Member of the performance company Station House Opera.

**Rustom Bharucha** is an independent writer, director, and cultural critic based in India. Author of several books, including *Theatre and the World* (1993), *The Question of Faith* (1993), *In the Name of the Secular* (1999), *The Politics of Cultural Practice* (2000), and *Rajasthan: An Oral History* (2003), he engages with issues relating to interculturalism and the politics of globalisation and development.

**Lyn Gardner** writes about theatre for *The Guardian*. Her first novel, *Into the Woods*, will be published by David Fickling Books in 2006.

**Naseem Khan** is a writer, broadcaster, policy developer/analyst and administrator who has been actively engaged in the area of cultural diversity for thirty years, receiving an OBE in 1999. Author of the pioneering report *The Arts Britain Ignores* (Calouste Gulbenkian Foundation, 1976), she was founder and co-ordinator of the first national umbrella body for all non-indigenous arts activities, MAAS (Minorities Arts Advisory Service), and Senior Policy Advisor to the Arts Council of England and Head of its Diversity Unit, 1996–2003.

**Dragan Klaić** is a Permanent Fellow of Felix Meritis, Amsterdam, theatre scholar and essayist. He teaches arts and cultural policy at Leiden University. His most recent work is *Europe as a Cultural Project* (Amsterdam, European Cultural Foundation, 2005).

**Peter Sellars** is a leading theatre, opera and festival director. A cultural activist, he is Professor of World Arts and Cultures at UCLA, and a lecturer in the Graduate School of Journalism at UC Berkeley.